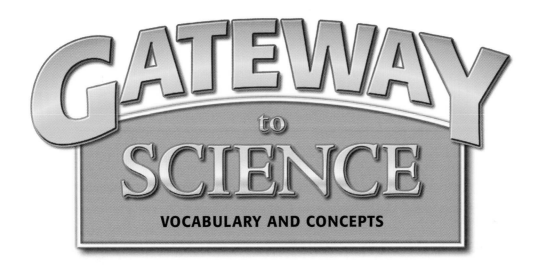

GATEWAY to SCIENCE

VOCABULARY AND CONCEPTS

Tim Collins

Mary Jane Maples

Science Consultants

David T. Crowther
Associate Professor Science Education
College of Education
University of Nevada
Reno, NV

Dr. Norman G. Lederman
Chair, Department of Mathematics and Science Education
Illinois Institute of Technology
Chicago, IL

George T. Ochs
Vice President
Gathering Genius, Inc.

David Bennum
Lecturer and Vice Chair of Physics
University of Nevada
Reno, NV

THOMSON

HEINLE

Australia • Canada • Mexico • Singapore • United Kingdom • United States

Gateway to Science
Tim Collins, Mary Jane Maples

Publisher, School ESL: *Phyllis Dobbins*
Director of Product Development: *Anita Raducanu*
Senior Development Editor: *Guy de Villiers*
Editorial Assistant: *Emily Dendinger*
Director of Product Marketing: *Amy Mabley*
Executive Marketing Manager: *Jim McDonough*

Production Manager: *Sally Giangrande*
Senior Production Editor: *Maryellen E. Killeen*
Senior Frontlist Buyer: *Mary Beth Hennebury*
Project Management, Design, and Composition:
InContext Publishing Partners

Printed in the United States of America.
1 2 3 4 5 6 7 8 9 10 — 11 10 09 08 07

For more information contact Thomson Heinle,
25 Thomson Place, Boston, Massachusetts
02210 USA, or you can visit our Internet site at
http://elt.thomson.com

Credits appear on pages 276–279, which constitutes
a continuation of the copyright page.

Student Edition (Hardcover)
ISBN-10: 1-4240-0331-8
ISBN-13: 978-1-4240-0331-0

Student Edition (Softcover)
ISBN-10: 1-4240-1621-5
ISBN-13: 978-1-4240-1621-1

Consultants and Reviewers

We gratefully acknowledge the contribution of the following educators who reviewed materials at various stages of development. Their input and insight provided us with valuable perspective and ensured the integrity of the program.

Science Consultants

David T. Crowther
Associate Professor Science Education
College of Education
University of Nevada
Reno, NV

Dr. Norman G. Lederman
Chair, Department of Mathematics
   and Science Education
Past-President, National Association
   for Research in Science Teaching
Illinois Institute of Technology
Chicago, IL

George T. Ochs
Vice President
Gathering Genius, Inc.

David Bennum
Lecturer and Vice Chair of Physics
University of Nevada
Reno, NV

Consultants

Grit Malkin
Parkview High School
Decatur, GA

Cheryl Trzasko
Palm Beach High School
Wellington, FL

Fran Zimmerman
La Jolla, CA

Reviewers

Sarah Campstrom
Madera High School North
Madera, CA

Karla Davis
Jonas Salk Middle School
Sacramento, CA

Traci Theis
Lewis Middle School
Atascadero, CA

Kathleen Sierra
Madera Unified High School
Madera, CA

Lorraine Vara
Azusa Pacific University
Azusa, CA

Steve Sloan
James Monroe High School
North Hills, CA

Jennifer L. Sharp
Highland High School
Bakersfield, CA

Elizabeth Campos
Long Beach Unified
Lakewood, CA

Karin Aguliar
LAUSD
Cerritos, CA

Allan Derr
Jefferson Middle School
Villa Park, IL

Bobbi Minogue
Jay Stream Middle School
Carol Stream, IL

Naeem Karriem
Chicago Public Schools
Chicago, IL

Cally Andriotis-Williams
Newcomers High School
Auburndale, NY

Libby DeLeon
Plano ISD
Plano, TX

M. Danielle Bragaw
Bedichek Middle School
Austin, TX

Malgorzata Stone
Franklin High School
Seattle, WA

Guadalupe Irene Rodriquez
Seattle Public Schools
Seattle, WA

Ramona Esparza
Clark County School District
Las Vegas, NV

Matthew Trillo
Naylor Middle School
Tuscon, AZ

Jeanette E. Page
Kennett Middle School
Kennett Square, PA

Rita Valentino Meskel
Lakewood Senior High School
Jefferson County
Lakewood, CO

Chris George
Herndon High School
Herndon, VA

Nancy Svedson
Stuart High School
Falls Church, VA

Contents

Gateway to Science Scope and Sequence Chart

Science Basics

Lesson Title	Science Vocabulary	Academic Vocabulary	Word Study	Concepts	Critical Thinking	Science Skill	National Science Education Standards
Thinking Like a Scientist	experimental design, observation, question, hypothesis, prediction, experiment, data, analyze, conclusion, descriptive design, correlational design, nectar, relationships	The scientist **saw/ noticed/ observed** the foods birds eat.	Word Parts: analyze Word Families: conclusion, conclude	Observing and Describing Finding Relationships Experimenting	Analyzing Information Hypothesizing	Looking at Relationships	Systems, order, and organization; Evidence, models, and explanation; Abilities necessary to do scientific inquiry; Understandings about scientific inquiry; Science and technology in society; Science as a human endeavor; Nature of science.
Science Tools	graduated cylinder, beaker, balance, test tube, petri dish, computer, anemometer, thermometer, microscope, telescope volume, meniscus, glass slide, stage, objective lens, eyepiece lens, coarse adjustment, medium power lens, high power lens, fine adjustment, satellites, GOES, geostationary	The lenses of a microscope **enlarge/ magnify** an object.	Word Parts: meter Word Origins: microscope, telescope	Finding Volume by Displacement A Compound Microscope GOES Weather Satellite	Making Inferences Applying Information	Reading Volume on a Graduated Cylinder	Change, constancy, and measurement; Abilities necessary to do scientific inquiry; Nature of science.
Metric Units of Measurement	milliliter (mL), liter (L), meter (m), centimeter (cm), millimeter (mm), kilometer (km), cubic centimeter (cm³), kilogram (kg), gram (g), degree Celsius (C) metric system, mass, length, volume, thermometer, temperature	The number 0.4 is **four tenths.** The number 200 is **two hundred.** The number .02 is **two hundredths.** The number 3,000 is **three thousand.** The number 0.003 is **three thousandths.**	Prefixes: kilo, deci, centi, milli Word Origins: thermometer	The Metric System Temperature Scales	Classifying Information Analyzing Information	Comparing and Contrasting	Systems, order, and organization; Change, constancy, and measurement; Abilities necessary to do scientific inquiry; Understandings about scientific inquiry; Nature of science; History of science.
Data Analysis	line graph, pie chart, bar graph, data table, flow chart, Venn diagram, map, map key organize, compare, title, rows, columns, earthworms, volume, percentages	A line graph **shows** relationships between numbers. A pie chart **is used** to compare the parts with the whole.	Multiple-Meaning Words: table	Understanding Tables Understanding Graphs Understanding Pie Charts	Comparing and Contrasting Applying Information	Organizing Data	Evidence, models, and explanation; Change, constancy, and measurement; Abilities necessary to do scientific inquiry; Nature of science.
Safety in the Lab	goggles, lab apron, gloves, soap and water, fire extinguisher, fire alarm, first aid kit	You can **avoid/ prevent** problems by following safety rules.	Syllabification: extinguisher Word Origins: experiment	Staying Safe Responding to Accidents Treatment of Living Things	Looking for Patterns Making Observations	Reading Safety Signs and Warnings	Abilities necessary to do scientific inquiry; Understandings about scientific inquiry.

Lesson Title	Science Vocabulary	Academic Vocabulary	Word Study	Concepts	Critical Thinking	Science Skill	National Science Education Standards
The Cell	cell, cytoplasm, cell membrane, chloroplast, vacuole, nucleus, endoplasmic reticulum, ribosome, Golgi complex, lysosome, mitochondria, cell wall organelles, microscope, bacteria	The cell membrane **controls/ is in charge of** motion in or out of the cell.	Multiple-Meaning Words: cell Word Origins: chloroplast	What Do Organelles Do? Robert Hooke Sees Cells Bacteria Cells	Making Inferences Integrating Information	Reading a Table	Systems, order, and organization; Evidence, models, and explanation; Form and function; Structure and function in living systems; Diversity and adaptation of organisms.
Single-Celled Organisms	pseudopod, amoeba, paramecium, cilia, protozoans, trichonympha, algae, dinoflagellate, flagella, fungus, yeast, bacteria chloroplasts, euglena, energy, trypanosome, sunlight, crust, tube worms	Protozoans **get/ obtain/ acquire** food by eating other cells.	Word Origins: pseudopod Irregular Plurals: bacteria	Kinds of Single-Celled Organisms Getting Energy Extreme Conditions for Life	Making Inferences Comparing and Contrasting	Comparing and Contrasting	Systems, order, and organization; Evidence, models, and explanation; Form and function; Structure and function in living systems; Populations and ecosystems; Diversity and adaptation of organisms.
Multicellular Organisms	cell, tissue, organ, organ system red blood cells, gases, white blood cells, cell division, chromosomes	Tissues **contain** many like cells. Organs **are made up of** different kinds of cells.	Word Parts: multicellular Phrasal Verbs: move away from	Kinds of Animal Cells How Cells Divide	Comparing and Contrasting Applying Information	Looking for Details	Systems, order, and organization; Form and function; Structure and function in living systems; Personal health.
Plants	flower, sunlight, stem, leaf, soil, root, cone, fruit, seed, spores rock, humus, nutrients, minerals, clay, sandy, loam, nitrogen, chemicals, digest	Rocks in soil **provide/ supply** plants with minerals.	Irregular Plurals: leaves Noncount Nouns: air, water, sunlight	Plant Parts What Is Soil? The Venus Flytrap	Analyzing Evidence Comparing and Contrasting	Reading Bar Graphs	Systems, order, and organization; Evidence, models, and explanation; Form and function; Structure and function in living systems; Populations and ecosystems; Diversity and adaptations of organisms; Populations, resources, and environments.
Kinds of Plants	vascular plants, ferns, flowering plants, conifers, cones, xylem, phloem, seeds, nonvascular plants, mosses, liverwort, leaves, stem, roots stamens, pistils, anther, pollen, pollination, ovule, fertilizes, spores, germinate, seedling	Ferns share **traits/ features/ characteristics** with both mosses and seed plants.	Word Parts: conifer Suffixes: -less	Flowering Plants What Is a Fern? How a Seed Works	Making Inferences Comparing and Contrasting	Reading Steps in a Sequence	Systems, order, and organization; Evidence, models, and explanation; Form and function; Structure and function in living systems; Diversity and adaptation of organisms.
Photosynthesis	sunlight, green plant, roots, leaves, chlorophyll, chloroplast, stems, photosynthesis, soil, guard cells, stomata, xylem, phloem carbon dioxide, glucose, oxygen, annual rings	Plants **produce** oxygen in photosynthesis. They **release** the oxygen as a waste product.	Word Origins: photosynthesis Multiple-Meaning Words: tissue	Photosynthesis Transport in a Plant Annual Tree Rings	Making Inferences Applying Information	Interpreting a Diagram	Systems, order, and organization; Evidence, models, and explanation; Form and function; Structure and function in living systems.

Life Science

Lesson Title	Science Vocabulary	Academic Vocabulary	Word Study	Concepts	Critical Thinking	Science Skill	National Science Education Standards
Life Science — Animals	backbone, air, water, octopus, shark, turtle, crab, duck, frog, grosbeak, nest, raccoon, shelter, deer, food worms, sponges, jellyfish, insects, birds, fish, reptiles, mammals, cells, senses, reproduce, brain, suckers, shellfish, funnel	An octopus **needs/ requires** food, air, water, and shelter.	Word Origins: animal Word Origins: octopus	Kinds of Animals What Is an Animal? The Amazing Octopus	Comparing and Contrasting Making Inferences	Reading a Pie Chart	Systems, order, and organization; Form and function; Structure and function in living systems; Diversity and adaptation of organisms; Populations, resources, and environments.
Invertebrates	backbone, invertebrates, basket sponge, jellyfish, tapeworm, heartworm, earthworm, beetle, centipede, spider, clam, shell, scallop, lobster, sea star arachnids, molting, metamorphosis, insects, caterpillar, chrysalis, pores	Caterpillars **develop into/ become/ change into** butterflies.	Multiple-Meaning Words: sponge Multiple-Meaning Words: stage	Arachnids Metamorphosis How Sponges Work	Integrating Information Making Observations	Reading a Cycle Diagram	Systems, order, and organization; Evidence, models, and explanation; Form and function; Structure and function in living systems; Diversity and adaptation of organisms; Populations, resources, and environments.
Vertebrates	backbone, vertebrates, fish, trout, seahorse, amphibians, frog, salamander, reptiles, crocodile, snake, birds, flamingo, penguin, mammals, bear, human warm-blooded, cold-blooded	Seahorses **belong to/ are part of/ are members of** the fish group of vertebrates.	Word Origins: amphibian Compound Words: warm-blooded, newborn	Warm-blooded and Cold-blooded Vertebrates Kangaroos Are Mammals with Pouches	Classifying Information Analyzing Information	Comparing and Contrasting	Systems, order, and organization; Evidence, models, and explanation; Form and function; Structure and function in living systems; Diversity and adaptation of organisms.
The Human Body	bones, muscles, blood vessels, heart, kidney, liver, stomach, intestines, brain, lungs, skin organ systems, energy	The excretory system **controls/ is responsible for/ is in charge of** removing wastes.	Word Meanings: heart Word Families: circular, circulate, circulation	Organ Systems The Circulatory System	Making Inferences Comparing and Contrasting	Concept Maps	Systems, order, and organization; Evidence, models, and explanation; Form and function; Structure and function in living systems; Personal health.
Asexual Reproduction	asexual reproduction, cell division/ mitosis, parent cell, nucleus, daughter cells, chromosome, leaf, stem, root, vegetative reproduction, bulb bacteria, amoebas, yeast, prophase, metaphase, anaphase, telophase, runners	Cellular reproduction occurs in a **series/ sequence** of stages.	Word Parts: reproduction Word Parts: prophase, metaphase, anaphase, telophase	Bacteria Reproduction Mitosis Vegetative Reproduction	Inferring from Evidence Analyzing Information	Looking for Patterns	Form and function; Evidence, models, and explanation; Structure and function in living things; Reproduction and heredity; Personal health.

Lesson Title	Science Vocabulary	Academic Vocabulary	Word Study	Concepts	Critical Thinking	Science Skill	National Science Education Standards
Sexual Reproduction	sexual reproduction, parent cell, chromosome, meiosis, cell division, daughter cells, sex cells process, crossing over, sperm, variations	**First**, matching chromosomes come close to one another. **Then**, crossing over can occur. **Finally**, two daughter cells form.	Prefixes: *a-*; Two-Word Verbs: line up	Meiosis and Sex Cells; Variations	Making Inferences	Reading a Flowchart	Systems, order, and organization; Evidence, models, and explanation; Form and function; Structure and function in living systems; Reproduction and heredity; Personal health.
Genetics	chromosome, gene, thymine, cytosine, adenine, guanine, trait, DNA, double helix; offspring, inherit, dominant, recessive, Punnett square	A dominant gene **controls/ is responsible for** tongue rolling.	Multiple-Meaning Words: base; Antonyms: dominant, recessive	Dominant and Recessive Traits; Punnett Squares	Inferring from Evidence; Applying Information	Reading a Punnett Square	Systems, order, and organization; Evidence, models, and explanation; Evolution and equilibrium; Reproduction and heredity; Diversity and adaptations of organisms.
Changes Over Time	organism, adaptation, beak, species, common ancestor, subspecies, variation, fossil; evolution, base, extinct, natural selection	Variations **happen/ develop/ occur** over time.	Suffixes: *-tion*; Multiple-Meaning Words: theory	The Theory of Evolution; Natural Selection	Interpreting Information; Recognizing Evidence	Reading a Tree Diagram	Systems, order, and organization; Evidence, models, and explanation; Evolution and equilibrium; Form and function; Understandings about scientific inquiry; Structure and function in living systems; Reproduction and heredity; Diversity and adaptations of organisms; Populations, resources, and environments; Nature of science.
Classification Systems	six kingdoms, eubacteria kingdom, bacteria, cyanobacteria, archeobacteria kingdom, halophiles, methanogens, protist kingdom, seaweed, protozoan, fungi kingdom, mushrooms, mold, plant kingdom, fern, pine tree, animal kingdom, worm, dog; phylum, class, order, family, genus, species, DNA, binomial nomenclature	A pine tree **belongs to/ is a member of/ is part of** the plant kingdom.	Multiple-Meaning Words: mushroom; Synonyms: alike, like, similar	Levels of Classification; Using DNA to Classify; Two-part Names	Comparing and Contrasting; Interpreting Information	Reading a Diagram	Systems, order, and organization; Heredity; Diversity of organisms.

Life Science

Life Science

Lesson Title	Science Vocabulary	Academic Vocabulary	Word Study	Concepts	Critical Thinking	Science Skill	National Science Education Standards
Biomes and Ecosystems	ecosystems, biomes, tundra, taiga, deciduous forest, rain forest, grassland, desert, community, population, species, ecological succession, temperature, rainfall, adapted, climate, habitat, kangaroo rats	Lizards and cactus plants are **equipped/ adapted** to live in deserts.	Word Origins: *deciduous* Word Origins: *ecosystem*	Ecological Succession Desert Biomes The Kangaroo Rat's Ecosystem	Applying Information Analyzing Evidence	Reading a Timeline	Systems, order, and organization; Evidence, models, and explanation; Evolution and equilibrium; Population and ecosystems; Diversity and adaptations of organisms; Populations, resources, and environments.
Energy Transfer in Living Things	consumer, producer, food chain, carnivore, food, herbivore, decomposer, food web, energy pyramid, heat, symbiosis, mutualism, commensalism, parasitism, host, intestines, predator, prey, hunt	Not all energy **moves to/ transfers to** the next level in a pyramid.	Word Origins: *carnivore, herbivore* Word Families: *-sis* and *-tic*	An Energy Pyramid Symbiosis Predators and Their Prey	Analyzing Evidence Applying Information	Interpreting an Illustration	Systems, order, and organization; Evidence, models, and explanation; Population and ecosystems; Populations, resources, and environments.
Cycles in Nature	evaporation, condensation, precipitation, runoff, groundwater, cycle, water, cloud, rain, snow nitrogen, bacteria, transpiration	Living things **give off/ release/ discharge** gases during the oxygen-carbon dioxide cycle.	Suffixes: *-ation* Nouns Used as Verbs: *cycle*	The Nitrogen Cycle The Oxygen/ Carbon Dioxide Cycle Plants in the Water Cycle	Making Inferences Thinking About Systems	Reading a Model	Systems, order, and organization; Evidence, models, and explanation; Form and function; Structure of the earth system; Populations, resources, and environments.
Responding to the Environment	migration, stimulus, response, estivation, hibernation, phototropism, gravitropism, behavior, reflex, learned behavior, instincts	Plants **respond/ react** to a source light.	Irregular Plurals: *stimuli* Word Parts: *phototropism*	Plant Responses Watching Plants Move Behavior by Instinct	Making Observations Intergrating Information	Interpreting Time-Lapse Photos	Systems, order, and organization; Regulation and behavior; Populations and ecosystems; Diversity and adaptation of organisms; Populations, resources, and environments.
Conservation	extinct species, dodo, dinosaur, seed fern, mammoth, quagga, endangered species, humpback whale, black rhino, whooping crane, mountain gorilla, giant panda, Siberian tiger, hedgehog cactus species, subspecies, habitat, medicines, rain forests, pollution	Pollution **caused** weak eggshells. Weak shells **resulted** in broken eggs.	Prefixes: *en-* Irregular Plurals: *species*	Tigers in Danger Saving Rain Forest Plants Bald Eagles Recover	Recognizing Cause and Effect Making Inferences	Reading a Map	Systems, order, and organization; Populations and ecosystems; Populations, resources, and environments.

	Lesson Title	Science Vocabulary	Academic Vocabulary	Word Study	Concepts	Critical Thinking	Science Skill	National Science Education Standards
Earth Science	**Space**	space, star, galaxy, solar system, planets, telescope, radio telescope astronomical units (AU), light-years, spiral, radio waves	The arms **contain/ consist of** stars, gases, and dust.	Multiple-Meaning Words: space Word Parts: telescope	Distances in Space The Milky Way Galaxy Telescopes	Comparing and Contrasting Applying Information	Reading Numbers in a Table	Systems, order, and organization; Evidence, models, and explanation; Earth in the solar system.
	Stars	nebula, star, main sequence star, red giant, supergiant, white dwarf, supernova, neutron star, black hole, constellations, sun magnitude, temperature	The H-R diagram **groups/ classifies/ arranges** stars by magnitude and temperature.	Antonyms: dwarf, giant Word Parts: magnitude	Star Magnitude The Hertzsprung-Russell Diagram Pictures in the Sky: Constellations	Comparing and Contrasting Applying Information	Reading a Diagram	Systems, order, and organization; Evidence, models, and explanation; Form and function; Earth in the solar system.
	Our Solar System	dwarf planet, orbit, moon, comet, sun, asteroid, meteoroid, Neptune, Uranus, Saturn, Jupiter, Mars, Earth, Venus, Mercury Great Red Spot, moons, Halley's comet	The moons **move around/ revolve around** Jupiter.	Word Origins: orbit Synonyms: detect, discover	Jupiter and Its Moons A Famous Comet Dwarf Planets	Comparing and Contrasting Making a Prediction	Interpreting an Illustration	Systems, order, and organization; Evidence, models, and explanation; Earth in the solar system.
	Earth, the Moon, and the Sun	sun, seasons, day, night, revolve, tilt, Earth, rotation, spin, rotate, axis, moon, orbit phases	The sun **seems/ appears** to move across the sky during the day.	Word Families: rotate, rotation Synonyms: revolve, orbit	Length of Day and Night Summer and Winter Seasons Phases of the Moon	Applying Information Making Inferences	Making Observations	Systems, order, and organization; Evidence, models, and explanation; Earth in the solar system.
	Eclipses and Tides	tides, eclipse, high tide, low tide, solar eclipse, partial eclipse, lunar eclipse, shadow, total eclipse tidal range, gravity, spring tide, neap tide	Earth's shadow **causes/ results in** a lunar eclipse.	Word Families: eclipse Word Origins: solar, lunar	High and Low Tides Total and Partial Eclipses How the Sun Affects Tides	Comparing and Contrasting Recognizing Cause and Effect	Contrasting Photos	Systems, order, and organization; Evidence, models, and explanation; Earth in the solar system.
	Space Exploration	space probe, satellite, space station, space shuttle, external fuel tank, booster rocket, spacecraft, launchpad, astronaut, space suit lunar module, command module	The space shuttle **carried/ transported** scientists into space.	Compound Words: space shuttle, space station, space suit, space probe Word Origins: astronaut	Early Space Exploration Walking on the Moon International Space Station	Comparing and Contrasting Integrating Information	Reading a Time Line	Systems, order, and organization; Evidence, models, and explanation; Earth in the solar system; Understandings about science and technology.

Earth Science

Lesson Title	Science Vocabulary	Academic Vocabulary	Word Study	Concepts	Critical Thinking	Science Skill	National Science Education Standards
Minerals and Rocks	minerals, feldspar, crystals, quartz, diamond, press together, rocks, igneous rocks, granite, basalt, sedimentary rocks, limestone, sandstone, layers, fossil, metamorphic rocks, marble, slate volcanoes, weathering, sediment, erosion	Heat and pressure can **change/ transform** rock.	Multiple-Meaning Words: rock Related words: hard/harden, press/pressure	Classifying Rocks The Rock Cycle	Making Observations Hypothesizing	Interpreting a Rock Cycle Diagram	Systems, order, and organization; Evidence, models, and explanation; Change, constancy, and measurement; Structure of the Earth system; Earth's history.
Earth's Structure	plates, plate boundaries, continent, fossil, crust, upper mantle, lower mantle, outer core, inner core Pangaea, continental drift, seafloor spreading, magma, oceanic ridge, plate tectonics, plate boundary	The mantle is the layer of Earth just **under/ below/ beneath** the crust.	Multiple-Meaning Words: plate Word Origins: tectonics	Continental Drift Seafloor Spreading Plate Tectonics	Comparing and Contrasting Applying Information	Reading a Map	Systems, order, and organization; Evidence, models, and explanation; Change, constancy, and measurement; Structure of the Earth system; Earth's history; Natural hazards.
Earth's Surface	plain, mesa, canyon, mountain, lake, oceans, delta, rivers, continents salt water, fresh water, groundwater, atmosphere, glaciers, landforms, hills	Soil and gravel **accumulate/ build up** to form a delta.	Superlative Adjectives: the highest, the most famous Word History: delta	Water on Earth Earth's Landforms Fresh Water Meets Salt Water	Interpreting Information Hypothesizing	Reading a Topographic Map	Systems, order, and organization; Evidence, models, and explanation; Change, constancy, and measurement; Structure of the Earth system.
Earthquakes and Volcanoes	plates, earthquakes, seismic waves, epicenter, focus, fault, tsunami, volcano, lava, eruption, magma, vent, crater plate boundaries, diverge, converge, waves, tsunami	Earthquakes form where plates **diverge** (pull apart). **converge** (come together).	Multiple-Meaning Words: fault Word Origins: tsunami	Where Do Earthquakes Happen? Surface Waves and Tsunamis Where Do Volcanoes Form?	Making Inferences Making Observations	Interpreting a Drawing	Systems, order, and organization; Evidence, models, and explanation; Change, constancy, and measurement; Structure of the Earth system; Earth's history; Natural hazards.
Our Changing Earth	erosion, soil, glacier, sand, weathering, abrasion, ice wedging, deposition, sand dune, moraine, delta mechanical weathering, chemical weathering, react	Weathering **happens/ occurs** when rock is broken down.	Suffixes: -tion or -sion Multiple-Meaning Words: deposit	Weathering Glaciers Erosion and Deposition	Analyzing Evidence Looking for Patterns	Recognizing Cause and Effect	Systems, order, and organization; Evidence, models, and explanation; Change, constancy, and measurement; Structure of the Earth system; Earth's history.
The Atmosphere	cloud, air, atmosphere, fog, pollution, water vapor, gas, particles, rain, wind oxygen, nitrogen, trace gases, carbon dioxide, layers, troposphere, exosphere	The atmosphere **is made of/ is composed of/ consists of** several gases.	Multiple-Meaning Words: gas Word Origins: atmosphere	Gases in the Atmosphere The Oxygen-Carbon Dioxide Cycle Layers of the Atmosphere	Applying Information Making Inferences	Reading a Pie Chart	Systems, order, and organization; Evidence, models, and explanation; Change, constancy, and measurement; Structure of the Earth system.

Lesson Title	Science Vocabulary	Academic Vocabulary	Word Study	Concepts	Critical Thinking	Science Skill	National Science Education Standards
Earth Science							
Weather and Climate	clouds, precipitation, rain, snow, hail, wind, fog, water vapor, air mass, cold front, warm front, weather map, temperature atmospheric pressure, isobars, dust, salt, gravity, climate, temperature, tropical, subtropical, polar	Some maps **show/ display** temperatures.	Multiple-Meaning Words: weather Word Origins: isobar	Weather Maps How Do Clouds and Rain Form? Weather and Climate	Looking for Patterns Interpreting Information	Reading a Weather Map	Systems, order, and organization; Evidence, models, and explanation; Change, constancy, and measurement; Structure of the Earth system.
Extreme Weather	thunderstorm, lightning, updraft, water vapor, downdraft, hail, waterspout, flood, tornado, rotation, hurricane, eye wall cloud, funnel, tropical disturbance, tropical depression, tropical storm, storm surges, watches, warnings	A watch **means/ indicates** that severe weather is possible.	Synonyms: hurricane, cyclone, typhoon Modal verbs: might	How Tornadoes Form Stages of a Hurricane Watches and Warnings	Comparing and Contrasting Analyzing Information	Interpreting a Model	Systems, order, and organization; Evidence, models, and explanation; Structure of the Earth system; Natural hazards.
Natural Resources	water energy, wind energy, geothermal energy, nuclear energy, solar energy, recycle, fossil fuels, natural gas, coal, petroleum, minerals renewable resources, biomass, nonrenewable resources, reduce, reuse	People **use/ consume** natural resources.	Word Origins: geothermal Prefixes: re	Renewable and Nonrenewable Resources Recycle, Reduce, and Reuse Wind Farms	Analyzing Information Comparing and Contrasting	Using Percentages	Systems, order, and organization; Evidence, models, and explanation; Change, constancy, and measurement; Structure of the Earth system; Populations and ecosystems; Populations, resources, and environments.
Physical Science							
Nature of Matter	senses, color, odor, taste, texture, chemical changes, burn, rust, states, gas, solid, liquid states, particles, volume, physical properties, chemical properties	You can **recognize/ identify** an object by its properties.	Multiple-Meaning Words: property Word Families: taste	States of Matter Observing Matter Physical and Chemical Properties	Analyzing Information Interpreting Information	Interpreting an Illustration	Systems, order, and organization; Properties and changes of properties in matter.
Measuring Matter	balance, mass, graduated cylinder, volume, melting point, freezing point, gas, thermometer, boiling point, liquid, solid, sink, float buoyant force, force of gravity, density	At its melting point, ice **changes to/ becomes** water.	Multiple-Meaning Words: volume Frequently Misused Words: mass, weight	Changes of State Buoyancy Mass, Volume, and Density	Applying Information Analyzing Evidence	Using Numbers to Compare	Systems, order, and organization; Change, constancy, and measurement; Abilities necessary to do scientific inquiry; Understandings about scientific inquiry; Properties and changes of properties in matter; Nature of science; History of science.
Atoms and Molecules	atom, electron, nucleus, proton, neutron, molecule, element, metal, gold, silver, nonmetal, oxygen, carbon nucleus, properties, liquid, gases, periodic table, symbol, atomic number	When two atoms **join together/ combine** they form a molecule.	Word History: names of elements Word History: symbols of elements	Structure of an Atom Molecules The Periodic Table of Elements	Visualizing Looking for Patterns	Interpreting a Diagram	Systems, order, and organization; Evidence, models, and explanation; Properties and changes of properties in matter.

Lesson Title	Science Vocabulary	Academic Vocabulary	Word Study	Concepts	Critical Thinking	Science Skill	National Science Education Standards
Compounds and Mixtures	pure substances, elements, oxygen, aluminum, compounds, water, sugar, mixtures, heterogeneous mixture, granite, homogenous mixture, air carbon dioxide, sodium, chlorine, suspension, solution, dissolves, physical changes, chemical change	Elements join to **make/ form/ produce** compounds.	Multiple-Meaning Words: solution Prefixes: *hetero*	Common Compounds Types of Mixtures Physical and Chemical Changes	Applying Information Making Inferences	Comparing and Contrasting	Systems, order, and organization; Change, constancy, and measurement; Properties and changes of properties in matter.
Chemical Reactions	equation, symbol, formula, element, burn, rust, compound, molecule, bond, atom, electron exothermic, endothermic, law of conservation of mass	Chemical equations **tell/ communicate/ express** what happens during a chemical reaction.	Multiple-Meaning Words: equation Word Origins: endothermic, exothermic	Chemical Bonds Chemical Equations Conservation of Mass	Looking for Patterns Applying Information	Reading an Equation	Systems, order, and organization; Evidence, models, and explanation; Change, constancy, and measurement; Properties and changes of properties in matter.
Radiation and Radioactivity	radioactive sample, radiation, radioactive symbol, alpha particles, beta particles, gamma rays, paper, aluminum, concrete, atom, nucleus uranium, decay, protons, neutrons, electron, half-life, X-rays, cancer, surgery	An atom decays when it **gives off/ releases/ emits** particles or energy.	Multiple-Meaning Words: particle Suffixes: *tion*	Discovery of Radioactivity Radioactive Decay Uses of Radiation	Making Inferences Applying Information	Comparing Data	Change, constancy, and measurement; Properties and changes of properties in matter; Transfer of energy; Understandings about scientific inquiry; Understandings about science and technology; Personal health; Natural hazards; Science and technology in society; History of science.
Forces	balanced, unbalanced, friction, push, pull, move, stop, gravity attraction, mass, weight, equilibrium	Friction **works against/ opposes** motion.	Multiple-Meaning Words: force Antonyms: push, pull; move, stop	Gravity Friction Balanced and Unbalanced Forces	Applying Information Inferring from Evidence	Using Numbers to Compare	Systems, order, and organization; Evidence, models, and explanation; Change, constancy, and measurement; Equilibrium; Motions and forces.
Forces and Motion	velocity, mass, force, speed, acceleration, action force, reaction force inertia, friction, meters per second (m/s), m/s per second (m/s/s), equal, opposite	Forces can **change/ affect** an object's motion.	Related Meanings: velocity, speed, acceleration Prefixes: *re*	Newton's First Law Newton's Second Law Newton's Third Law	Analyzing Information Applying Information	Using Math to Solve Problems	Systems, order, and organization; Evidence, models, and explanation; Change, constancy, and measurement; Equilibrium; Motions and forces.
Work, Power, and Machines	load, simple machines, lever, inclined plane, wedge, screw, pulley, wheel and axle, fulcrum work, effort force, compound machines	Machines reduce the force you **use/ apply/ exert** to do work.	Homonyms: plane, plain Multiple-Meaning Words: work	Force and Distance The Wedge Compound Machines	Applying Information Drawing Conclusions	Interpreting a Simple Machine Diagram	Systems, order, and organization; Evidence, models, and explanation; Change, constancy, and measurement; Equilibrium; Motions and forces.

Physical Science

Physical Science

Lesson Title	Science Vocabulary	Academic Vocabulary	Word Study	Concepts	Critical Thinking	Science Skill	National Science Education Standards
Waves	waves, transverse waves, crest, trough, wavelength, amplitude, water waves, longitudinal waves, sound waves, compression, rarefaction matter, medium, X-rays, radio waves, electromagnetic waves, electromagnetic spectrum	Light waves can **move/ travel** through empty space.	Multiple-Meaning Words: wave Multiple-Meaning Words: medium	Longitudinal and Transverse Waves Electromagnetic Spectrum Uses of Electromagnetic Waves	Making Inferences Comparing and Contrasting	Interpreting a Model	Systems, order, and organization; Evidence, models, and explanation; Change, constancy, and measurement; Equilibrium; Motions and forces.
Light	transparent, translucent, opaque, light source, stars, sun, natural light, candle, lamp, artificial light, reflect, refract, absorb, prism, colors	A prism **divides/ separates** light into different colors.	Multiple-Meaning Words: reflect Antonyms: reflect, absorb, natural, artificial	Reflection and Refraction Seeing Colors Transparent, Translucent, or Opaque	Making Observations Classifying Information	Interpreting Photos	Systems, order, and organization; Evidence, models, and explanation; Change, constancy, and measurement; Transfer of energy.
Forms of Energy	renewable energy, nonrenewable energy, sound energy, thermal energy, light energy, chemical energy, electrical energy, mechanical energy, potential energy, kinetic energy replace, hydropower, fossil fuels, vibrates, molecules	You can **classify/ group** energy and energy sources different ways.	Word Families: heat Prefixes: re-	Potential and Kinetic Energy Renewable and Nonrenewable Energy Sound Energy	Making Inferences Applying Information	Visualizing	Systems, order, and organization; Evidence, models, and explanation; Change, constancy, and measurement; Transfer of energy.
Energy Transformations	thermal energy, sound energy, electrical energy, chemical energy, heat, potential energy, kinetic energy, light energy, temperature conduction, convection, radiation, law of conservation of energy	A toaster **changes/ converts/ transforms** electrical energy into thermal energy.	Suffixes: -ation Word Origins: transfer	Heat and Temperature Heating Matter Conservation of Energy	Applying Information Inferring from Evidence	Thinking about Systems	Systems, order, and organization; Evidence, models, and explanation; Change, constancy, and measurement; Equilibrium; Motions and forces.
Energy and Life	leaf, sun, light energy, chemical energy, photosynthesis, cellular respiration, chloroplast, chlorophyll glucose, mitochondria	The sun **provides/ supplies** energy that living things need.	Syllabification: photosynthesis, respiration Word Origins: chlorophyll	Living Things Use the Sun's Energy Photosynthesis Cellular Respiration	Making Inferences	Making Observations	Systems, order, and organization; Transfer of energy; Structure and function in living systems; Regulation and behavior.
Electricity and Magnetism	static electricity, charge, electron, conductor, insulator, electromagnet, magnetic poles, magnet, magnetic field, electric generator, electric current, circuit current electricity, energy source, battery, flashlight, wire, lightbulb, switch, copper wire, insulator	The metal wire is **covered by/ enclosed in** plastic.	Multiple-Meaning Words: positive, negative Multiple-Meaning Words: conductor	Static and Current Electricity Circuits Conductors and Insulators	Understanding Cause and Effect Integrating Information	Reading a Circuit Diagram	Systems, order, and organization; Evidence, models, and explanation; Change, constancy, and measurement; Transfer of energy; Abilities of technological design; Understandings about science and technology.

Scientifically Based Research in *Gateway to Science*

The National Center for Educational Statistics (NCES) states that between 1979 and 2004 the number of students aged 5 to 7 who are English Language Learners (ELLs) grew from 3.8 million to 9.9 million, or from 9% to 19% of all school aged children (2006a). Over the same 25 year period the school aged population (ages 5 to 17) increased 18%; however, the ELL student population grew 162%. The number of school-age children who spoke English with difficulty also increased from 1.3 million to 2.8 million (or 5 percent) over the same time period. In the 2003–2004 school year, English language services were provided to 3.8 million students representing 11% of all students (NCES 2006b). At the same time, state and federal legislation require schools to ensure that all students meet grade-level content standards and to place ELLs in mainstream classes on very short timelines. The content, instructional design, and accompanying ancillary materials for *Gateway to Science* are designed to help schools and teachers reach this growing population.

Standards-Based Content

In order to ensure learners achieve grade-level science standards and to prepare them for mainstream classes and textbooks, *Gateway to Science* is based upon the National Science Education Standards and is compatible with science standards for ELLs issued by TESOL and by the WIDA Consortium.

Research-Based Instructional Design

The instructional design of *Gateway to Science* is based upon the most recent scientifically based research, as well as time-tested strategies and methods for teaching and learning content and language. These are outlined below.

Content-Matter Learning

Schleppegrell (2004) identifies the challenges ELLs experience when facing science content. Volumes such as Echevarria, Vogt, & Short (2004), Reiss (2005), and Ulh Chamot & O'Malley (1994) summarize copious scientifically based research that supports the scaffolding and language development approach used in *Gateway to Science*. *Gateway to Science*, therefore, is fully compatible with approaches such as SIOP (Sheltered Instruction Observation Protocol) and CALLA (Cognitive Academic Language Learning Approach). Studies such as Fathman & Crowther (2006) and Carr, Sexton & Lagunoff (2006) present extensive scientifically based research specifically related to science for ELLs. These studies demonstrate that for students to be able to read and comprehend content science, they need activation of prior knowledge (see the Focus Question at the beginning of each lesson and the Teacher Edition); development of content vocabulary (see the first two pages of each lesson) and academic vocabulary (see the Academic Vocabulary section in each lesson); development of graphic literacy (see the numerous charts, tables and graphs in the Science Skills section in each lesson), hands-on active learning techniques (see the lab in each Workbook lesson and the activities in the Teacher Edition); and a variety of means to build and check comprehension (see the Check Your Understanding sections in each lesson) found in *Gateway to Science*.

Vocabulary Development

Numerous studies detail the importance of vocabulary in reading and success in school, and provide research-based evidence in support of the use of the visual approach employed in *Gateway to Science* to develop learners' vocabulary. Carlo, et al. (2004) and Blachowicz & Fischer (2000) make clear cases for the relationship between vocabulary development and reading success. Kinsella (2004) strongly recommends the practice of developing key vocabulary prior to reading, and calls this process "frontloading" or "preloading" vocabulary. Blachowicz & Fischer (2000), Decarrico (2001) and Stockdale (2004) all provide evidence in support of the approach in *Gateway to Science* of presenting both labeled pictures as well as illustrations of concepts accompanied by prose explanation of them, so that students can learn both the meaning of the new terms and how they are used in context (see the vocabulary list, illustrations, and Vocabulary in Context sections in the first two pages of each lesson).

Carlo, et al. (2004) provides empirical evidence that ELLs reading comprehension benefits from systematic instruction in the vocabulary and vocabulary-related skills (deriving meaning from context, using word parts) presented in *Gateway to Science* (see the Word Study sections in each lesson). Volumes such as Marzano & Pickering (2005) and studies such as Coxhead (2000) stress the importance of developing students' academic vocabulary and provide criteria on selecting appropriate lexical items (see the Academic Vocabulary section in each lesson).

Nation (2001) and Nation (2005) give support for the variety of vocabulary development activities included in the Teacher Edition and Workbook.

Best Practices in Teaching English Language Learners

Gateway to Science is compatible with Best Practices for Teaching ELLs recommended in studies such as Echevarria, Vogt, & Short (2004), Fathman & Crowther (2006), Carr, Sexton & Lagunoff (2006), Crowther, Robinson, Edmondson (in press), Douglas, Klentschy, Watts and Binder (2006). These best practices include:

- Providing clear science and language objectives (see the Teacher Edition).

- Building on students' prior knowledge (see the Focus Question in each lesson and the Set the Stage activity in the Teacher Edition).

- Using hands-on inquiry and activities (see the Research and Inquiry questions in each lesson, the labs in each Workbook lesson).

- Introducing key vocabulary in context (see the Vocabulary in Context section in each lesson).

- Providing scaffolding for learning complex content and vocabulary (see the progression from vocabulary in the first two pages in each lesson to the concepts in the second two pages in each lesson).

- Developing key science concepts (see the second two pages in each lesson).

- Building knowledge based upon big ideas (see the Focus Question at the beginning of each lesson).

- Using cooperative groups (see activities in the Teacher's Edition).

- Assessing learning, including alternative, formative and summative assessment (see the *Assessment Book* and the *Teacher Resource CD-ROM with Exam-View® Pro*).

- Addressing the needs of different proficiency levels (see the Teacher's Edition).

- Integrating science and language instruction (see each lesson in *Gateway to Science*).

- Developing students' graphic literacy, science skills, vocabulary skills, and academic vocabulary (see the Science Skill, Word Study, and Academic Vocabulary sections in each lesson).

- Incorporating reading, writing, listening, speaking and critical thinking into every lesson (see the readings on the second spread of each lesson, the Audio selections for each lesson, activities in the Teacher Edition, the Critical Thinking questions in the Check Your Understanding sections in each lesson, and the Writing section in each lesson).

Because best practices for teaching English Language Learners parallel those for teaching inquiry-based science, *Gateway to Science* can be used in a variety of classroom settings and instructional models, including inquiry-based science classrooms; push-in, pull-out, or self-contained ESL classroom models; sheltered science classes; or team teaching situations. In addition, *Gateway to Science* is appropriate for students who are not reading at grade level or who have other special needs.

Finally, because science standards spiral from upper elementary school to middle school to high school, *Gateway to Science* may be used with English language learners at all levels who lack the prerequisite language or science skills to succeed in mainstream classrooms or textbooks.

Sources Consulted

Content-Matter Learning

Brinton, D., Snow, M., & Wesche, M. (1989). *Content-based second language instruction*. Boston: Heinle.

Case, R. (2002). The intersection of language, education, and content. The Clearing House. Nov./Dec. 2002.

Echevarria, J., Vogt, M., & Short, D. (2004). *Making content comprehensible for English learners: The SIOP model*. Boston: Pearson Allyn & Bacon.

Reiss, J. (2005). *Teaching content to English language learners*. White Plains, New York: Longman.

Richard-Amato, P. & Snow, M. (2005). *Academic success for English language learners: Strategies for K–12 mainstream teachers*. White Plains, New York: Longman.

Schleppegrell, M. J. (2004). *The Language of schooling: A functional linguistics perspective*. Mahwah, NJ: Erlbaum.

Uhl Chamot, A. & O'Malley, J. (1994). *The CALLA handbook*. White Plains, New York: Longman.

Content-Matter Learning in Science

Crowther, D., Robinson, M., Edmondson, A. & Colburn, A. (in Press). Preparing English language learners in the science classroom, in A. Kerson (Ed.) *Interdisciplinary language arts and science instruction in elementary classrooms: Applying research to practice*. Mahwah, NJ: Lawrence Erlbaum Press.

Carr, J.; Sexton, U.; & Lagunoff, R. (2006). *Making science accessible to English language learners: A guidebook for teachers*. San Francisco: West Ed.

Douglas, R.; Klentschy, M.; Worth, K.; & Binder, W. (2006). Linking science & literacy in the K–8 Classroom. Arlington, VA. NSTA Press.

Fathman, A. & Crowther, D. T. (2006). Science for English language learners: K–12 classroom strategies. Arlington, VA: NSTA Press.

Schleppegrell, M. (2002). Challenges of the science register for ESL students: Errors and meaning-making. In *Developing advanced literacy in first and second languages*, pp. 119–142. Mahwah, NJ: Lawrence Erlbaum Associates.

Hands-On Science

Amaral, O., Garrison, L., & Klentschy, M. (2002, Summer). Helping English learners increase achievement through inquiry-based science instruction. *Bilingual research journal, 26*, 213–239.

Population and Demographics

Kindler, A. (2002). *Survey of the states' limited English proficient students and available educational programs and services 2000–2001 summary report*. Washington, D.C.: NCELA.

NCES (2006a). *The Condition of Education 2006*. Retrieved online at: http://nces.ed.gov/programs/coe/2006/section1/indicator07.asp

NCES (2006b) *Public and Secondary Students, Staff, Schools, and School Districts: School Year 2003–2004*. Retrieved online at: http://nces.ed.gov/pubsearch/pubsinfo.asp?pubid=2006307

Vocabulary Development

Blachowicz, C.L.Z., & Fisher, P. (2000). Vocabulary instruction. In M.L. Kamil, P.B. Mosenthal, P.D. Pearson, & R. Barr (Eds.), *Handbook of reading research: Vol. 3* (pp. 503–523). Mahwah, NJ: Lawrence Erlbaum.

Carlo, M.S., August, D., McLaughlin, B., Snow, C.E., Dressler, C., Lippman, D.N., Lively, T.J., & White, C.E. (2004). Closing the Gap: Addressing the vocabulary needs of English-language learners in bilingual and mainstream classrooms. *Reading Research Quarterly, 39*(2), 188–215.

Coxhead, A. (2000). A new academic word list. TESOL Quarterly, 2, 213–238.

Decarrico, J. (2001). Vocabulary learning and teaching. In M. Celce-Murcia, *Teaching English as a second or foreign language*. 3rd ed. Boston: Heinle.

Jiang, N. (2004). Semantic transfer and its implications for vocabulary teaching in a second language. *The modern language journal, 88* (3), 416–431.

Kinsella, K. (2004). Vocabulary front-loading strategies to support diverse learners in content-area classrooms. Burlingame, CA: Best Practices for Teacher Leaders.

Lively, T.J., & White, C.E. (2004). Closing the gap: Addressing the vocabulary needs of English-language learners in bilingual and mainstream classrooms. *Reading Research Quarterly, 39*(2), 188–215. doi:10.1598/RRQ.39.2.3

www.reading.org/publications/journals/rrq/v39/i2/abstracts/RRQ-39-2-Carlo.html Marzano, R. & Pickering, D. (2005). Building academic vocabulary teachers' manual. Alexandria, Virginia: Association for Supervision and Curriculum Development.

Moudraia, O. (2001). The lexical approach to second language learning. ERIC Digest ED455698. Retrieved at www.ericdigests.org/2002-2/lexical.htm.

Nation, P. (2001). Learning vocabulary in another language. Cambridge, Cambridge University Press.

Nation, P. (Ed.) (2005). *New ways of teaching vocabulary*. Washington, DC: TESOL.

Stockdale, J. (2004). Definition plus collocation in language teaching and learning. *The internet TESOL journal*. May, 2004. Retreived at iteslj.org/Articles/Stockdale-Vocabulary.html.

— Tim Collins
Associate Professor, ESL
  and Bilingual Education
National College of Education
National-Louis University
Chicago, IL

— David T. Crowther
Associate Professor, Science
  Education
College of Education
University of Nevada
Reno, NV

Welcome to
GATEWAY TO SCIENCE

The **Focus Question** shows the main idea of the lesson. Use the question to focus your work during the lesson.

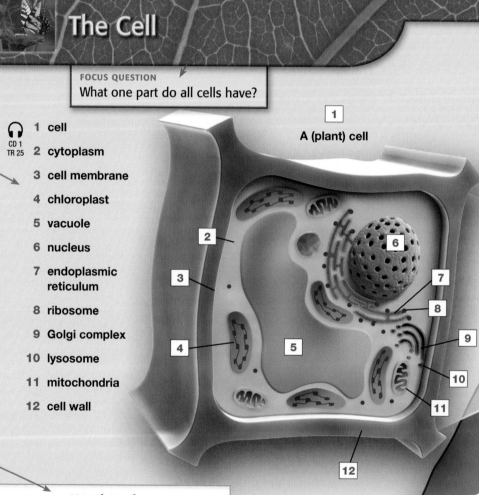

The Cell

FOCUS QUESTION
What one part do all cells have?

The **Vocabulary** list presents the most important words in the lesson. Use the list to learn key vocabulary.

CD 1
TR 25

1 cell
2 cytoplasm
3 cell membrane
4 chloroplast
5 vacuole
6 nucleus
7 endoplasmic reticulum
8 ribosome
9 Golgi complex
10 lysosome
11 mitochondria
12 cell wall

1
A (plant) cell

Word Study presents vocabulary skills. Use the Word Study box to build your vocabulary.

Word Study

Multiple-Meaning Words

The word **cell** has different meanings.

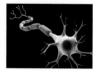

A **cell** is "a small room locked from the outside."

People in jail are kept in **cells.**

A **cell** is the "basic unit of living things."

Your body is made up of many **cells.**

⏵ For information on living things made of single cells, see pages 26–29.

22

Vocabulary in Context presents the new vocabulary in a short reading. Use the reading to help you understand the new vocabulary.

Vocabulary in Context 🎧 CD 1 TR 26

All living things are made up of one or more **cells.** Cells are the smallest unit of life. All cells have a **cell membrane.** It controls what moves into and out of a cell. Most cells have other parts, such as a **nucleus, vacuoles, ribosomes,** and **lysosomes.** The nucleus controls all activity in the cell. Vacuoles store water, food, and waste. Ribosomes build proteins. Lysosomes break down, or digest, material.

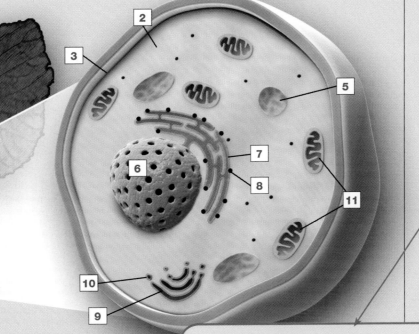

1

An (animal) cell

Check Your Understanding presents several questions. Use these questions to make sure you understand the new information.

✓ Check Your Understanding

1. Look at the plant cell and animal cell. Name five parts that both cells have.

2. What does the nucleus do?

3. What one part do all cells have?

Critical Thinking Making Inferences
4. Why do cells have many different parts?

▶ For information on living things made of many cells, see pages 30–33.

📖 Workbook page 21

The Cell

For information on how plants make their own food, see pages 42–45.

What Do Organelles Do? CD 1 TR 27

Cell parts are called **organelles.** Organelles perform life activities as seen below.

Column

Head

Row

Organelle	Job or Life Activity
nucleus	The nucleus controls all cell activities.
chloroplast	Chloroplasts are in charge of making food from sunlight. Animal cells do not have chloroplasts.
cytoplasm	This jelly-like material is inside the cell membrane, but outside the nucleus. It contains all the other cell parts.
lysosome	The lysosomes digest or break down material.
endoplasmic reticulum	The endoplasmic reticulum moves chemicals around the cell.
Golgi complex	The Golgi complex packages or processes proteins.
cell wall	The stiff cell wall holds up the plant.
mitochondria	Mitochondria make energy from food.

■ What Organelles Do

Science Skill Reading a Table

First, look carefully at the heads of each column in the table above. They tell you what information is found in the table. Then look at the information in the table.

1. Which part of the cell contains all the other parts?
2. Which part of a plant cell makes food?
3. Which part of the cell provides energy for other cell activities?

■ Robert Hooke's Drawing of a Cell

For information about microscopes, see page 6.

Robert Hooke Sees Cells CD 1 TR 28

The picture shows an early drawing of a cell. A scientist named Robert Hooke drew it. He studied cork from a cork oak tree under a **microscope.** He saw the empty cell walls. He invented the name *cell* for his discovery.

Academic Vocabulary

The cell membrane	controls is in charge of	motion in or out of the cell.

Bacteria Cells CD 1 TR 29

Bacteria are very simple cells. Like all cells, a bacteria cell has cytoplasm and a cell membrane. The cell membrane is very thick. A bacteria cell does not have a nucleus or other organelles. It still performs all the life activities of a cell.

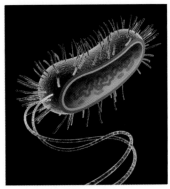

■ A Bacteria Cell

▶ For information on bacteria, see pages 26–29.

Word Study
Word Origins
Chloroplast comes from two Greek words.
- **Chloros** means "green."
- **Plastikos** means "to form or mold."

    Chloroplasts are the organelles in green plants that make food.

✅ Check Your Understanding
1. What do organelles do? Give a few examples.
2. What did Robert Hooke see under the microscope?
3. What does a bacteria have that all cells have?

Critical Thinking Integrating Information
4. Which kind of cell has the most kinds of organelles: a plant cell, an animal cell, or a bacteria cell?

 Research and Inquiry Use the internet, the library, or your science book to answer these questions.
1. How large can cells become? What limits their size?
2. What scientist first studied living cells?
3. What did the botanist Robert Brown add to what we know about cells?

 Writing How does a cell work? Write a short paragraph. Tell the role of the nucleus, cell membrane, cytoplasm, and mitochondria.

Research and Inquiry presents topics to study on the internet, at the library, or in your science book. Use this section to study on your own and learn more about the lesson topic.

Writing contains a writing topic. Use this section to build writing skills for science class and for all subjects at school.

 Workbook pages 22–23 — **25**

1

Thinking Like a Scientist

1

FOCUS QUESTION

How do scientists learn about the world around us?

CD 1
TR 1

1 **experimental design**

2 **observation**

3 **question**

4 **hypothesis**

5 **prediction**

6 **experiment**

7 **data**

8 **analyze**

9 **conclusion**

10 **descriptive design**

11 **correlational design**

a. Make an observation and ask a question.

My phone is not working. What's wrong with it?

2 3

b. Form a hypothesis and predict an outcome.

I think the battery is dead. If I charge the battery, then the phone will work.

4 5

c. Gather data and test your hypothesis.

The battery is charging.

6 7

10

Word Study

Word Parts

Analyze comes from Greek:

The word part **ana** means "break up."

The word part **lyze** means "to loosen."

To **analyze** something, you "break it apart" and look at the separate parts. You look closely at each detail to find out what it means.

▶ For information on data analysis tools, see pages 14–17.

2

d. Study the test results.

I'll try to call someone.

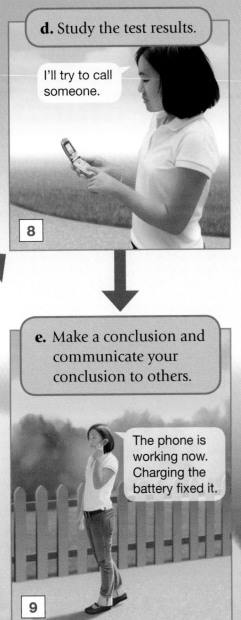

8

e. Make a conclusion and communicate your conclusion to others.

The phone is working now. Charging the battery fixed it.

9

11

Vocabulary in Context CD 1 TR 2

Scientists learn about the world around us in different ways. Sometimes scientists use a **descriptive design.** They observe and describe animals, plants, planets, or rocks. Sometimes their observations lead them to new questions. Then they might use a **correlational design.** A scientist observes dead fish in a stream. She wonders, "Is something in the water killing the fish?" She tests some water from the stream. She wants to see if there is a relationship between the water and the dead fish.

Another way scientists learn is by using an **experimental design.** They make **observations,** ask **questions,** form a **hypothesis,** make **predictions,** and gather **data.** Then they study their results and draw **conclusions.**

Observation: "My cell phone is not working."

Question: "Why doesn't my cell phone work?"

Hypothesis: "The battery needs to be charged."

Prediction: "If I charge the battery, then the phone will work."

Gather data: **Experiment** by charging the battery.

Study the test result: The phone works.

Make a **conclusion** and communicate the results: If the phone works, the hypothesis is supported. In this case, the hypothesis is correct.

Tell others how you solved the problem.

✔ Check Your Understanding

1. Look at the pictures. What observation does the student make in the first picture?

2. Was the hypothesis proved or disproved? How do you know?

3. How do scientists learn about the world around us?

Critical Thinking Analyzing Information

4. Imagine that the student recharged the phone, and it still doesn't work. What's another possible hypothesis?

■ A Scientist Observing Nature

Observing and Describing 🎧 CD 1 TR 3

One example of a descriptive design is observing the foods birds eat. One scientist observed birds in a state park. She wrote notes about each bird's food. She observed that warblers ate caterpillars on the tree leaves. She saw that hummingbirds visited flowers. They drank **nectar** from the flowers. She also noticed them visiting spider webs. They took tiny insects—and sometimes even the spider—from the webs. Sparrows ate the seeds from sunflowers. Woodpeckers drilled holes in trees to find insects to eat.

📖 Academic Vocabulary		
The scientist	**observed**	the foods birds eat.
	saw	
	noticed	

Finding Relationships 🎧 CD 1 TR 4

Correlational designs look for **relationships** in data. An example of correlational design is the relationship between birds' beak types and what they eat. Scientists have identified how beak types are related to what birds eat.

| Sparrows have short, thick beaks for cracking seeds. | Woodpeckers have long, sharp beaks for drilling into wood to get insects, such as termites and ants. | Hummingbirds have long, thin beaks for reaching nectar in flowers. | Warblers have thin, pointed beaks for catching caterpillars and flying insects. |

■ Types of Bird Beaks

Science Skill Looking at Relationships

When you look at relationships, you look at how one thing affects another thing. The chart shows the relationship between the type of beak a bird has and the foods it eats.

1. What type of beak does a sparrow have? How is its beak type related to what it eats?
2. How is a woodpecker's beak type related to what it eats?
3. Warblers catch and eat flying insects. What type of beak do they have?

Experimenting CD 1 TR 5

Scientists answer questions that can be tested. A group of science students asked, "Which material will keep ice frozen the longest at 35°C?" They did an experiment to answer their question. The results from their experiment are in the table below. Each material is listed in the left column. The time the ice stayed frozen is shown across the top. The group concluded that packing foam kept ice frozen the longest.

Word Study
Word Families

Conclusion is a noun.

His **conclusion** was that he liked blue best.

Conclude is a verb.

She **concluded** that the baseball broke the window.

Insulation Material	Number of Minutes									
	10	20	30	40	50	60	70	80	90	100
shredded newspaper	√	√	√	√	√	√				
bubble wrap	√	√	√	√						
packing foam	√	√	√	√	√	√	√	√		

■ Bar Graph of the Ice Experiment

● For information on graphs and tables, see pages 14–17.

✔ Check Your Understanding

1. What is an example of a descriptive design?
2. What does a correlational design look for?
3. What kinds of questions do scientists answer?

Critical Thinking Hypothesizing

4. What is an example of a question you could test? How would you test it?

 Research and Inquiry Use the internet, the library, or your science book to answer these questions.

1. Who was Louis Pasteur? How did he use experimental design?
2. What did Jane Goodall study? What kind of design did she use?
3. What did William Harvey use correlational design to discover?

 Writing Think of a time when you had a question about something. Describe how you could use one of the scientific methods to find the answer to your question. Write a paragraph.

Science Tools

FOCUS QUESTION
What are some tools that scientists use?

CD 1
TR 6

1 graduated cylinder

2 beaker

3 balance

4 test tube

5 petri dish

6 computer

7 anemometer

8 thermometer

9 microscope

10 telescope

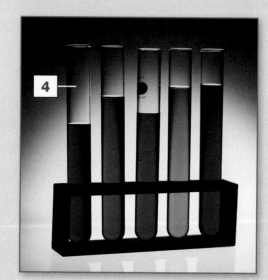

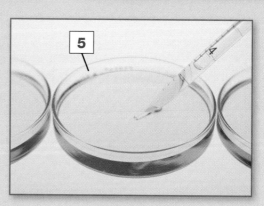

Word Study

Word Parts

The word part **meter** comes from the Greek word **metron,** which means "measure."

A word ending in **meter** names a tool for measuring.

A **thermometer** is a tool that measures temperature.

An **anemometer** is a tool that measures wind speed.

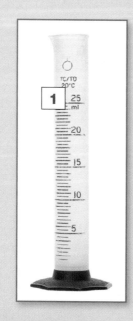

▶ For information on measurement, see pages 10–13.

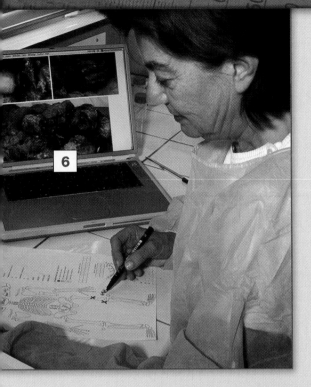

6

Vocabulary in Context CD 1 TR 7

Scientists use many tools. They use **graduated cylinders, beakers,** and **balances** to measure things. They use **petri dishes** and **test tubes** to hold things they are testing. They often store data from experiments in **computers.** Scientists use several tools to track the weather. A **thermometer** measures air temperature. An **anemometer** measures wind speed. Scientists use **telescopes** to take a closer look at stars, moons, and planets. Scientists use **microscopes** to study things that we can't see with only our eyes.

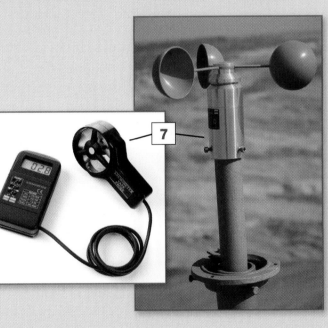

7

8

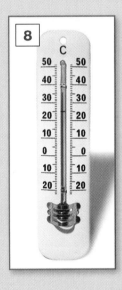

9

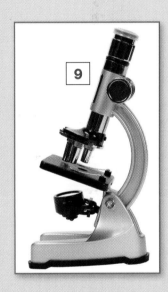

10

✅ Check Your Understanding

1. Look at the pictures. Which tools can scientists use to measure things?

2. Which tool do scientists use to study the stars?

3. What are some tools that scientists use?

Critical Thinking Making Inferences

4. Which of these tools might scientists use outside of a lab?

📖 Workbook page 5

(volume of water + rock) − volume of water = volume of rock

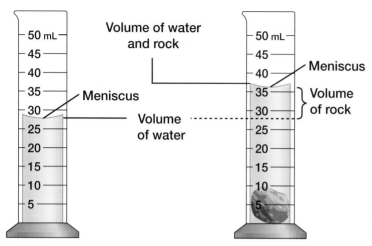

Volume of water and rock

Meniscus

Meniscus

Volume of water

Volume of rock

■ Finding Volume by Displacement

Finding Volume by Displacement 🎧 CD 1 TR 8

You measure the **volume** of a solid, such as a rock, by using water. Choose a graduated cylinder that the rock will fit into. Fill the empty graduated cylinder about half full. Put 28 mL of water in the cylinder. Record this as Volume 1. Next carefully put the rock in the water. Make sure the rock is completely under water. Then read the volume again. Suppose you read the volume as 36 mL. Record this as Volume 2. Finally, subtract Volume 1 from Volume 2: 36 mL − 28 mL = 8 mL. The volume of the rock is 8 mL.

Science Skill Reading Volume on a Graduated Cylinder

Look at the drawings. The surface of the water curves down in the center. The **meniscus** is the curved line made by the water. Read the numbers from the bottom of the meniscus to find the volume of water.

1. Read the volume of the water in the cylinder on the left. What is the volume?

2. Read the volume of the water plus the rock in the cylinder on the right. What is the volume?

A Compound Microscope 🎧 CD 1 TR 9

A compound light microscope helps you to see small objects. You place a small, thin object on a **glass slide** over a hole in the **stage.** A mirror or lamp directs light up toward the object. An **objective lens** enlarges the object. The object is magnified again by the **eyepiece lens.** Turn the **coarse adjustment** knob to make the object clear. Switch to the **medium** or **high power lens.** Then turn the **fine adjustment** knob to make the object clearer.

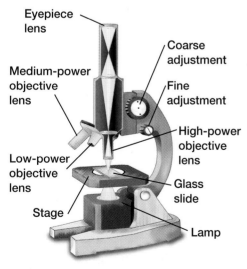

Eyepiece lens

Coarse adjustment

Medium-power objective lens

Fine adjustment

Low-power objective lens

High-power objective lens

Stage

Glass slide

Lamp

■ A Compound Microscope

Academic Vocabulary

The lenses of a microscope	**enlarge**	an object.
	magnify	

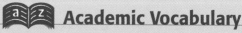

Word Study

Word Origins

Micro comes from a Greek word meaning "small."

Tele comes from a Greek word meaning "far."

A **microscope** helps us see small things.

A **telescope** helps us see things far away.

GOES Weather Satellite CD 1 TR 10

Not all science tools are in labs. Weather scientists use **satellites** that orbit, or circle, Earth in space. **GOES** stands for Geostationary Operational Environmental Satellite. **Geostationary** means the satellite moves at the same speed as Earth moves. This makes it stay above the same place on Earth all the time. GOES measures weather conditions such as air temperature and winds. Scientists use the satellite to take pictures of clouds and watch for bad weather.

■ A GOES Weather Satellite in Space

❯ For information on weather, see pages 150–153.

❯ For information on orbits, see pages 110–113.

✅ Check Your Understanding

1. What tool do you use to measure the volume of a solid?
2. You are using a compound microscope. Where do you put the glass slide?
3. Why does GOES stay above the same place on Earth all the time?

Critical Thinking Applying Information
4. How would you find the volume of a small toy car?

 Research and Inquiry Use the internet, the library, or your science book to answer these questions.

1. Who was Julius Richard Petri? What did he add to the scientist's toolbox?
2. What are some ways that scientists use hand magnifiers?
3. How is an electron microscope different from a light microscope?

 Writing You put a flower seed on a microscope slide. Describe what happens when someone uses a microscope to view the flower seed. How does the microscope work? How does it bring the image into focus? Write a paragraph.

Metric Units of Measurement

FOCUS QUESTION
What do scientists measure?

CD 1
TR 11

1 milliliter (mL)

2 liter (L)

3 meter (m)

4 centimeter (cm)

5 millimeter (mm)

6 kilometer (km)

7 cubic centimeter (cm³)

8 kilogram (kg)

9 gram (g)

10 degrees Celsius (C)

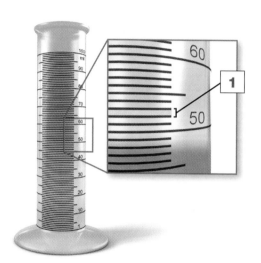

3

100 cm = 1 m

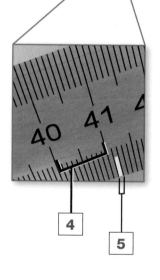

4

5

Word Study

Prefixes

A prefix is a letter or group of letters added to the beginning of a word. The prefix changes the word's meaning.

Prefix	Meaning
kilo	thousand (1,000)
deci	tenth (0.1)
centi	hundredth (0.01)
milli	thousandth (0.001)

The prefix **kilo** added to the word **meter** forms **kilometer.** A kilometer equals 1,000 meters.

1,000 m = 1 km

6

▶ For information on measuring mass, volume, and density, see page 169.

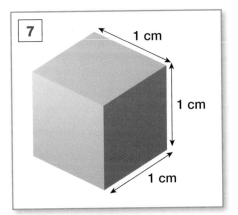

7

1 cm

1 cm

1 cm

Vocabulary in Context

 CD 1 TR 12

Every day we talk about measurements. "How tall is that building? How heavy is that box? How cold is it?" Scientists answer these questions with units. A unit is an amount that never changes. Scientists use different units to measure different things. They measure length or distance in **millimeters, centimeters, meters,** and **kilometers.** They measure how much space things occupy in **cubic centimeters, milliliters,** and **liters.** They measure mass, or how much matter is in an object, in **grams** and **kilograms.** Finally, they measure how hot or cold something is in **degrees Celsius.**

8

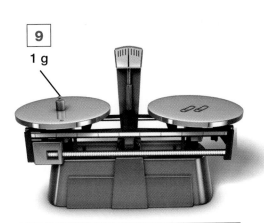

9

1 g

| 1 kg | = | 1,000 g |

10

✅ Check Your Understanding

1. Look at the pictures. How many centimeters are in a meter? How many grams are in a kilogram?

2. What do scientists use units for?

3. What do scientists measure?

Critical Thinking Classifying Information

4. What units do scientists use to measure (a) the length of a soccer field, (b) the mass of a bag of fruit, and (c) the amount of juice in a bottle?

📖 Workbook page 9

Metric Units of Measurement

■ Distances to Towns Measured in Kilometers

The Metric System CD 1 TR 13

We use the **metric system** to measure **mass, length,** and **volume.** The metric system works on a system of bases:
- The base unit for mass is the gram.
- The base unit for length is the meter.
- The base unit for volume is the liter.

We use a system of prefixes to show smaller and larger units. The prefix *kilo* means "1,000." So a kilogram is 1,000 grams. The prefix *centi* means "one hundredth" (.01). So a centimeter is one hundredth (.01) of a meter.

The metric system was invented in France. Before the metric system, people in different cities and countries used different measurement systems. People often didn't understand each other's measurement system. After the metric system was invented, many countries began to use it. Scientists began to use it too. Today most countries use the metric system. The United States uses feet, miles, inches, gallons, and pounds. But scientists in the United States use the metric system.

Kind of Measurement	Base Unit	Other Units
length or distance	meter (m)	kilometer (km) = 1,000 meters centimeter (cm) = .01 meters millimeter (mm) = .001 meters
mass	gram (g)	kilogram (kg) = 1,000 grams
volume	liter (L)	centiliter (cL) = .01 liters

■ Some Metric Units

🔤 Academic Vocabulary

The number 0.4 is **four tenths.**

The number 200 is **two hundred.**

The number .02 is **two hundredths.**

The number 3,000 is **three thousand.**

The number 0.003 is **three thousandths.**

Temperature Scales CD 1 TR 14

A **thermometer** measures how hot or cold something is. Most people in the United States use the Fahrenheit **temperature** scale. However, most of the world uses the Celsius temperature scale. Scientists also use the Celsius scale.

Science Skill Comparing and Contrasting

When you compare, you tell how two things are alike. When you contrast, you tell how two things are different. Look at the temperature scales on the two thermometers.

1. What do both scales measure?

2. At what temperature does water freeze on each scale?

3. At what temperature does water boil on each scale?

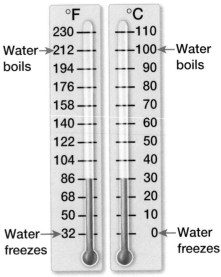

Fahrenheit Celsius

■ Temperature Scales

◆ For more information on thermometers and other science tools, see pages 6–9.

Word Study
Word Origins

Thermometer is made from two word parts.

- The Greek word **therme** means "heat."
- The Latin word **metrum** means "to measure."

    A **thermometer** is a tool used to measure the temperature of objects.

✅ Check Your Understanding

1. An abbreviation is a short way to write something. What are the abbreviations for the base units of the metric system?

2. What measurement system do scientists use in the United States?

3. What tool do scientists use to measure temperature? What scale do scientists use?

Critical Thinking Analyzing Information

4. Why do scientists use meters and centimeters and not feet and inches?

 Research and Inquiry Use the internet, the library, or your science book to answer these questions.

1. What measuring systems did early civilizations such as Egypt use? What standards were they based on?

2. What tools do scientists use to make measurements?

3. How much do a mile and a gallon measure in the metric system?

 Writing You are on your way to school in the morning. Describe your trip. Include three examples of how you might use measurements during the trip. Write a paragraph.

Data Analysis

FOCUS QUESTION
What are seven ways to show data?

CD 1
TR 15

1 line graph

2 pie chart

3 bar graph

4 data table

5 flowchart

6 Venn diagram

7 map

8 map key

1

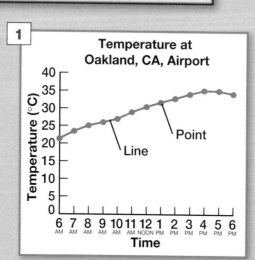

Temperature at Oakland, CA, Airport

Line

Point

2

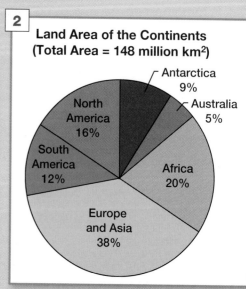

Land Area of the Continents
(Total Area = 148 million km²)

- Antarctica 9%
- Australia 5%
- North America 16%
- South America 12%
- Europe and Asia 38%
- Africa 20%

3

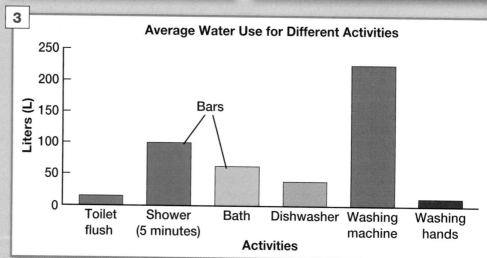

Average Water Use for Different Activities

Bars

Activities: Toilet flush, Shower (5 minutes), Bath, Dishwasher, Washing machine, Washing hands

Word Study
Multiple-Meaning Words

Table has different meanings.

A **table** is a piece of furniture.
Put your books on the **table**.

Average Math Grades per Quarter	
Grading Quarter	Average Grade
First	73
Second	79
Third	83
Fourth	87

Table can also mean "a display of numbers."

This **table** shows math grades during each quarter.

4

Average Monthly Temperatures in Cities A and B		
Month	Temperature (°C) in City A	Temperature (°C) in City B
January	−7	−6
February	−6	−6
March	−1	−2
April	6	4
May	12	9
June	17	15

Row —

Column

14

5

An Ocean Food Chain

6

Comparing Plant and Animal Cells

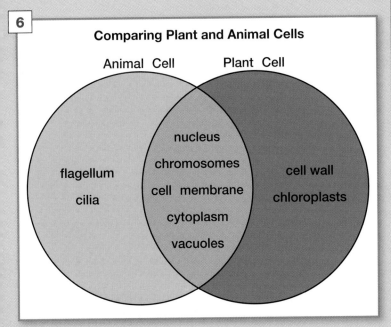

Animal Cell   Plant Cell

flagellum

cilia

nucleus

chromosomes

cell membrane

cytoplasm

vacuoles

cell wall

chloroplasts

7

Weather for November 21

Seattle

Winnipeg

Portland

Quebec

Omaha   Chicago

Boston

New York

Las Vegas

Los Angeles

Phoenix

Dallas

Atlanta

New Orleans

Miami

N

- Clear
- Partly cloudy
- Cloudy

Snow

Rain

Warm front   Cold front

Honolulu

Juneau

8

Vocabulary in Context CD 1 TR 16

We show data or information in different ways. Then we can study it. We can show data in **tables** and **graphs.** The data in a table can be numbers or words. We often make graphs of the information in tables.

The most common graphs are **bar graphs, line graphs,** and **pie charts.** The bar graph on page 14 uses long or short bars to compare water usage. The line graph on page 14 uses points and a line to show temperature changes over time. A pie chart shows parts of something. The pie chart on page 14 shows the total land area of Earth divided into continents.

A **flowchart** uses drawings to show steps in a process. A **Venn diagram** uses circles. It shows how things are the same and different. The Venn diagram on page 15 shows what is the same and different between animal cells and plant cells.

A **map** shows Earth's surface. There are many kinds of maps. The map on page 15 gives data about weather. The **map key** helps you understand the map.

✔ Check Your Understanding

1. Look at the pictures. Which one shows part of Earth's surface?
2. What are three kinds of graphs?
3. What are seven ways to show data?

Critical Thinking Comparing and Contrasting
4. How are bar graphs and line graphs the same? How are they different?

📖 Workbook page 13

15

Data Analysis

Average Monthly Temperatures	
Month	**Temperature (°C)**
April	6
May	12
June	17

■ A Table

Understanding Tables 🎧 CD 1 TR 17

A table is a way to **organize** data. It is also a way to **compare** the data. The **title** tells the data that is being compared. Tables are made of a series of rows and columns. **Rows** go across the table. **Columns** go up and down. This table shows the change in temperature over three months. Read across a row to see the temperature for that month.

Word Study

Suffix

A suffix is added to the end of a word. The suffix **est** means "the most."

> The **hottest** month had the most hot temperatures.

> The **coldest** month had the most cold temperatures.

Science Skill Organizing Data

Tables are made up of data. Tables let you look at each piece of information. They let you compare pieces of information. Look at the temperature table.

1. What is the average temperature in June?
2. Which month was the hottest?
3. Which month was the coldest?

Understanding Graphs 🎧 CD 1 TR 18

A graph is a way to picture data. Two kinds of graphs are bar graphs and line graphs. This bar graph shows rainfall during a year. The length of the bar shows the amount of rain that fell each month. It makes comparison between the months easy.

A line graph connects points with a line. The line graph shows how the number of **earthworms** relates to the **volume,** or amount, of water in soil. The number of earthworms went up with the amount of water.

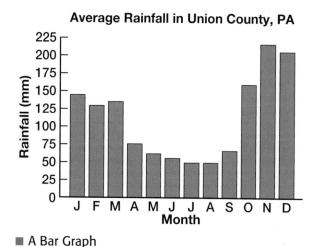

Average Rainfall in Union County, PA

■ A Bar Graph

Number of Earthworms vs. Volume of Water in Soil

Earthworm

■ A Line Graph

Understanding Pie Charts CD 1 TR 19

A pie chart shows a circle divided into parts. The parts are called sections or slices. A pie chart is used to compare the size of the parts. A pie chart is a good way to show data that is in **percentages.** The parts add up to 100, or 100 percent. This pie chart shows where fresh water is found on Earth. Look at the largest slice of the pie. Over 77% of this fresh water is ice.

Fresh Water on Earth

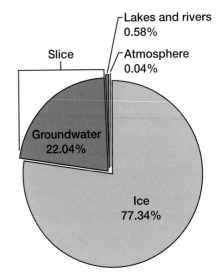

- Lakes and rivers 0.58%
- Slice
- Atmosphere 0.04%
- Groundwater 22.04%
- Ice 77.34%

■ A Pie Chart

Academic Vocabulary

A line graph **shows** relationships between numbers.

A pie chart **is used** to compare the parts with the whole.

✓ Check Your Understanding

1. Look at the temperature table. What is a row? What is a column?

2. Look at the bar graph of rainfall. Compare the bars. Use a ruler. When was the rainfall more than 200 mm? When was the rainfall the lowest?

3. Look at the pie chart showing fresh water on Earth. What percent of the fresh water is groundwater? What is the smallest slice?

Critical Thinking Applying Information

4. You plant 100 flowers. Only 38 percent of them grow. What kind of graph could you use to show your results?

Heights of Animals

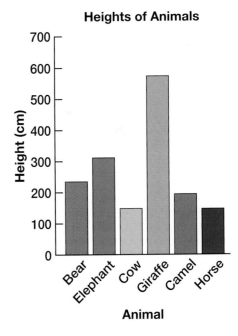

Height (cm) vs Animal (Bear, Elephant, Cow, Giraffe, Camel, Horse)

 Research and Inquiry Use the internet, the library, or your science book to answer these questions.

1. What does a cartographer do? Who uses a cartographer's work?

2. How could a graph be used to map the ocean floor?

3. When was the first moon map made? How are moon maps made today?

 Writing The graph above was made as part of a scientific study of animals. Which animal is the tallest, the second tallest, the shortest, and so on? Write a paragraph.

Safety in the Lab

FOCUS QUESTION
How do we stay safe during science experiments?

CD 1
TR 20

1 **goggles**

2 **lab apron**

3 **gloves**

4 **soap and water**

5 **fire extinguisher**

6 **fire alarm**

7 **first aid kit**

Word Study
Syllabification

You can break **extinguisher** into syllables to make it easier to read and say.

extinguisher = ex • **tin** • guish • er

The fire **extinguisher** is on the wall.

1

2

3

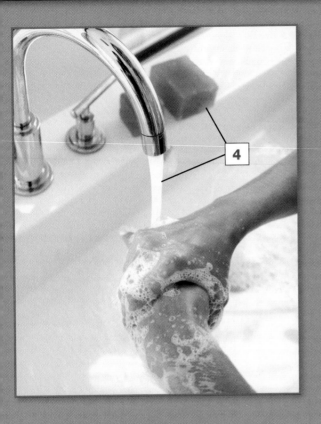

Vocabulary in Context

CD 1
TR 21

You must be careful in the lab. First, you should always wear **goggles.** They protect your eyes. Your teacher may want you to wear **gloves** and a **lab apron,** too. They protect your hands, clothing, and body.

If you get hurt, tell your teacher right away. If you touch a chemical, wash the area right away in plenty of **soap and water.** If you get a burn, wash it in plenty of cold water. Other equipment also helps keep you safe if something goes wrong. A lab should have a **fire alarm** and a **fire extinguisher** or fire blanket in case of emergency.

> For more information on performing science experiments, see pages 2–5.

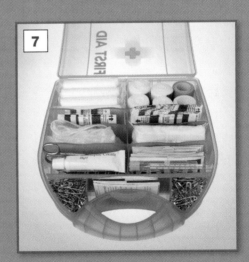

✅ Check Your Understanding

1. Look at the pictures. What safety equipment protects your eyes?

2. What should you do if you spill a chemical on your arm?

3. How do we stay safe during science experiments?

Critical Thinking Looking for Patterns

4. Think of all the places where you usually see first aid kits. Make a list.

Workbook page 17

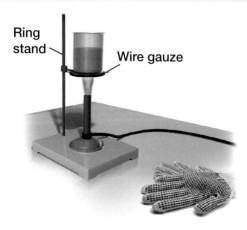

Ring stand

Wire gauze

■ Keep anything that could catch fire away from an open flame. When heating a liquid in a beaker, use a ring stand and a wire gauze. Use heatproof gloves to remove the item after the burner is turned off.

■ Hot glass looks just like cold glass. Use heatproof gloves when touching glass objects that have been heated.

■ Tell your teacher about any problem.

Staying Safe

CD 1
TR 22

You might work with chemicals in some science experiments. In others, you might use an open flame or a hot plate. Staying safe during science experiments is important.

You can avoid injuries by wearing goggles, gloves, and a lab apron. You should always follow directions. Read all safety signs and warnings. Never start an experiment until your teacher says it is okay.

ELECTRIC SHOCK

SHARP OBJECT

CORROSIVE CHEMICAL

■ Safety Signs and Warnings

Science Skill Reading Safety Signs and Warnings

Safety signs and warnings help you prevent accidents. Look at the safety signs and warnings above.

1. What does the Electric Shock sign tell you?
2. What can happen with sharp objects?
3. You see the Corrosive Chemical sign. What clothes should you wear?

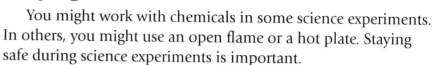

Academic Vocabulary

| You can | avoid | problems by following safety rules. |
| | prevent | |

Responding to Accidents

CD 1
TR 23

Accidents can happen during experiments even if you are careful. If something goes wrong, tell your teacher right away. Then follow your teacher's instructions. You may need to use soap and water if you touch a chemical. You can use a first aid kit for treating cuts and burns.

Treatment of Living Things

🎧 CD 1 TR 24

Some science experiments can involve plants, animals, or other living things. It is important not to harm living things in lab work or outside of class. You don't always need to bring living things to class. Sometimes you can bring pictures. That way, you avoid disturbing nature.

❯ For information on plants, see pages 34–37.

❯ For information on animals, see pages 46–49.

■ Taking a Picture for a Science Experiment

✓ Check Your Understanding

1. How can you protect your hands from burns?
2. There is an accident in an experiment. What is the first thing you do?
3. You want to avoid using living things in science experiments. What can you do?

Critical Thinking Making Observations

4. Name one piece of safety equipment in your science room.

🔍 **Research and Inquiry** Use the internet, the library, or your science book to answer these questions.

1. Find three examples of safety signs and warnings that are not on this page.
2. Make a list of rules that should be in a guide about safety in science class.
3. What are the differences between Class A, Class B, and Class C fire extinguishers?

 Writing Describe a science experiment from your science class. Explain the safety gear you use during the experiment. Write a paragraph.

The Cell

CD 1
TR 25

What one part do all cells have?

1 cell

2 cytoplasm

3 cell membrane

4 chloroplast

5 vacuole

6 nucleus

7 endoplasmic reticulum

8 ribosome

9 Golgi complex

10 lysosome

11 mitochondria

12 cell wall

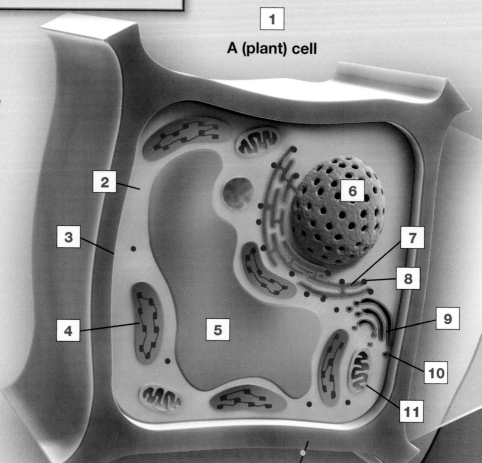

A (plant) cell

Word Study

Multiple-Meaning Words

The word **cell** has different meanings.

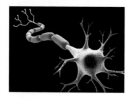

A **cell** is "a small room locked from the outside."

People in jail are kept in **cells**.

A **cell** is the "basic unit of living things."

Your body is made up of many **cells**.

▶ For information on living things made of single cells, see pages 26–29.

Vocabulary in Context
 CD 1 TR 26

All living things are made up of one or more **cells.** Cells are the smallest unit of life. All cells have a **cell membrane.** It controls what moves into and out of a cell. Most cells have other parts, such as a **nucleus, vacuoles, ribosomes,** and **lysosomes.** The nucleus controls all activity in the cell. Vacuoles store water, food, and waste. Ribosomes build proteins. Lysosomes break down, or digest, material.

An (animal) cell

✅ Check Your Understanding

1. Look at the plant cell and animal cell. Name five parts that both cells have.

2. What does the nucleus do?

3. What one part do all cells have?

Critical Thinking Making Inferences

4. Why do cells have many different parts?

▶ For information on living things made of many cells, see pages 30–33.

📖 Workbook page 21

The Cell

For information on how plants make their own food, see pages 42–45.

What Do Organelles Do? CD 1 TR 27

Cell parts are called **organelles.** Organelles perform life activities as seen below.

Column

Head — **Row** —

Organelle	Job or Life Activity
nucleus	The nucleus controls all cell activities.
chloroplast	Chloroplasts are in charge of making food from sunlight. Animal cells do not have chloroplasts.
cytoplasm	This jelly-like material is inside the cell membrane, but outside the nucleus. It contains all the other cell parts.
lysosome	The lysosomes digest or break down material.
endoplasmic reticulum	The endoplasmic reticulum moves chemicals around the cell.
Golgi complex	The Golgi complex packages or processes proteins.
cell wall	The stiff cell wall holds up the plant.
mitochondria	Mitochondria make energy from food.

■ What Organelles Do

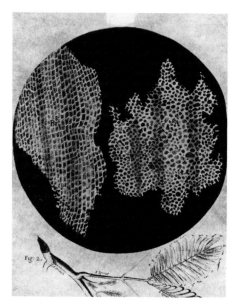

■ Robert Hooke's Drawing of a Cell

Science Skill Reading a Table

First, look carefully at the heads of each column in the table above. They tell you what information is found in the table. Then look at the information in the table.

1. Which part of the cell contains all the other parts?
2. Which part of a plant cell makes food?
3. Which part of the cell provides energy for other cell activities?

Robert Hooke Sees Cells CD 1 TR 28

The picture shows an early drawing of a cell. A scientist named Robert Hooke drew it. He studied cork from a cork oak tree under a **microscope.** He saw the empty cell walls. He invented the name *cell* for his discovery.

For information about microscopes, see page 6.

Academic Vocabulary

The cell membrane	controls / is in charge of	motion in or out of the cell.

Bacteria Cells CD 1 TR 29

Bacteria are very simple cells. Like all cells, a bacteria cell has cytoplasm and a cell membrane. The cell membrane is very thick. A bacteria cell does not have a nucleus or other organelles. It still performs all the life activities of a cell.

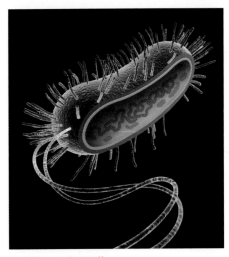

■ A Bacteria Cell

❯ For information on bacteria, see pages 26–29.

Word Study

Word Origins

Chloroplast comes from two Greek words.

- **Chloros** means "green."
- **Plastikos** means "to form or mold."

    Chloroplasts are the organelles in green plants that make food.

✔ Check Your Understanding

1. What do organelles do? Give a few examples.
2. What did Robert Hooke see under the microscope?
3. What does a bacteria have that all cells have?

Critical Thinking Integrating Information
4. Which kind of cell has the most kinds of organelles: a plant cell, an animal cell, or a bacteria cell?

 Research and Inquiry Use the internet, the library, or your science book to answer these questions.

1. How large can cells become? What limits their size?
2. What scientist first studied living cells?
3. What did the botanist Robert Brown add to what we know about cells?

 Writing How does a cell work? Write a short paragraph. Tell the role of the nucleus, cell membrane, cytoplasm, and mitochondria.

Single-Celled Organisms

CD 1
TR 30

1 pseudopod
2 amoeba
3 protozoans
4 cilia
5 paramecium
6 trichonympha
7 algae
8 dinoflagellate
9 flagella
10 fungus
11 yeast
12 bacteria

3 | Protozoans

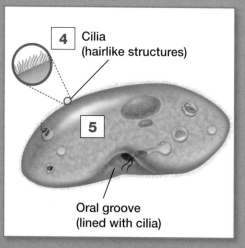

4 | Cilia (hairlike structures)

5

Oral groove (lined with cilia)

1

2

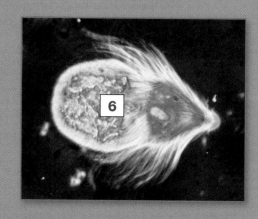

6

Word Study

Word Origins

Pseudopod is from two Greek words.

- **Pseudo** means "false" or "pretend."
- The word **pod** means "foot."

An amoeba uses its **pseudopod** to move and to get food.

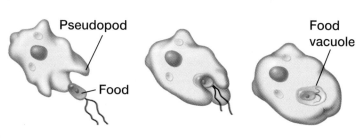

Pseudopod

Food

Food vacuole

▶ For information about vacuoles, see pages 22–23.

7 Algae

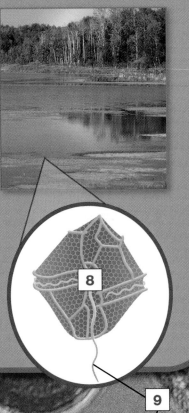

8

9

Euglena

Vocabulary in Context CD 1 TR 31

Do you know that most living things are just one cell in size? These cells are so small you cannot see them with your naked eyes. All one-celled living things live in wet places. They need water. Otherwise, they dry out.

Single-celled organisms include **protozoans,** some **algae, yeast,** and **bacteria.** Protozoans use **flagella, cilia,** or **pseudopods** to move. Some use pseudopods to feed. **Dinoflagellates** are one-celled algae. They use sunlight to make their own food. Yeast is a one-celled kind of **fungus.** Yeast is helpful to humans. People use it to make bread and other products. Bacteria are also one-celled organisms. Some bacteria can cause disease. Bacteria are different shapes. There are rod, round, and spiral bacteria.

10 Fungus

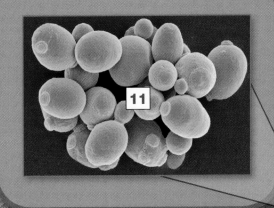

11

12 Bacteria

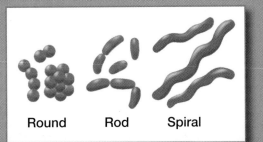

Round   Rod   Spiral

✓ Check Your Understanding

1. Look at the pictures. What are the names of some single-celled organisms?
2. What do single-celled organisms need to live?
3. What are some single-celled organisms?

Critical Thinking Making Inferences

4. What happens if you take some algae out of the water it lives in?

Workbook page 25

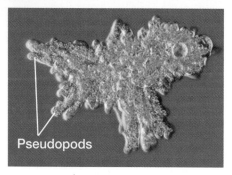

Pseudopods

■ An amoeba uses pseudopods to move and get food.

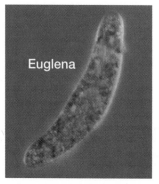

Euglena

■ A euglena can find food or make its own food with sunlight and chlorophyll.

❯ For information on the parts of a cell, see pages 22–23.

❯ For information on how plants make food from sunlight, see pages 42–43.

Kinds of Single-Celled Organisms CD 1 TR 32

There are many kinds of single-celled organisms. Algae use light to make their own food like plants do. These organisms have **chloroplasts** inside their cells. The green chemical in chloroplasts helps the cells make their own food. Some, such as **euglena,** have features of both plants and animals. When there is sunlight, they can make their own food with chlorophyll. Without sunlight, euglena find food to eat. An amoeba moves by forming pseudopods. It can also get food using pseudopods.

| **Science Skill** | Comparing and Contrasting |

When we compare, we find ways things are the same. When we contrast, we find ways things are different. The photos show a euglena and an amoeba. Both live in fresh water. Look at them carefully. See how they are alike and how they differ.

1. Which cell is able to make its own food?
2. Which cell can't make its own food? Which features help that cell get food?
3. How are these two organisms alike? How are they different?

Getting Energy CD 1 TR 33

Protozoans eat other cells to get **energy.** Some protozoans get food by catching it with their cilia. Other protozoans obtain food by catching it with their pseudopods. The **trypanosome** in the picture acquires energy from eating blood cells.

Some single-celled organisms are called algae. Algae are grouped as green, red, or gold. Like plants, algae make their own food. They get their energy from **sunlight.**

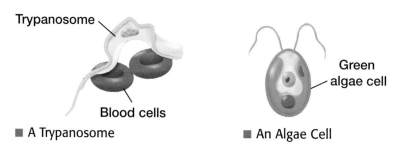

Trypanosome

Blood cells

■ A Trypanosome

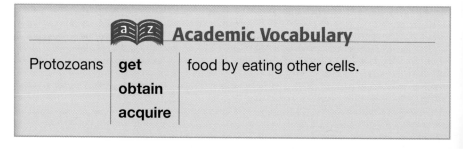

Green algae cell

■ An Algae Cell

🔤 Academic Vocabulary

Protozoans	**get**	food by eating other cells.
	obtain	
	acquire	

Extreme Conditions for Life CD 1 TR 34

Like you, most bacteria need water and air to live. But some bacteria live only where a few other organisms can live. Some bacteria live in places with no air, such as inside a cow's stomach.

Other bacteria live deep in the ocean. They live in places where materials in Earth's **crust** make the water very hot. Millions of bacteria live inside giant **tube worms** in this hot ocean water. Some of these worms are more than 2.5 meters long. Other kinds of bacteria live only where the water is very salty.

■ Some bacteria live in giant tube worms.

▶ For information on Earth's crust, see pages 130–131.

Word Study

Irregular Plurals

Bacteria is an irregular plural. Irregular plurals don't end in **s** or **es**. The singular is **bacterium.**

- Singular: One cell by itself is a **bacterium.**
- Plural: Two or more cells are called **bacteria.**

Euglena is also an irregular plural. The singular and plural are both **euglena.**

   A **euglena** is a single-celled organism.

   Euglena are similar to both plants and animals.

Check Your Understanding

1. What are euglena?
2. How do protozoans get food? How do algae get food?
3. Name three extreme conditions some bacteria live in.

Critical Thinking Comparing and Contrasting

4. How are humans and single-celled organisms alike? How are they different?

Research and Inquiry Use the internet, the library, or your science book to answer these questions.

1. Some bacteria live in geysers at Yellowstone National Park. What are living conditions there like?
2. What other living things are found around thermal vents deep in the ocean?
3. What organisms cause a red tide? What are its effects?

Writing Choose one of the organisms in the chapter. Describe the organism. Tell how it moves and gets food. Describe conditions where it lives. Write a paragraph.

Multicellular Organisms

FOCUS QUESTION
What is a multicellular organism?

CD 1
TR 35

1 cell

2 tissue

3 organ

4 organ system

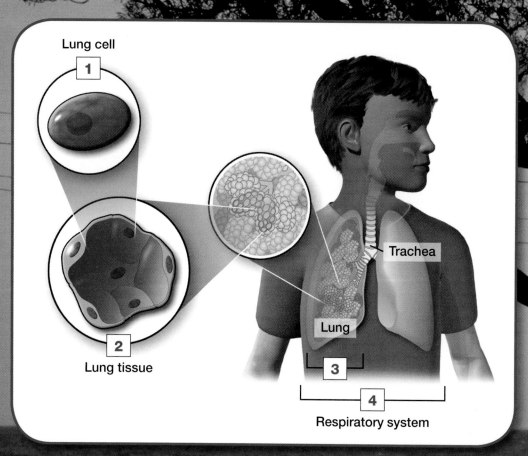

Lung cell

1

2

Lung tissue

Trachea

Lung

3

4

Respiratory system

Word Study

Word Parts

Multicellular is made up of two word parts.

The prefix **multi** can mean "much" or "many."

The word **cellular** can mean "made of cells."

A **multicellular** animal is made up of many cells.

▶ For information about plant tissues, see pages 38–39.

▶ For more information on cells, see pages 22–25.

▶ For more information on organs and organ systems, see pages 58–61.

Vocabulary in Context 🎧 CD 1 TR 36

Trees, people, and many other living things are made up of many **cells.** They are multicellular organisms. Groups of the same kind of cell form **tissues.** All the cells in a tissue do the same kind of work. For example, lung tissue helps you breathe. Tubes in plant stems carry things between the roots and leaves. Those tubes are a tissue.

Two or more different tissues that work together form an **organ.** A lung is an animal organ. A leaf is a plant organ. Several organs that work together form **organ systems.** For example, your lungs form part of your respiratory system. The leaves, stems, and flowers on a plant are in the plant's shoot system.

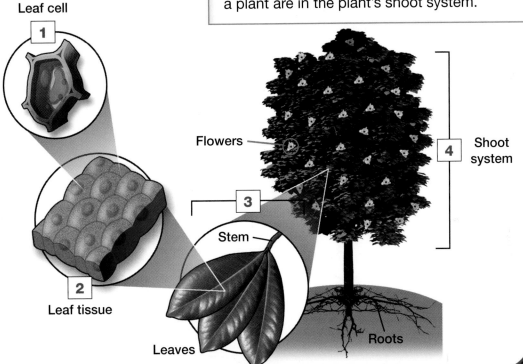

Leaf cell
1

2 Leaf tissue

Flowers

Stem

3

Leaves

4 Shoot system

Roots

✔ Check Your Understanding

1. Look at the pictures. What are tissues made of?

2. Give two examples of organs. Give two examples of organ systems.

3. What is a multicellular organism?

Critical Thinking Comparing and Contrasting

4. How are tissues different from organs?

Kinds of Animal Cells CD 1 TR 37

Multicellular animals contain many different kinds of cells. Each kind of cell has a certain job. No other kind of cell can do that job. For example, **red blood cells** collect **gases** in the lungs. **White blood cells** protect the body against disease. They cannot collect gases in the lungs.

Kind of Cell	What does this kind of cell do?
cardiac muscle cell	The heart is made up of cardiac muscle cells. This kind of cell causes the heart to beat.
skeletal muscle cell	Skeletal muscle cells are connected to bones. This kind of cell forms tissues that help move bones.
smooth muscle cell	This kind of cell forms organs that help move food in the digestive system. It also lines blood vessels and the airways of the lungs.
bone cell	The skeleton is made up of bone cells. This kind of cell provides support and allows the body to move.
skin cell	This kind of cell protects the outside of the body from injury and germs.
red blood cell	This kind of cell carries gases to other cells in the body.
white blood cell	This kind of cell fights disease in the body. White blood cells hunt and eat germs and bacteria.

■ Animal Cells and Their Jobs

Science Skill Looking for Details

A table presents information in rows and columns. Sometimes a table will present details. Details are small, important pieces of information.

1. Which two cells help protect the body? Which two cells help the body move?

2. What are three jobs that muscle cells have in the body?

3. Which cell causes the heart to beat?

Academic Vocabulary

Tissues	contain	many like cells.
Organs	are made up of	different kinds of cells.

How Cells Divide CD 1 TR 38

Cell division is the way an organism makes new cells or repairs an injury.

First, the cell copies its **chromosomes.** Chromosomes are in the cell's nucleus. Chromosomes have information on how to make new cells. Next, the two sets of chromosomes move away from each other. Finally, the cell separates into two new cells. Each new cell gets one set of chromosomes.

Word Study

Phrasal Verbs

Phrasal verbs are made up of two or three words.

Move away from means "to go to a different place."

Two sets of chromosomes **move away from** each other when a cell divides.

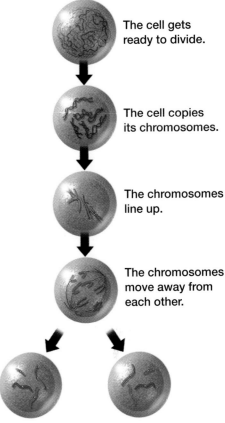

The cell gets ready to divide.

The cell copies its chromosomes.

The chromosomes line up.

The chromosomes move away from each other.

The cells divide.

■ Cell Division

● For more information on cell division, see pages 62–65.

✓ Check Your Understanding

1. How do red blood cells help the body?
2. How do bone cells help the body?
3. What are three important steps in cell division?

Critical Thinking Applying Information
4. You get a small cut. What do cells do to help your skin heal?

 Research and Inquiry Use the internet, the library, or your science book to answer these questions.

1. Why is the skin an organ system?
2. Why is an artificial heart not an organ?
3. How do skeletal muscles make bones move?

 Writing Suppose you fall and scrape your knee. How do your white blood cells help you heal? Write a paragraph.

Plants

CD 1
TR 39

1	flower	7	cone
2	sunlight	8	fruit
3	stem	9	seed
4	leaf	10	spores
5	soil		
6	root		

1

2

3

4

5

6

Word Study

Irregular Plurals

Leaf has an irregular plural form. The final **f** changes to **ves.** The plural of **leaf** is **leaves.**

The **leaves** of a plant make food for the plant.

7

Vocabulary in Context

 CD 1
TR 40

Leaves use energy from **sunlight** to make food. Food, water, and other materials move through **stems.** **Roots** store food. Roots take in water from **soil.** They also hold a plant in place in the soil. Soil gives a plant the materials it needs to build its parts.

Some plants use **flowers** to reproduce, or make new plants. Flowering plants make **fruits.** A fruit contains one or more **seeds.** New plants grow from seeds. Some plants make seeds in **cones.** Other plants, such as mosses and ferns, make **spores** instead of seeds. Spores are cells that make new plants.

▶ For information about food made by plants, see pages 42–43.

▶ For information about mosses and ferns, see pages 38–39.

8

9

Pomegranate

10

✅ Check Your Understanding

1. Look at the pictures. Which plant part are leaves joined to?

2. Name three jobs that roots perform.

3. What are the parts of a plant?

Critical Thinking Analyzing Evidence

4. What do plants need to live?

Workbook page 33

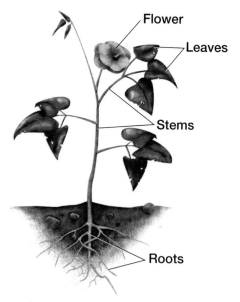

Flower

Leaves

Stems

Roots

■ Plant Parts

● For information about seeds, see page 41.

Plant Parts 🎧 CD 1 TR 41

The parts of a plant work together to help the plant stay alive. The leaves use sunlight to make food for the plant. Stems carry water, minerals, and food between the leaves and the plant roots. Stems also support the plant so that the leaves can get sunlight.

Plant roots grow away from the stem to find water. Roots take in water and minerals from soil. Roots hold plants firmly in the ground. Roots also store food. Seeds and spores help plants reproduce. Flowers are the parts of plants that make seeds. Cones and fruits protect the seeds until they can grow.

What Is Soil? 🎧 CD 1 TR 42

Soil is a mixture of small pieces of **rock, humus,** air, and water. Humus is a dark brown material made from dead plants and animals. Humus is rich in the **nutrients** plants need to grow. Plants need air, water, and **minerals.** The bits of rock provide the minerals.

There are different kinds of soil. **Clay** soil is made of very small particles. Water and air can't flow through it. **Sandy** soil is light and made of large particles. Water runs through it quickly. **Loam** is soil made of humus, sand, clay, and the right mixture of air and water. It is a mixture of large and small particles. It usually supplies many minerals. Plants grow well in loam.

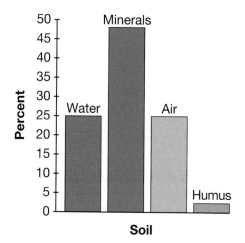

■ The Composition of a Soil Sample

Science Skill Reading Bar Graphs

A bar graph shows quantities using bars of different lengths. When you read a bar graph, place your ruler across the top of each bar. That will make it easier to read the numbers. Look at this bar graph about the composition of a soil sample.

1. Which material makes up the largest part of this soil sample? How much of the sample is this material?

2. How much of the soil sample is water?

3. What percent of the sample is air and humus?

Academic Vocabulary

Rocks in soil	**supply**	plants with minerals.
	provide	

The Venus Flytrap CD 1 TR 43

Most green plants get nutrients from the soil. **Nitrogen** is a nutrient. A Venus flytrap lives in places where the soil does not supply nitrogen. The flytrap has leaves that help the plant get nitrogen. Insects contain nitrogen. When an insect steps on the flytrap's leaves, the leaves snap shut. The leaves make **chemicals** that **digest** the insect. The flytrap gets the nitrogen it needs.

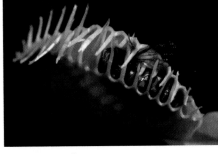

■ A Venus Flytrap

Word Study

Noncount Nouns

Noncount nouns do not form plurals with **s. Air, water,** and **sunlight** are noncount nouns. Do not use *a/an* with these words.

Plants need **water, air,** and **sunlight** to grow.

✅ Check Your Understanding

1. What jobs do plant stems do?
2. Where do the minerals in soil come from?
3. What nutrient does a Venus flytrap get from an insect?

Critical Thinking Comparing and Contrasting

4. How are loam and clay soil the same? How are loam and clay soil different?

 Research and Inquiry Use the internet, the library, or your science book to answer these questions.

1. Soils are mixtures of different kinds of materials. What is the soil in your region like?
2. How do plant materials become coal?
3. How does a pitcher plant trap its food?

 Writing You are a reporter for the *Daily Flypaper.* You see an insect on a Venus flytrap. Describe what happens to the insect. Write a newspaper article.

Kinds of Plants

CD 1
TR 44

1 **vascular plants**

2 **ferns**

3 **flowering plants**

4 **conifers**

5 **cones**

6 **xylem**

7 **phloem**

8 **seeds**

9 **nonvascular plants**

10 **mosses**

11 **liverwort**

12 **leaves**

13 **stem**

14 **roots**

| 1 | Vascular Plants |

Word Study

Word Parts

The word **conifer** is made up of two parts: the word **cone** and the suffix **fer.**

The suffix **fer** is from the Latin **ferre.** It means "to bear" or "produce."

The whole word means "cone-bearing."

A **conifer** is a seed plant that produces seeds in cones.

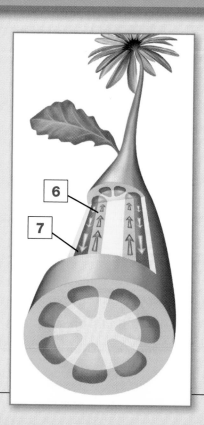

▶ For information about how plants make food in their leaves, see pages 42–45.

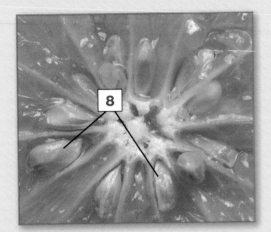
8

Vocabulary in Context 🎧 CD 1 TR 45

Ferns, flowering plants, and **conifers** (plants with **cones**) are **vascular plants.** Vascular plants have tubes in their **stems.** These tubes are called **xylem** and **phloem.** Xylem moves water and minerals from the **roots** to the **leaves.** Phloem moves food from the leaves to other parts of the plant. These tubes help vascular plants stand tall and upright. Vascular plants can live in dry or wet places. **Mosses** are **nonvascular plants.** Nonvascular plants do not have tubes or roots. They are small and low to the ground. They live in dark, wet places. Some live in water.

Many plants produce **seeds.** Other plants such as ferns and mosses are **seedless** plants.

9 Nonvascular Plants

10

11

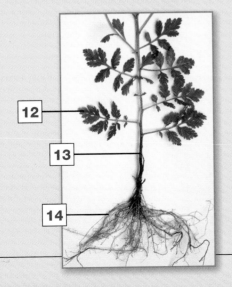
12
13
14

✔ Check Your Understanding

1. Look at the pictures. What nonvascular plants do you see?
2. Where do nonvascular plants live?
3. What are vascular plants?

Critical Thinking Making Inferences
4. Why are nonvascular plants low to the ground?

📖 Workbook page 37

39

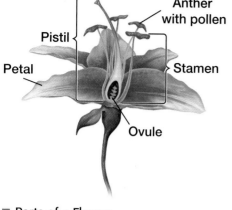

Anther with pollen

Pistil

Petal

Stamen

Ovule

■ Parts of a Flower

Flowering Plants
CD 1 TR 46

The flower is the part of a flowering plant that helps the plant make new plants. A flower contains **stamens** and one or more **pistils.** The top part of the stamen is called the **anther.** The anther makes **pollen,** a yellow powder. A pistil has eggs in it.

Pollination happens when pollen lands on the sticky top of the pistil. A tube then grows from the top of the pistil down to the **ovule** inside the pistil. The pollen travels down the tube. The pollen then **fertilizes** an egg in the ovule. A seed develops from the egg.

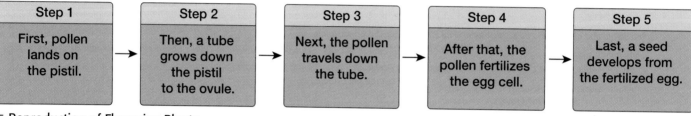

Step 1	Step 2	Step 3	Step 4	Step 5
First, pollen lands on the pistil.	Then, a tube grows down the pistil to the ovule.	Next, the pollen travels down the tube.	After that, the pollen fertilizes the egg cell.	Last, a seed develops from the fertilized egg.

■ Reproduction of Flowering Plants

▶ For more information on the parts of plants and how they work, see pages 42–45.

▶ For more information on sexual reproduction, see pages 66–69.

Science Skill   Reading Steps in a Sequence

Steps in a sequence tell you the order in which things happen. Words like "first," "then," "next," "after that," and "last" show the order of the steps. Look at the steps that a flowering plant goes through when it reproduces.

1. What is the first step in reproduction in a flower?

2. What happens after the tube grows down to the ovule?

3. What happens last in the reproduction of the plant?

What Is a Fern?
CD 1 TR 47

Ferns are plants that share some traits with mosses. They share other features with flowering plants and conifers. Ferns and mosses are both seedless plants. They reproduce by making **spores.** A spore is one cell that develops into a new plant. But ferns also share characteristics with seed plants. They have roots and xylem and phloem. This makes them like flowering plants and conifers.

Spores

■ Fern Spores

Academic Vocabulary

Ferns share	traits	with both mosses and seed plants.
	features	
	characteristics	

Word Study

Suffixes

A suffix is a word part that is added to the end of a word. A suffix changes the meaning of the word it is added to. The suffix **less** means "without."

Ferns and mosses are both **seedless** plants.

The word **seedless** tells you that ferns and mosses are without seeds.

How a Seed Works CD 1 TR 48

When some seeds fall from their parent plant, they **germinate,** or start growing, right away. Other seeds must rest before they germinate. Some seeds have to travel away from their parent plant. This happens in different ways. The wind can carry seeds far from the plant. Some seeds have tiny hooks that make them stick to animals' fur.

When a seed is ready to germinate, it absorbs water. This makes the seed's hard outer shell break. A root grows out of one end of the seed. A stem grows out of the other end. The new plant is called a **seedling.**

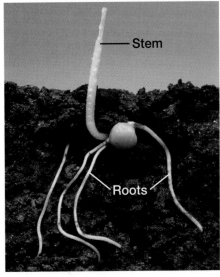

Stem

Roots

■ A Sprouting Seed

✅ Check Your Understanding

1. What is pollen? Which part of the flower makes pollen?

2. How do ferns reproduce?

3. What are two ways a seed can be carried away from its parent plant?

Critical Thinking Comparing and Contrasting

4. How are ferns like mosses? How are they different from mosses?

 Research and Inquiry Use the internet, the library, or your science book to answer these questions.

1. What are the oldest living trees? How old are they?

2. What are evergreen plants? Are all evergreen plants conifers? Explain.

3. What plant has the largest flower in the world? Where does it live? What does it smell like?

 Writing Think of a plant that you know. It might be a tree at your school or some moss on the sidewalk. Describe the plant. Where does it grow? Is it vascular? Is it seedless or seed-bearing?

Photosynthesis

CD 1
TR 49

FOCUS QUESTION
What is photosynthesis?

1 sunlight
2 green plant
3 roots
4 leaves
5 chlorophyll
6 chloroplast
7 stems
8 photosynthesis
9 soil
10 guard cells
11 stomata
12 xylem
13 phloem

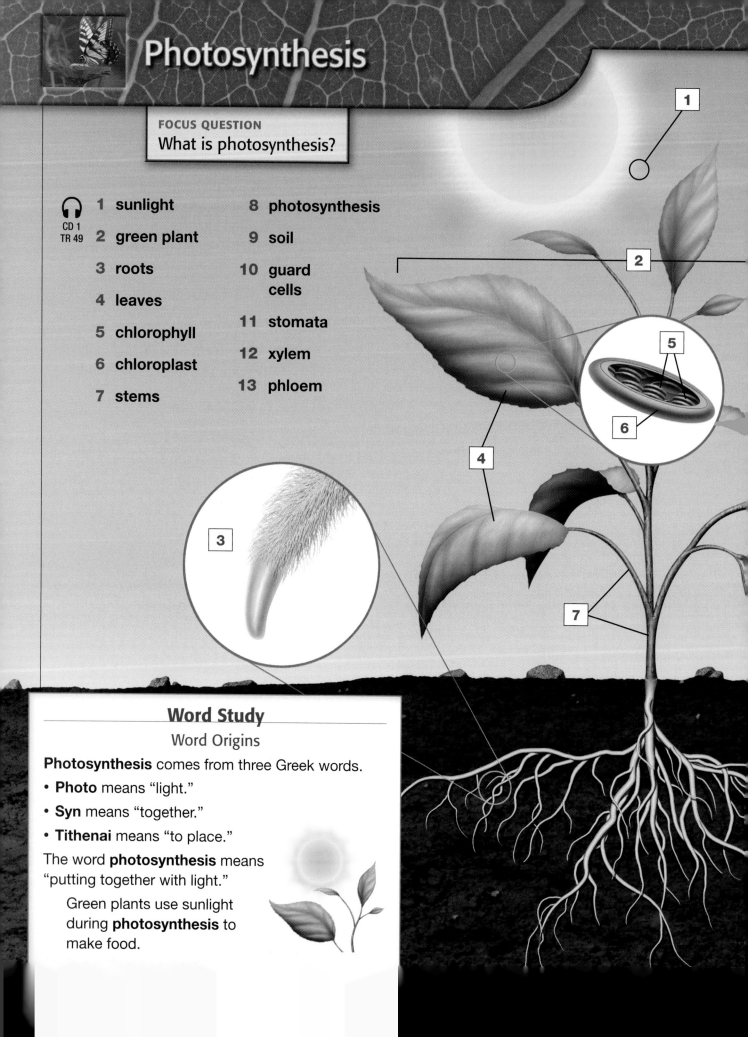

Word Study
Word Origins

Photosynthesis comes from three Greek words.

- **Photo** means "light."
- **Syn** means "together."
- **Tithenai** means "to place."

The word **photosynthesis** means "putting together with light."

Green plants use sunlight during **photosynthesis** to make food.

8

$$\text{carbon dioxide + water} \xrightarrow[\text{chlorophyll}]{\text{sunlight}} \text{sugar + oxygen}$$

Vocabulary in Context CD 1 TR 50

Green plants use **sunlight,** water, and carbon dioxide to make their food (a kind of sugar). This process is **photosynthesis.** Photosynthesis happens in **leaves,** in the **chloroplasts** of leaf cells. **Chlorophyll** is in the chloroplasts. Chlorophyll uses the energy in sunlight to make food. Photosynthesis releases oxygen as waste.

Other plant parts help make and store food. Water from **soil** travels up from the **roots** through tubes in the **stems** and leaves called **xylem.** Carbon dioxide and oxygen enter and leave the plant through the **stomata,** on the underside of leaves. **Guard cells** in leaves open and close the stomata. Food travels to the rest of the plant through **phloem,** tubes in the stems and leaves.

▶ For information about oxygen and carbon dioxide, see page 148.

▶ For information on chemical reactions, see pages 178–181.

12

13

Carbon dioxide   Oxygen

9

10

11

✅ Check Your Understanding

1. Look at the pictures. Where do carbon dioxide and oxygen from the air enter and leave the leaf?

2. What does a plant need to make food?

3. What is photosynthesis?

Critical Thinking Making Inferences

4. Why will a plant make less food on a very cloudy day?

Workbook page 41

Photosynthesis

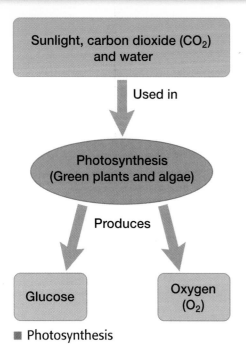

Sunlight, carbon dioxide (CO$_2$) and water

↓ Used in

Photosynthesis (Green plants and algae)

Produces

Glucose

Oxygen (O$_2$)

■ Photosynthesis

Photosynthesis CD 1 TR 51

Plants are organisms that can make their own food. Most other organisms get their food from plants or from organisms that eat plants. In photosynthesis, plants use sunlight to combine **carbon dioxide** (CO$_2$) with water and turn them into **glucose,** a kind of sugar. Plants release **oxygen** (O$_2$) as a waste product.

H$_2$O

H$_2$O

■ Transport in a Plant

Transport in a Plant CD 1 TR 52

How do materials move around in a plant? Tiny round cells link from end to end to form tubes.

Water in the soil enters the plant roots. The water is pulled up to the leaves through tubes called xylem.

Other tubes, called phloem, carry the food made in plant leaves. This phloem tissue carries food to growing roots, stems, and leaves.

Academic Vocabulary

Plants	**produce**	oxygen in photosynthesis.
They	**release**	the oxygen as a waste product.

Annual Tree Rings CD 1 TR 53

Tree trunks are the woody stems of trees. They contain the plant's xylem and phloem tissue. The outer bark is dead phloem cells. Just under the bark is the live phloem tissue. The xylem is found inside the phloem tissue.

Each year a tree grows a new ring of xylem and phloem. If you study a cross section of a tree trunk, you see its **annual rings.** These rings are made of old xylem tissue. The rings may be wide or narrow. Wide rings are a sign of a year with a lot of rain. You can tell the age of a tree by counting the rings.

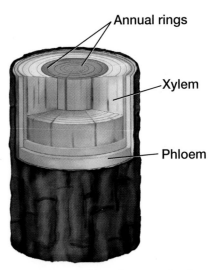

■ A Cross-section of a Tree Trunk Showing Annual Rings

Word Study

Multiple-Meaning Words

The word **tissue** has different meanings.

Tissue can mean "a paper product such as a paper handkerchief."

When I sneeze, I use a **tissue.**

Tissue can mean "a group of cells that all do a certain job."

Xylem and phloem are plant **tissues.**

✔ Check Your Understanding

1. What is glucose?
2. What tubes bring water to the leaves?
3. What are tree trunks? What do they contain?

Critical Thinking Applying Information

4. A tree is cut down in your yard. How can you figure out the age of the tree? Explain.

Research and Inquiry Use the internet, the library, or your science book to answer these questions.

1. How important are oceans in providing oxygen for animals?
2. What tree does maple sugar come from? How do people make maple syrup?
3. Why do leaves change color in the fall? How does this affect photosynthesis?

Writing Explain how the xylem and phloem of plant stems help the plant make food. Think about the things plants need for photosynthesis and the jobs that these tubes do. Write a paragraph.

Animals

FOCUS QUESTION
What do all animals need?

CD 1
TR 54

1 backbone	9 frog
2 air	10 grosbeak
3 water	11 nest
4 octopus	12 raccoon
5 shark	13 shelter
6 turtle	14 deer
7 crab	15 food
8 duck	

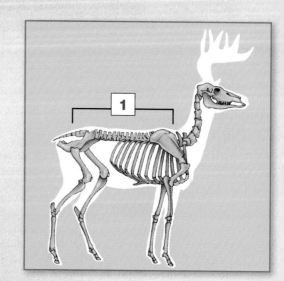

Word Study
Word Origins

Animal has Latin and Greek origins.

- The Latin word **animus** means "spirit."
- The Greek word **anemo** means "wind."
- The Latin word **anima** means "breath."

The origins of this word show the importance of air to this group of living things.

Vocabulary in Context 🎧 CD 1 TR 55

All animals have the same basic needs. Animals need **air** and **water** to live. Many animals use the oxygen in air. **Sharks** and **octopuses** get oxygen from the water around them. Water keeps animals' bodies from drying out. It keeps them cool.

Animals also need **food** and **shelter.** Food provides energy. Land animals such as **deer** or **raccoons** get water by drinking or from their food. A shelter is a safe place to live. Birds and raccoons live in trees. Octopuses live in caves or hide among rocks.

▶ For information on where animals live, see pages 82–85.

Grass

✔ Check Your Understanding

1. Look at the pictures. Which animals live in the water? Which ones live on land? Do any live in both? Explain.

2. How do land animals get water?

3. What do all animals need?

Critical Thinking Comparing and Contrasting

4. What are different ways animals meet their needs? Give examples.

📖 Workbook page 45

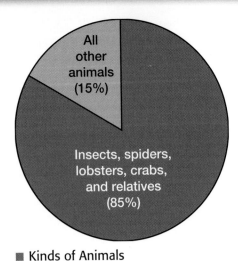

All
other
animals
(15%)

Insects, spiders,
lobsters, crabs,
and relatives
(85%)

■ Kinds of Animals

◆ For more information on animals with backbones, see pages 54–57.

◆ For more information on living things built from many cells, see pages 30–33.

Kinds of Animals CD 1 TR 56

Animals are divided into many groups. Most do not have backbones to support their bodies. Animals such as **worms, sponges,** and **jellyfish** have soft bodies. Animals such as **insects** and crabs have tough outer shells. The animals that are well known to you (**birds, fish, reptiles,** and **mammals**) are less than 5 percent of animals.

Science Skill   Reading a Pie Chart

A pie chart shows the parts of something. The pie is cut into slices. Each slice shows an amount. A bigger slice means a greater amount. When you read a pie chart, read the labels carefully. The numbers in parentheses ( ) tell you the percentages of each slice of the pie. Look at the pie chart.

1. Which group of animals is the largest?
2. Are humans members of the largest group of animals?

What Is an Animal? CD 1 TR 57

Animals have a number of common features. All animals are made of many **cells.** Animals eat food for energy. Most animals move about freely during part of their lives. Most have **senses** to help them respond to things around them. Their senses help them get the food, shelter, and water they need to live. Animals **reproduce** (make new baby animals like themselves) in different ways.

■ An owl eats mice for food.

The Amazing Octopus CD 1 TR 58

The octopus is a soft-bodied sea animal with a big **brain** and excellent eyesight. An octopus has eight arms covered with rows of **suckers.** The octopus uses its arms to catch **shellfish** it requires as food. It also uses its arms to walk along the ocean floor. Under its head is a **funnel.** If the octopus needs to move quickly, it forces a jet of water out of this funnel. It can hide by squirting out a cloud of black ink.

Suckers

■ An Octopus

Word Study
Word Origins

Octopus comes from Greek word roots.

- **Octo** means "eight."
- **Pod** means "foot."

  Octopus has two plurals: a regular plural form **(octopuses)** and a plural form from Greek **(octopi).**

 Academic Vocabulary

| An octopus | **needs** | food, air, water, and shelter. |
| | **requires** | |

✅ Check Your Understanding

1. You see a bird and an insect. Which animal belongs to the most common animal group?
2. How can you tell that a deer and a crab are animals?
3. What two ways can an octopus move?

Critical Thinking Making Inferences
4. Why does an octopus need to hide?

 Research and Inquiry Use the internet, the library, or your science book to answer these questions.

1. The cheetah is the fastest animal in the world. What are some other world record holders in the animal world?
2. Why do scientists think the octopus is a very smart animal?
3. How is a shark's body different from other fish?

 Writing Think of an animal that you know well. It might be a pet or one you have seen in the park or at a zoo. Tell how it meets its needs. Write a paragraph.

Invertebrates

CD 2
TR 1

1 backbone

2 invertebrates

3 basket sponge

4 jellyfish

5 tapeworm

6 heartworm

7 earthworm

8 beetle

9 centipede

10 spider

11 clam

12 shell

13 scallop

14 lobster

15 sea star

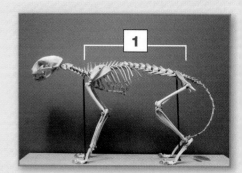

2 | Invertebrates

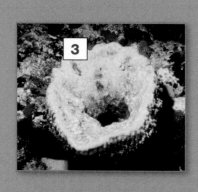

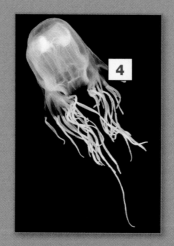

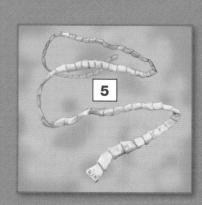

Word Study

Multiple-Meaning Words

The word **sponge** has different meanings.

Sponge can mean "a cleaning tool used to soak up water."

Luisa cleaned the table with a **sponge.**

Sponge can also mean "a simple animal that lives in water."

Many **sponges** are brightly colored.

Vocabulary in Context 🎧 CD 2 TR 2

Invertebrates are animals that don't have **backbones.** A backbone is a series of bones. It goes down the middle of an animal's back. Many invertebrates, such as **beetles,** have a hard, strong body case. Some invertebrates have **shells.**

More than 95% of all kinds of animals are invertebrates. Invertebrates live everywhere—in soil, in buildings, and even in other animals. **Earthworms** live in the ground. **Heartworms** and **tapeworms** live inside other animals. But invertebrates are most common in the sea. **Sponges, clams, jellyfish, sea stars, scallops,** and **lobsters** all live in the sea.

▶ For more information on classification systems, see pages 78–81.

✅ Check Your Understanding

1. Look at the pictures. What are three invertebrates that do not have legs?
2. What are three invertebrates that live in the sea?
3. What are invertebrates?

Critical Thinking Integrating Information
4. What kinds of invertebrates have you seen? Where have you seen them?

📖 Workbook page 49

Arachnids CD 2 TR 3

Arachnids include scorpions, spiders, and ticks. All arachnids have eight legs. An arachnid's body is divided into two sections. A hard, tough case covers the body. This case comes off as the animal gets larger. Then a new case grows. This is called **molting.** Spiders, like other arachnids, lay eggs. The spider eggs hatch into tiny spiders. The young spiders molt several times before they become adults.

■ Tick   ■ Scorpion

■ A chrysalis

Metamorphosis CD 2 TR 4

Metamorphosis is a process in which an animal's body shape changes as it grows. Most **insects** develop through metamorphosis. A butterfly starts as an egg. The egg hatches into a **caterpillar.** The caterpillar eats and grows. Then it forms a **chrysalis.** A chrysalis is a hard covering. Inside the chrysalis, the caterpillar changes into a butterfly. At last, the chrysalis opens and an adult butterfly comes out.

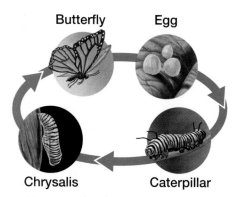

Butterfly   Egg

Chrysalis   Caterpillar

■ Metamorphosis

| **Science Skill** | Reading a Cycle Diagram |

A cycle diagram shows a number of connected events. These events happen again and again in the same order. Look at the diagram.

1. What are the four stages in a butterfly's life?
2. How is a butterfly's body different from a caterpillar's body?
3. Where do the eggs in the diagram come from?

a–z Academic Vocabulary

Caterpillars	**become**	butterflies.
	change into	
	develop into	

Word Study

Multiple-Meaning Words

The word **stage** has different meanings.

Stage can mean "a place for actors to perform."

He walked onto the **stage.**

Stage can also mean "a step in a process."

A chrysalis is a **stage** in a butterfly's life.

How Sponges Work CD 2 TR 5

Young sponges swim in water. Then they settle on objects and develop into adults. Adult sponges live in one place. They can't move. A sponge's body is a hollow tube. The tube is closed at the bottom and open at the top. Its body is covered with tiny openings called **pores.** Sponges pull in water through their pores. They get food from the water. Then the water leaves the sponge's body through the top opening.

Waterflow

Pores

■ An Adult Sponge

✔ Check Your Understanding

1. Name three kinds of arachnids.
2. A butterfly egg changes as it develops. What is this process called?
3. How do sponges get their food?

Critical Thinking Making Observations

4. What arachnids have you seen? Where have you seen them?

 Research and Inquiry Use the internet, the library, or your science book to answer these questions.

1. What other animals belong to the same group of invertebrates as jellyfish?
2. What are some kinds of worms that are harmful to people or pets?
3. What are some social insects? Why are they called social insects?

 Writing Imagine you are a butterfly egg. What will happen to you during your life? Write a paragraph.

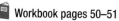

Vertebrates

FOCUS QUESTION
What groups of animals are vertebrates?

CD 2
TR 6

1 backbone

2 vertebrates

3 fish

4 trout

5 seahorse

6 amphibians

7 frog

8 salamander

9 reptiles

10 crocodile

11 snake

12 birds

13 flamingo

14 penguin

15 mammals

16 bear

17 human

| 1 |

| 2 | Vertebrates |

| 3 | Fish |

| 4 |

| 5 |

| 6 | Amphibians |

| 7 |

| 8 |

Word Study

Word Origins

The word **amphibian** comes from two Greek words.

- **Amphi** means "of two kinds."
- **Bios** means "way of life."

  Amphibians live both in water and on land.

Vocabulary in Context 🎧 CD 2 TR 7

Vertebrates are animals with **backbones.** There are five groups of vertebrates. **Trout** and **seahorses** are **fish. Frogs** and **salamanders** are **amphibians. Crocodiles** and **snakes** are **reptiles. Flamingos** and **penguins** are **birds. Bears** and **humans** are **mammals.**

▶ For information on how animals are grouped, see pages 78–79.

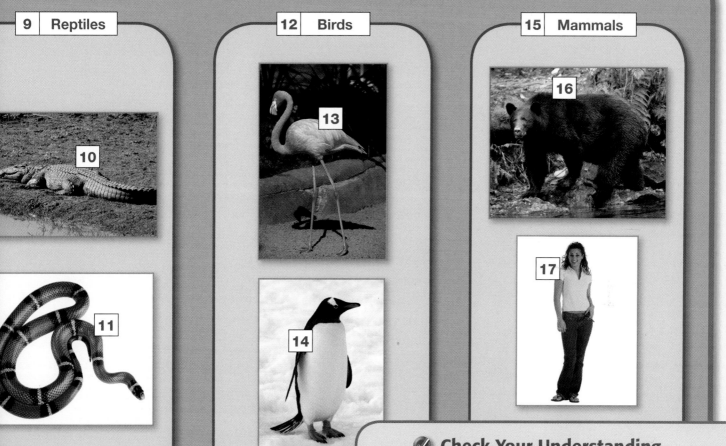

9	Reptiles
12	Birds
15	Mammals

10

11

13

14

16

17

✔ Check Your Understanding

1. Look at the pictures. What members of the reptile group are shown in the pictures?

2. What do all vertebrates have?

3. What groups of animals are vertebrates?

Critical Thinking Classifying Information

4. What group does a dog belong to? What group does a robin belong to? Think of another vertebrate. What group does it belong to?

📖 Workbook page 53

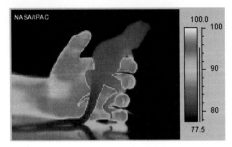

NASA/IPAC 100.0

■ This picture shows heat from an animal's body. Look at the cold blues of a reptile's body. Then look at the warm reds of the human hand.

▶ For information on how animals use food to make energy, see pages 86–87.

Warm-blooded and Cold-blooded Vertebrates 🎧 CD 2 TR 8

Some animals have body temperatures that always stay about the same. These animals are **warm-blooded.** They make body heat from the food they eat. Mammals and birds belong to this group.

Cold-blooded animals have body temperatures that change. Fish, amphibians, and reptiles are part of this group. These animals get their heat from what is around them. Reptiles move around to control their temperatures. They lie in the sun to warm up. They move into the shade to cool down.

Warm-blooded Vertebrates	Cold-blooded Vertebrates
Mammals and birds are warm-blooded.	Fish, amphibians, and reptiles are cold-blooded.
Body temperature stays about the same.	Body temperature changes.
They make body heat from the food they eat.	They get body heat from their surroundings.
They have backbones.	They have backbones.

■ Characteristics of Warm-blooded and Cold-blooded Vertebrates

Science Skill   Comparing and Contrasting

When you compare, you tell how two things are the same. When you contrast, you tell how two things are different. Look at the chart.

1. Which groups of vertebrates are cold-blooded? Which are warm-blooded?
2. Where does a mammal's body heat come from?
3. How are a bird's and a reptile's body temperatures different?
4. What feature do warm-blooded vertebrates and cold-blooded vertebrates both have?

📖 Academic Vocabulary

Seahorses	belong to	the fish group of vertebrates.
	are part of	
	are members of	

Kangaroos Are Mammals with Pouches

 CD 2 TR 9

Kangaroos are members of a group of mammals with pouches. A kangaroo baby grows inside its mother's body for only a short time. The tiny newborn crawls across its mother's fur into her pouch. The baby is called a joey. The joey lives in its mother's pouch. It drinks its mother's milk and grows bigger. It rides in the pouch until it is nine months old.

■ A Mother Kangaroo with a Joey in Her Pouch

Word Study

Compound Words

Compound words are made of two words put together.

Some compound words are hyphenated.

Bears are **warm-blooded.**

Some compound words are not hyphenated.

A **newborn** joey crawls into its mother's pouch.

✔ Check Your Understanding

1. A turtle is a reptile. How can it warm up its body?

2. Are humans warm-blooded or cold-blooded? How do you know?

3. What does a baby kangaroo do while living in its mother's pouch?

Critical Thinking Analyzing Information

4. Which groups of animals probably do not live where it is very cold? Explain.

■ A Turtle

Research and Inquiry Use the internet, the library, or your science book to answer these questions.

1. How are seahorses different from other fish?

2. How do frogs and toads change as they grow?

3. What are some birds that cannot fly? Where do they live?

 Writing Imagine that you are a cold-blooded animal. How will a summer day in your life be different from a summer day in your life as a warm-blooded animal? How will your daily activities change? Write a paragraph.

The Human Body

CD 2
TR 10

1 bones

2 muscles

3 blood vessels

Organs

4 heart

5 kidney

6 liver

7 stomach

8 intestines

9 brain

10 lungs

11 skin

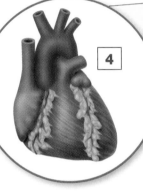

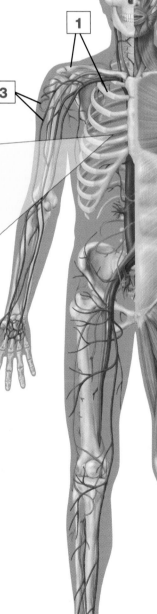

Word Study

Word Meanings

The **heart** is an organ of the body. Many English speakers connect the heart with love. For example, on Valentine's Day, people may send each other cards with hearts on them.

Vocabulary in Context 🎧 CD 2 TR 11

The human body is made of many different parts. **Bones** support your body. **Muscles** help your body move. The **heart** is an **organ.** An organ is a part of the body that has a special job. The heart's job is to pump blood. **Lungs** are organs that take in and let out air. **Skin** is the largest body organ. It protects the body. These body parts all work together.

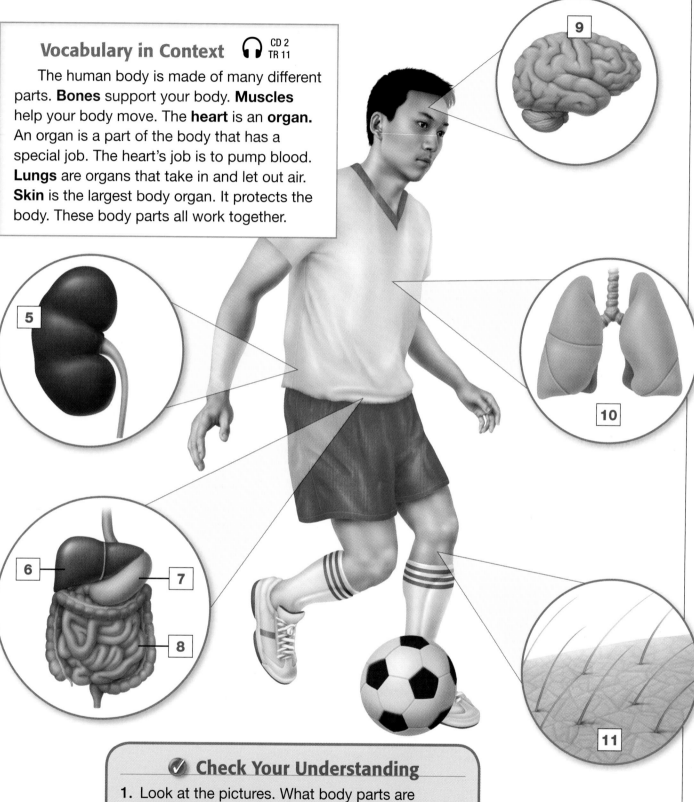

✅ Check Your Understanding

1. Look at the pictures. What body parts are connected to the heart?

2. What is the heart's job?

3. What are some organs of the human body?

Critical Thinking Making Inferences

4. You're running. What body parts and organs are you using? Make a list.

▶ For more information on organs, see pages 30–31.

📖 Workbook page 57

59

Organic Systems

● For more information on cells, tissues, and organs, see pages 30–31.

● For information on energy in living things, see pages 86–88.

Organ Systems

CD 2
TR 12

Organs are made of two or more tissues. Tissues are made of the same kinds of cells. Each organ has at least one job to do for the body. For example, the heart pumps blood. **Organ systems** are groups of organs that work together. Your body has eleven organ systems. Some of the jobs these systems do are carry things to and from all your cells, sense the outside world and react to it, help you move, change food into **energy,** and get rid of wastes.

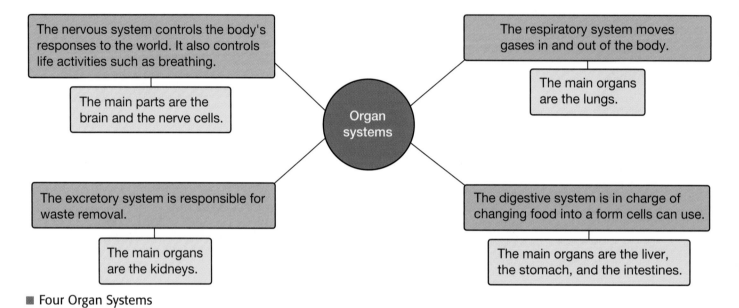

The nervous system controls the body's responses to the world. It also controls life activities such as breathing.

The main parts are the brain and the nerve cells.

The excretory system is responsible for waste removal.

The main organs are the kidneys.

Organ systems

The respiratory system moves gases in and out of the body.

The main organs are the lungs.

The digestive system is in charge of changing food into a form cells can use.

The main organs are the liver, the stomach, and the intestines.

■ Four Organ Systems

Science Skill   Concept Maps

A concept map organizes information. The main idea is in the middle. The boxes show related ideas. The concept map above contains information about some of the main systems in your body.

1. What job does the digestive system perform? What are its main organs?
2. Which organ system helps you get air?
3. Which organ system controls your responses to the outside world?

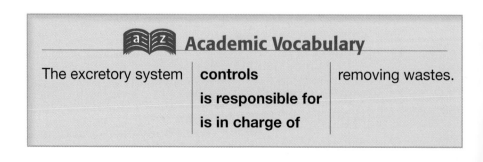

Academic Vocabulary

The excretory system	controls	removing wastes.
	is responsible for	
	is in charge of	

The Circulatory System

CD 2
TR 13

The circulatory system is the body's transport system. It takes food and gases to every cell. Small tubes called blood vessels act like pipelines that carry the blood.

The heart is the main part of the circulatory system. It is divided into two halves. The right side pumps blood to the lungs. Then the blood returns to the left side of the heart. The left side pumps blood out to the body through the blood vessels. Blood flows into a web of smaller and smaller tubes to reach each cell. Then it flows into blood vessels that return it to the right side of the heart. Look at the picture. Red lines show blood moving away from the heart. Blue lines show blood returning to the heart.

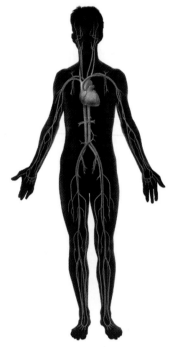

■ The circulatory system moves food and gases throughout the body. Red lines show blood moving away from the heart. Blue lines show blood returning to the heart.

Word Study
Word Families

Circular means "round."

Circulate means to "flow around" or to "pass around."

Blood **circulates** through the body.

Circulation means "movement in a circular path."

Good blood **circulation** is important to your health.

✓ Check Your Understanding

1. Name the main parts of the nervous system.
2. What is the job of the respiratory system?
3. What do blood vessels do?

Critical Thinking Comparing and Contrasting
4. How are the jobs of the two sides of the heart different? How are they the same?

Research and Inquiry Use the internet, the library, or your science book to answer these questions.

1. How do doctors replace damaged bones in joints, such as knees or hips?
2. What is homeostasis?
3. Find out what the scientist William Harvey discovered about the heart.

Writing Select an item in your classroom that is part of a system. What system does it belong to? How does it help make that system work? Write a paragraph.

Asexual Reproduction

FOCUS QUESTION
What is mitosis?

CD 2
TR 14

1 asexual reproduction

2 cell division/mitosis

3 parent cell

4 nucleus

5 daughter cells

6 chromosome

7 leaf

8 stem

9 root

10 vegetative reproduction

11 bulb

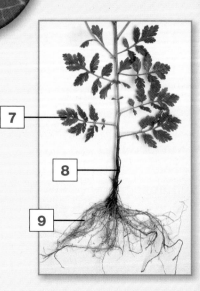

---

1 Asexual Reproduction

2 Cell Division/Mitosis

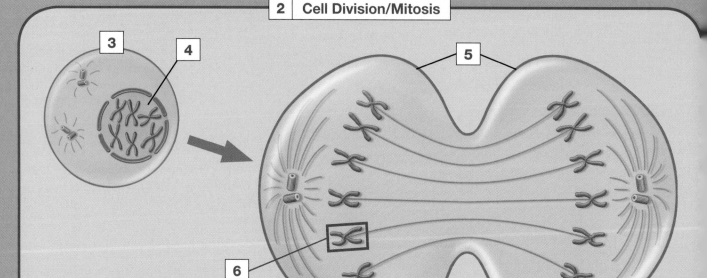

Word Study

Word Parts

The word **reproduction** has three parts.

- The prefix **re** means "again."
- The word **produce** means "to make" or "to create."
- The suffix **tion** refers to a process.

Put the word parts together. **Reproduction** is a life process. It means "the process of making again" or making offspring.

For more information on cells, see pages 22–25.

Vocabulary in Context 🎧 CD 2 TR 15

Your body makes new cells all the time. Cells use **cell division,** also called **mitosis,** to make new cells. In mitosis, a **parent cell** divides to make two new **daughter cells.** The daughter cells are exactly alike. That is because the cell copies its **chromosomes** before dividing. Chromosomes provide the instructions to make new cells. Each daughter cell has the same set of chromosomes as the parent cell.

All living things use mitosis, but only some, such as bacteria, use it to reproduce. Mitosis is a kind of **asexual reproduction.** Some plants use another kind of asexual reproduction. These plants make special **roots, bulbs, stems,** or **leaves.** These plant parts can form new plants. For example, new kalanchoe plants grow along the leaves of the parent plant. The tiny plants drop off the leaves, fall to the ground, and take root. This kind of reproduction is called **vegetative reproduction.** An onion plant also uses vegetative reproduction. An onion plant can grow a new bulb. A new plant can grow from this new bulb.

10 | Vegetative Reproduction

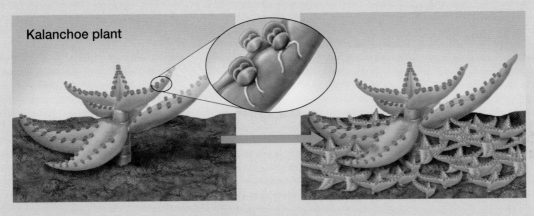

Kalanchoe plant

Onion plant

11

✔ Check Your Understanding

1. Look at the pictures of the cell. What is the cell doing?
2. What information do chromosomes provide?
3. What is mitosis?

Critical Thinking Inferring from Evidence

4. A parent cell has 8 chromosomes. After mitosis, how many chromosomes will each daughter cell have?

📖 Workbook page 61

63

Asexual Reproduction

Minutes	Number of Bacteria
0	1
15	2
30	4
45	8
60	16
75	32

■ Bacteria reproduce at a high rate.

▶ For information on single-celled organisms, see pages 26–29.

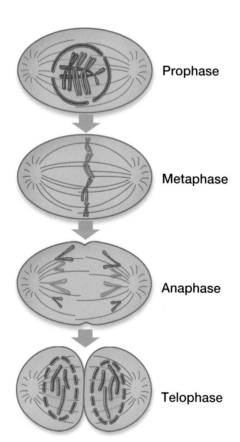

■ The Stages of Mitosis

Prophase

Metaphase

Anaphase

Telophase

▶ For information on chromosomes and genetics, see pages 70–73.

Bacteria Reproduction CD 2 TR 16

Many living things make offspring by asexual reproduction. This is how **bacteria, amoebas,** and **yeast** reproduce. Cell division occurs very quickly. Amoebas and yeast divide in a few hours. Most bacteria reproduce even faster. They make new cells in a few minutes. One bacteria cell can produce more than 16 million new bacteria in one day.

Science Skill Looking for Patterns

When you see numbers in a table, you can look for patterns. You can see the numbers going up or down. You can see if the numbers are changing quickly or slowly. You can see if the change is steady or irregular. Look at the table.

1. How many bacteria are there after 30 minutes have passed? How many are there after 75 minutes?

2. How often can a bacteria cell divide? What does this mean for a bacteria population?

3. What does the chart tell you about the speed at which bacteria can reproduce?

Mitosis CD 2 TR 17

Mitosis occurs in a series of stages, or phases. The first stage is **prophase.** The chromosomes double and pair up. The wall around the nucleus goes away. The chromosome pairs get ready to move.

The second stage is **metaphase.** All the chromosomes move to the middle of the cell.

The third stage is **anaphase.** The chromosome pairs pull apart. They move away from each other.

The last stage is **telophase.** The chromosomes are at opposite ends of the dividing cell. The wall of the nucleus forms around each set of chromosomes.

The sequence of cell division finishes. The cell divides, and two new cells form.

📖 Academic Vocabulary

Cellular reproduction occurs in a	**series**	of stages.
	sequence	

Word Study
Word Parts

The word part **phase** means "stage."

The prefix **pro** means "before."

    Prophase is the first stage in mitosis.

The prefix **meta** means "after."

    Metaphase is the next stage in mitosis.

The prefix **ana** means "up."

    Anaphase is when the chromosomes move apart.

The prefix **telo** means "end."

    Telophase is the last stage in mitosis.

Vegetative Reproduction CD 2 TR 18

Some plants reproduce asexually from their roots, stems, or leaves. This is vegetative reproduction. The new plants are the same as the parent.

Strawberry plants have stems that grow along the top of the soil. These stems are called **runners.** New plants grow at special places where a runner touches the ground.

Runners

■ Strawberry plants use runners to reproduce.

✅ Check Your Understanding

1. Name some living things that make offspring by asexual reproduction.

2. What are the four stages of mitosis? Give them in order from first to last.

3. What is a runner? What is one plant that uses runners to reproduce?

Critical Thinking Analyzing Information

4. Mitosis mainly affects one cell part. Which part is it?

 Research and Inquiry Use the internet, the library, or your science book to answer these questions.

1. What are some different ways that plants can reproduce asexually?

2. How does asexual reproduction help a starfish? Describe two ways.

3. Why is asexual reproduction important for medical research?

 Writing Imagine you are using a special microscope. You are watching bacteria reproduce. What do you see over a few hours? Write a paragraph.

CD 2
TR 19

FOCUS QUESTION
What happens during meiosis?

1 **sexual reproduction**

2 **parent cell**

3 **chromosome**

4 **meiosis**

5 **cell division**

6 **daughter cells**

7 **sex cells**

Chromosomes are copied.

Chromosomes line up in pairs.

Chromosomes pull apart.

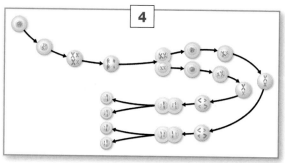

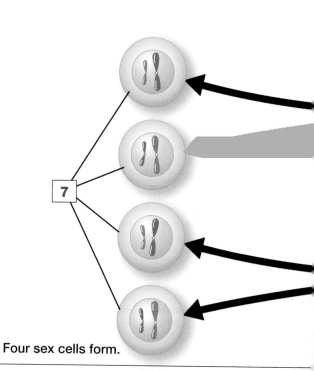

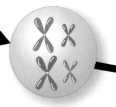

Four sex cells form.

Word Study

Prefixes

What is the difference between the terms **sexual reproduction** and **asexual reproduction**?

The difference is the short prefix **a**.

The prefix **a** means "without" or "not."

Sexual reproduction requires sex cells. **Asexual reproduction** happens without sex cells.

○ For information on chromosomes, see pages 70–71.

○ For information on asexual reproduction, see page 62.

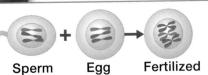

Sperm cell (from father) + Egg cell (from mother) → Fertilized cell

Vocabulary in Context

CD 2
TR 20

All living things reproduce, or make offspring. Many plants and animals reproduce by **sexual reproduction.** These offspring have two parents. The offspring are different from both parents. Some plants and animals can reproduce by asexual reproduction. These offspring have one parent. The offspring are identical to the parent.

Sex cells are important for sexual reproduction. Sex cells form through **meiosis.** In meiosis, a cell goes through **cell division** two times. The result is a set of four sex cells. Each sex cell has half the **chromosomes** of the **parent cell.** Chromosomes are in the cell nucleus. They provide the instructions to make new cells. One sex cell from each parent join together to create the offspring. Each fertilized cell has a complete set of chromosomes.

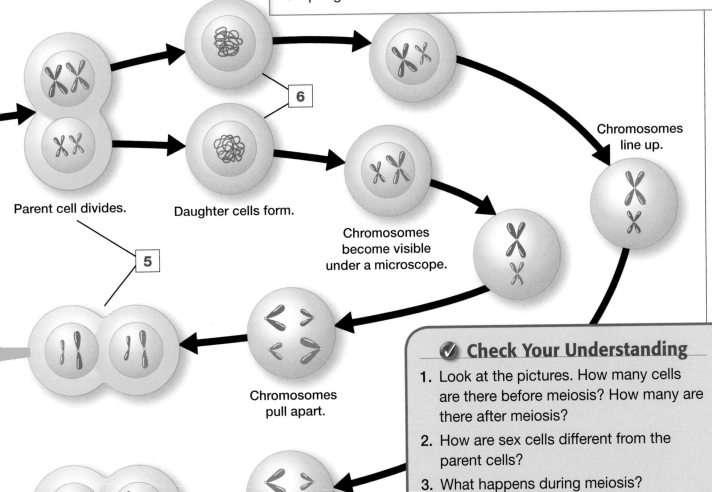

Parent cell divides.

5

Daughter cells form.

6

Chromosomes become visible under a microscope.

Chromosomes line up.

Chromosomes pull apart.

Daughter cells divide.

✓ Check Your Understanding

1. Look at the pictures. How many cells are there before meiosis? How many are there after meiosis?

2. How are sex cells different from the parent cells?

3. What happens during meiosis?

Critical Thinking Making Inferences

4. A cat has kittens. Why aren't all the kittens exactly like their mother?

📖 Workbook page 65

Meiosis and Sex Cells CD 2 TR 21

Meiosis is a **process** with many steps. First, pairs of matching chromosomes line up together. When the chromosomes line up, small sections of the chromosomes can switch places with one another. This is called **crossing over.** During crossing over, the chromosomes in the daughter cells become different from the chromosomes in the parent cell. As a result, the offspring will be different from their parents.

Meiosis ends when four new cells form from the parent cell. If the parent cell came from a female, then one of the sex cells becomes an egg cell. If the parent cell came from a male, then all the sex cells become **sperm** cells.

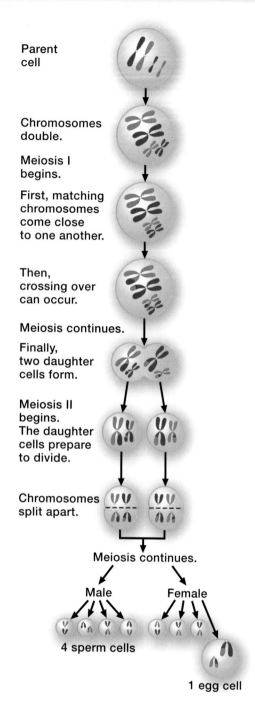

Parent cell

Chromosomes double.

Meiosis I begins.

First, matching chromosomes come close to one another.

Then, crossing over can occur.

Meiosis continues.

Finally, two daughter cells form.

Meiosis II begins. The daughter cells prepare to divide.

Chromosomes split apart.

Meiosis continues.

Male   Female

4 sperm cells

1 egg cell

■ Meiosis

Science Skill   Reading a Flowchart

A flowchart shows steps in a process. Arrows help you follow the steps. Most flowcharts show more than one path. Usually there is at least one place where the path branches. A branch means that more than one result is possible. Follow the path of the flowchart.

1. How many cells start this process?
2. Do chromosomes double in meiosis I? Do they double in meiosis II?
3. What are two possible results at the end of the process?

Word Study

Two-Word Verbs

Up can mean "the opposite of down."

The balloon flew **up** into the sky.

When **up** is used as part of a two-word verb, it often does not mean "the opposite of down."

Line up means "get into a line."

Matching pairs of chromosomes **line up.**

Academic Vocabulary

Words such as **first, then,** and **finally** can show the order, or sequence, in which events happen.

First, matching chromosomes come close to one another.

Then, crossing over can occur.

Finally, two daughter cells form.

Variations

CD 2
TR 22

Variations are differences. These puppies show variations in their markings. Sexual reproduction can cause changes in chromosomes. This sometimes happens during meiosis, when chromosomes cross over. It always happens when two sex cells from different parents join together and form a fertilized cell. The fertilized cell makes a new living thing. This new living thing has some chromosomes from each parent.

■ Variations Among Puppies

✓ Check Your Understanding

1. When during meiosis do chromosomes cross over?
2. What happens to chromosomes in daughter cells during crossing over?
3. What are variations? What are two ways sexual reproduction causes variations?

Critical Thinking Making Inferences
4. A set of four male cells is produced at the end of meiosis. What does this tell you about the parent cell?

 Research and Inquiry Use the internet, the library, or your science book to answer these questions.

1. Why is the variation produced by sexual reproduction an advantage?
2. Choose two animals. How many chromosomes are in the body cells of each animal? How many chromosomes are in the sex cells of each animal?
3. What are the stages of meiosis called? What happens in each stage? How are the stages of meiosis different from the stages of mitosis?

 Writing Choose an animal. Write a paragraph describing a variation that can occur because of sexual reproduction. Explain how this variation helps or harms the animal's chance of survival.

Genetics

FOCUS QUESTION
What do genes do?

CD 2
TR 23

1 **chromosome**

2 **gene**

3 **thymine**

4 **cytosine**

5 **adenine**

6 **guanine**

7 **trait**

8 **DNA**

9 **double helix**

Red

Brown

| 1 |
| 2 |
| 3 |
| 4 |
| 5 |
| 6 |
| 8 |

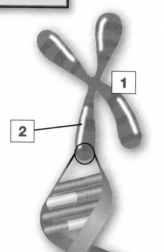

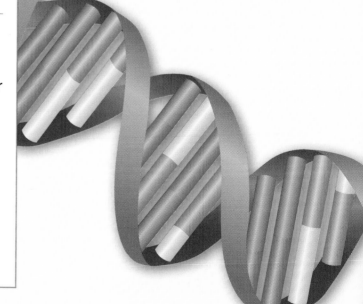

Word Study

Multiple-Meaning Words

The word **base** has different meanings.

In baseball, a **base** is one of four squares touched by runners.

The runner was out because he did not touch the **base.**

In science, a **base** is one kind of chemical compound.

DNA contains the **base** guanine.

● For information on chromosomes, see pages 66–69.

● For information on cells, see pages 24–27.

7

Blond

— Eye color

— Hair color

Vocabulary in Context 🎧 CD 2 TR 24

Eye and hair color are **traits.** Parents pass on traits to their children in their **genes.** Different genes control different traits. Genes are found on **chromosomes.** Chromosomes are in the nucleus of cells. Chromosomes are made from **DNA.** DNA provides the chemical recipe that builds your traits. DNA contains instructions on how to build each part of your body.

DNA is in the shape of a **double helix.** A double helix looks like a twisted ladder. The "rungs" of the ladder are made of four bases. They are **adenine, thymine, guanine,** and **cytosine.**

9

— Rung

✓ Check Your Understanding

1. Look at the pictures. What is DNA made from?
2. Where are genes found?
3. What do genes do?

Critical Thinking Inferring from Evidence

4. Why do children look like their parents or other relatives?

📖 Workbook page 69

Dominant and Recessive Traits CD 2 TR 25

Offspring receive, or **inherit,** pairs of genes from their parents. Each gene controls a certain trait. One gene in each pair comes from the one parent. The other gene comes from the other parent.

Sometimes, one trait appears in offspring while the other one stays hidden. A **dominant** gene controls a trait. A dominant gene allows people to roll their tongues. The trait appears whenever this gene is present. A **recessive** gene is in charge of a trait that only appears when two genes in a pair are recessive. Only people with two recessive genes cannot roll their tongues. When a pair of genes contains a dominant and a recessive gene, offspring show the dominant trait. Those offspring can roll their tongues.

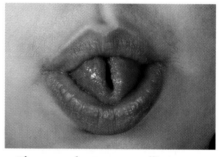

■ The gene for tongue rolling is dominant.

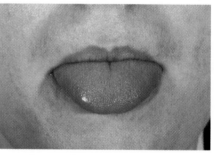

■ Only people with two recessive genes cannot roll their tongues.

Word Study

Antonyms

Antonyms are words with opposite meanings.

Dominant and **recessive** have opposite meanings in science.

Dominant means "having greater power."

Recessive means "hiding" or "without power."

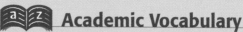 **Academic Vocabulary**

| A dominant gene | controls | tongue rolling. |
| | is responsible for | |

Punnett Squares CD 2 TR 26

A **Punnett square** shows how genes from two parents are responsible for producing traits. It helps predict which traits are likely to appear in their offspring. One parent's genes are across the top. The other parent's genes are listed on the side. This Punnett square tells about one trait of pea plants—whether they are tall or short. Tall (T) is the dominant gene. Short (t) is the recessive gene. A plant will be short only if it gets two recessive genes. Each offspring can get different genes. The different possible genes are in the boxes.

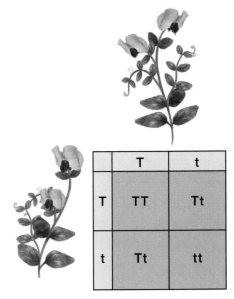

	T	t
T	TT	Tt
t	Tt	tt

■ In pea plants, tall (T) is the dominant trait.

Science Skill | Reading a Punnett Square

A Punnett square organizes information about the genes from two parents. The letters in the diagram stand for genes. Capital letters stand for a dominant gene (T). Small letters stand for a recessive gene (t). Look at the Punnett square.

1. Are the parent plants tall or short? How do you know?

2. Can the parent plants have short offspring? How do you know?

3. Can the plant with TT genes have short offspring? Explain.

✓ Check Your Understanding

1. What is a dominant gene? What is a recessive gene?

2. Is the gene for tongue rolling dominant or recessive?

3. What is a Punnett square?

Critical Thinking Applying Information

4. Two short pea plants reproduce. Can any of the offspring be tall? Why?

 Research and Inquiry Use the internet, the library, or your science book to answer these questions.

1. Who invented the Punnett square?

2. Which scientists figured out the double helix shape of DNA?

3. What is incomplete dominance? Give an example.

 Writing Black fur is a dominant trait in rabbits. Brown fur is recessive. A rabbit with two genes for black fur and a rabbit with two genes for brown fur mate. Will the offspring be black or brown? Why? Write a paragraph.

Changes Over Time

CD 2
TR 27

FOCUS QUESTION

What are variations? What are adaptations?

1 organism

2 adaptation

3 beak

4 species

5 common ancestor

6 subspecies

7 variation

8 fossil

| 1 |

| 2 | Adaptation |

An adaptation helps an animal survive.

■ Pouched beaks help pelicans scoop fish from the water to eat.

■ Crossed beaks help red crossbills pull seeds from pinecones.

■ Long, thin beaks help herons catch fish.

■ Short, strong beaks help grosbeaks eat seeds.

Word Study

Suffixes

The verb **adapt** means "to change." The suffix **tion** can be added to **adapt** to form the noun **adaptation.**

In life science, an **adaptation** is a change in an organism that helps the organism live. Scientists

believe that the shape of a duck's beak is an example of an adaptation. The shape of the beak helps the duck get food from the water.

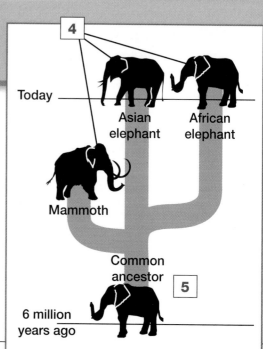

| 4 |

Today

Asian elephant

African elephant

Mammoth

Common ancestor

| 5 |

6 million years ago

Vocabulary in Context 🎧 CD 2 TR 28

Birds and other **organisms** have differences called **variations.** A variation that helps an organism survive is an **adaptation.** For example, birds have different **beaks.** Throughout history, birds lived in different places and found different food. Over time, the birds' beaks changed. The variations in beaks helped the birds eat the food they found. Thick, strong beaks helped grosbeaks eat seeds. Long, thin beaks helped herons catch fish. Birds whose beaks helped them find and eat food survived. Birds with different beaks died out.

Some kinds of birds have many adaptations. They become different from related birds. The birds can't reproduce together. Birds that can't reproduce together are members of different **species.**

Birds of the same species can have variations, too. For example, some seaside sparrows are different colors. Some have different markings. These birds can reproduce with one another. These birds are members of different **subspecies.**

6 | Subspecies

Seaside sparrows

8

Seaside sparrow

Marking

7

Louisiana seaside sparrow

Cape Sable seaside sparrow

✅ Check Your Understanding

1. Look at the pictures of the sparrows. Look at patterns and colors. What variations do you see?

2. What is a species? What is a subspecies?

3. What are variations? What are adaptations?

Critical Thinking Interpreting Information

4. Look at the birds on page 74. How do the adaptations help the birds?

▶ For information on birds, see pages 54–57.

📖 Workbook page 73

The Theory of Evolution

CD 2
TR 29

● For information on reproduction and genetics, see pages 66–69.

The theory of **evolution** explains how organisms change. Evolution means "change over time." This theory states that new species develop from earlier species. Over time, new variations occur. The variations help species adapt in order to survive. Eventually, new species appear. For example, fossils show that about 200 million years ago, there were no birds on Earth. But there were dinosaurs. Later fossils show some dinosaurs evolving into birds. Fossil evidence supports the theory that birds' common ancestor is a dinosaur.

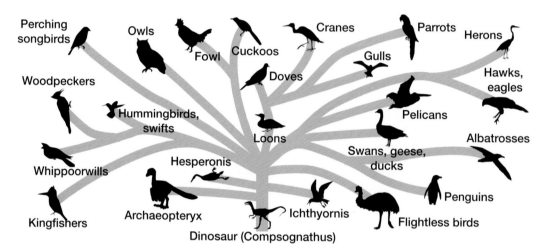

■ Birds' Common Ancestor

Science Skill   Reading a Tree Diagram

This tree diagram shows how scientists believe birds evolved. The **base,** or bottom, of the tree names the common ancestor. The first bird species branch off near the base. These birds are **extinct.** They don't exist today.

Look at all the tree branches. Find the birds at the ends of the branches. You can see how different types of birds are related.

1. What kind of bird is most closely related to hummingbirds? Explain.

2. Which four kinds of birds have the loon as a common ancestor? Explain.

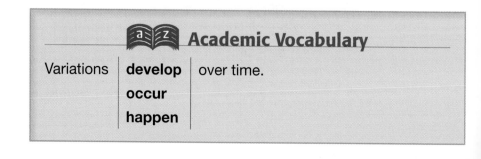

🔤 Academic Vocabulary

Variations	develop	over time.
	occur	
	happen	

Word Study
Multiple-Meaning Words

The word **theory** has an everyday meaning and a scientific meaning.

In everyday speech, a theory is an idea or guess. It is based on limited knowledge. It might or might not be true.

He can't prove his **theory** that cats can think.

In science, a theory is an explanation of how things happen. A theory is based on careful observation and hypotheses that scientists have tested and retested many times with scientific methods.

Fossil evidence supports the **theory** that birds' common ancestor is a dinosaur.

Natural Selection CD 2 TR 30

Organisms have many variations. Over time, some variations help the organisms survive. Those organisms live and reproduce. The result is an adaptation. This process is called **natural selection.**

Natural selection explains how organisms that are best adapted to their conditions survive. Two kinds of moths are a good example. The picture shows two subspecies of moths on a tree trunk. The dark moths were easy to see on light tree trunks. Birds and other insects saw and ate the dark moths. These moths became less common.

In the 1800s, coal dust darkened the tree trunks. The dark moths were hard to see. Birds and other insects stopped eating the dark moths. Dark moths became more common. The larger numbers of dark moths was the result of natural selection.

⊙ For more information on scientific methods, see pages 2–5.

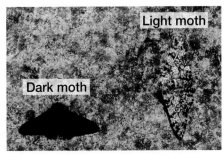
Light moth
Dark moth

■ Light and Dark Peppered Moths on a Light Tree Trunk

■ Green Moss

✅ Check Your Understanding

1. What is the theory of evolution?
2. What animal is birds' common ancestor?
3. Why did dark moths become more common than light moths?

Critical Thinking: Recognizing Evidence
4. What evidence can scientists use to show that birds developed from dinosaurs?

Research and Inquiry Use the internet, the library, or your science book to answer these questions.

1. Who was Charles Darwin? What led him to think of the theory of evolution by natural selection?
2. What is the geologic time scale? What does it show about how species of organisms have changed over time?
3. How have bacteria changed because of antibiotics?

 Writing Imagine that a moss starts growing on tree trunks. What kind of adaptation will help the moths? Write a paragraph.

Classification Systems

FOCUS QUESTION
What is a classification system?

CD 2
TR 31

1 six kingdoms

2 eubacteria kingdom

3 bacteria

4 cyanobacteria

5 archeobacteria kingdom

6 halophiles

7 methanogens

8 protist kingdom

9 seaweed

10 protozoan

11 fungi kingdom

12 mushrooms

13 mold

14 plant kingdom

15 fern

16 pine tree

17 animal kingdom

18 worm

19 dog

| 1 | Six Kingdoms |

| 2 | Eubacteria Kingdom |

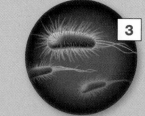
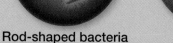

3

4

Rod-shaped bacteria

| 5 | Archeobacteria Kingdom |

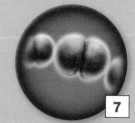

6

7

| 8 | Protist Kingdom |

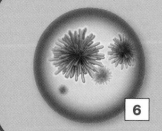
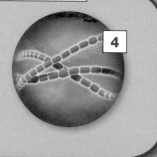

9

10

Word Study

Multiple-Meaning Words

The word **mushroom** has several meanings.

Mushroom means "an organism that is part of the fungi kingdom."

All **mushrooms** have a stem and a cap.

Mushroom can also mean "to grow quickly and in great numbers."

The population of the United States **mushroomed** from 181,000,000 in 1960 to 227,000,000 in 1980.

Vocabulary in Context

 CD 2
TR 32

A classification system organizes things into groups. Scientists classify living things into **six kingdoms. Worms,** fish, and **dogs** are part of the **animal kingdom. Pine trees,** roses, **ferns,** and mosses are in the **plant kingdom. Mushrooms** and **molds** are in the **fungi kingdom.**

Members of the **protist kingdom** live in wet places. **Seaweeds** are large, many-celled protists. Many other protists, such as **protozoans,** are made of only one cell. All members of the **eubacteria kingdom** are **bacteria.** They are made of only one cell. Members of the **archeobacteria kingdom** are bacteria that live in places where other organisms can't live. **Halophiles** live in very salty water. **Methanogens** live in animals' stomachs.

▶ For information on kinds of plants, see page 38.

▶ For information on invertebrates, see pages 50–53.

▶ For information on vertebrates, see pages 54–57.

▶ For information on single-cell organisms, see pages 26–29.

| 11 | **Fungi Kingdom** |

13

12

| 17 | **Animal Kingdom** |

18

19

| 14 | **Plant Kingdom** |

15

16

✔ Check Your Understanding

1. Look at the pictures. Name the different kingdoms of living things.

2. Where do protists live?

3. What is a classification system?

Critical Thinking Comparing and Contrasting

4. How are eubacteria and archeobacteria alike? How are they different?

📖 Workbook page 77

Levels of Classification 🎧 CD 2 TR 33

Each kingdom is divided into smaller and smaller groups. The next group after kingdom is the **phylum.** Then come **class, order,** and **family.** Finally, the smallest groups are **genus** and **species.** The living things that belong to a species group are all the same kind. Each species is a member of a genus.

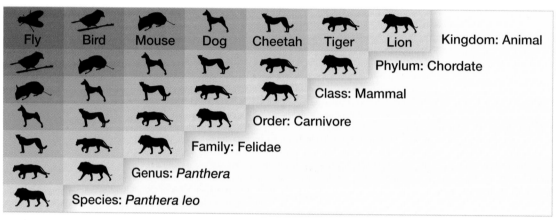

| | | | | | | | Kingdom: Animal |
| Fly | Bird | Mouse | Dog | Cheetah | Tiger | Lion | |

Phylum: Chordate

Class: Mammal

Order: Carnivore

Family: Felidae

Genus: *Panthera*

Species: *Panthera leo*

■ Classifying a Lion

Science Skill — Reading a Diagram

The diagram above shows how the lion is classified. From top to bottom, the groups get smaller and smaller. The smaller the group, the more alike the animals are. Look at the diagram.

1. Which animal is part of the same genus as the lion?
2. Which groups do both dogs and lions belong to?

🔖 Academic Vocabulary

A pine tree	belongs to	the plant kingdom.
	is a member of	
	is part of	

■ Working with DNA

▶ For information on chromosomes, see pages 70–73.

Using DNA to Classify 🎧 CD 2 TR 34

Scientists classify living things by how they are related to one another. They compare the **DNA** in body cells. Chromosomes are made of DNA. Chromosomes contain instructions on how to make new cells. Closely related species have DNA that is similar. Scientists sometimes discover a new plant or animal. Studies of DNA help scientists classify it.

Two-part Names

CD 2
TR 35

Carolus Linnaeus created the classification system used today. His system gives each species its own two-part name. The first part is the genus name. The second part is the species name. Scientists call this system **"binomial nomenclature."** The clouded leopard's name is *Neofelis nebulosa*. The leopard's name is *Panthera pardus*. The jaguar's name is *Panthera onca*.

■ A Clouded Leopard
(Neofelis nebulosa)

Word Study

Synonyms

Synonyms are words that have the same meaning. **Alike, like,** and **similar** are synonyms.

alike	The jaguar cubs look **alike.**
like	A leopard is more **like** a jaguar than a clouded leopard.
similar	A jaguar and a leopard are **similar**.

✅ Check Your Understanding

1. What is the genus and species name of a lion?
2. A new species is discovered. How do scientists decide how to classify it?
3. What did Carolus Linnaeus do?

Critical Thinking Interpreting Information

4. Which animal, a bird or a mouse, is more like a lion? How do you know?

 Research and Inquiry Use the internet, the library, or your science book to answer these questions.

1. What is the seven-group classification of *Tyrannosaurus rex?*
2. Some species, such as tigers, are divided into subspecies. How are subspecies named?
3. Scientists organize the six kingdoms into three large domains. What are the domains? Which kingdoms are in each domain?

 Writing People organize and classify many things in their homes. What is one example of a classification system in your home? Write a paragraph.

Biomes and Ecosystems

FOCUS QUESTION
Where do plants and animals live?

CD 2
TR 36

1 ecosystems

2 biomes

3 tundra

4 taiga

5 deciduous forest

6 rain forest

7 grassland

8 desert

9 community

10 population

11 species

| 1 | Ecosystems |

| 2 | Biomes |

Word Study

Word Origins

Deciduous comes from a Latin word, **decidere,** which means "to fall off."

Deciduous trees lose their leaves in the fall.

Deer antlers are **deciduous.** Deer lose their antlers each year.

► For information on relationships within communities, see pages 86–89.

Vocabulary in Context CD 2 TR 37

A **biome** is an area where plants and animals live. Different plants and animals live in different biomes. Some live in dry **grasslands.** Others live in **deserts.** Some live in the cold **tundra** or **taiga.** Others live in wet **rain forests.** Many live in **deciduous forests,** where there are four seasons. Each of these large areas is a biome. The living and nonliving parts of a biome form an **ecosystem.** Plants and animals are living things. Nonliving things include rocks, water, and soil. An ecosystem can be large or small.

Living things in ecosystems are divided into smaller units. Each kind of living thing is called a **species.** All the members of a species living in an area form a **population.** Two or more populations of living things from the same area form a **community.**

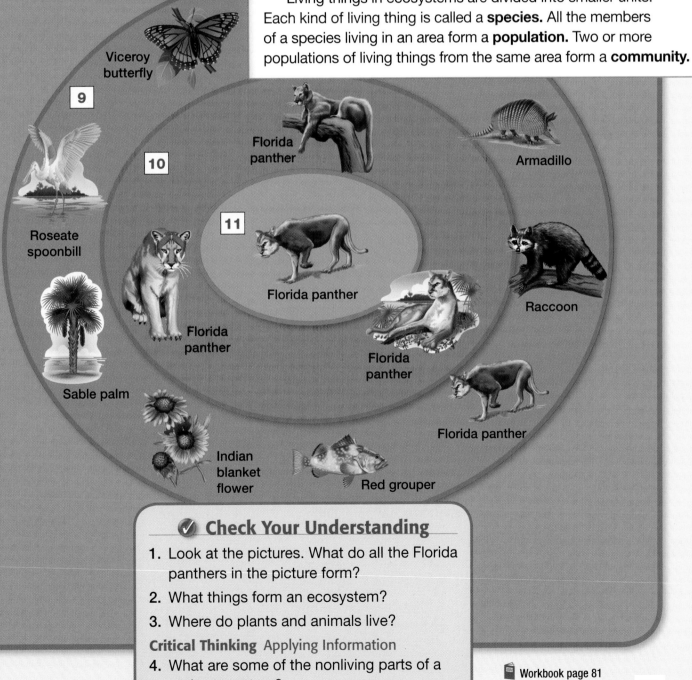

Viceroy butterfly

9

10

11

Florida panther

Armadillo

Roseate spoonbill

Florida panther

Florida panther

Florida panther

Raccoon

Sable palm

Florida panther

Indian blanket flower

Red grouper

✓ Check Your Understanding

1. Look at the pictures. What do all the Florida panthers in the picture form?

2. What things form an ecosystem?

3. Where do plants and animals live?

Critical Thinking Applying Information

4. What are some of the nonliving parts of a park ecosystem?

📖 Workbook page 81

Ecological Succession 🎧 CD 2 TR 38

All ecosystems change. A fire changes an area very quickly. But most change in nature is slow. **Ecological succession** is usually a slow change in the plants and animals in a community. This change may take many years. Look at the pond succession shown below. Over time, the pond changes to a forest community.

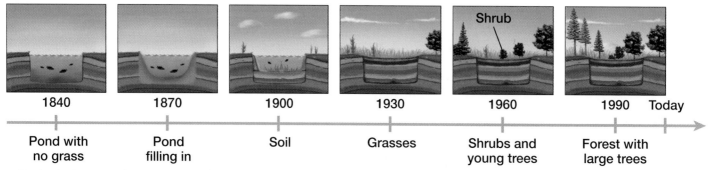

1840	1870	1900	1930	1960	1990	Today
Pond with no grass	Pond filling in	Soil	Grasses	Shrubs and young trees	Forest with large trees	

■ Ecological Succession: From Pond to Forest

Science Skill Reading a Timeline

A timeline shows things that take place over time. Read a timeline from left to right. Answer the questions using the timeline and the pictures above.

1. When was the pictured area a pond community without grasses? When did the pond begin to fill in?
2. When did grasses start to move into the area?
3. How many years did it take for the area to change from a pond to a forest with large trees?

Desert Biomes 🎧 CD 2 TR 39

A biome is a large area on Earth with a certain **temperature** and **rainfall.** Deserts are one kind of biome. Temperatures are from 20°C to 30°C. Rainfall is less than 25 cm a year. The living things there are **adapted** to that **climate.** Lizards and cactus plants are equipped to live in the desert. For example, cactus plants have special places for keeping water.

■ A Lizard and a Cactus Plant in a Desert Biome

▶ For more information on adaptations, see pages 74–77.

🔤 Academic Vocabulary

| Lizards and cactus plants are | adapted | to live in deserts. |
| | equipped | |

The Kangaroo Rat's Ecosystem

CD 2
TR 40

An ecosystem is made up of living things and nonliving things. Each species lives where it finds the things it needs. That place is its **habitat,** or home. The living things are adapted to live in that place. **Kangaroo rats** live in burrows (holes in the ground) in hot, dry, desert conditions. They do not have to drink water. They get all their water from seeds that they eat.

■ A Kangaroo Rat in Its Habitat

Word Study
Word Origins

Ecosystem is made up of two word parts.

- **Eco** comes from the Greek word **oikos,** which means "house."

- **System** comes from the Greek word **systema,** which means "to bring together."

  An **ecosystem** brings together, or is made of, all the living and nonliving parts of a living thing's home.

✔ Check Your Understanding

1. What is ecological succession?

2. How much rain falls each year in a desert biome?

3. What nonliving thing do kangaroo rats get from seeds?

Critical Thinking Analyzing Evidence

4. How are kangaroo rats adapted to live in the desert ecosystem? Explain your answer.

 Research and Inquiry Use the internet, the library, or your science book to answer these questions.

1. What is a cold desert? Where are cold deserts located?

2. What kinds of plants or animals are in a pond ecosystem? What nonliving things are part of this ecosystem?

3. Choose a biome. Make a list of the plants and animals in that biome.

 Writing Write about an ecosystem that you know well. Describe the living and nonliving things in the ecosystem. How big is it? How do the living things there stay alive? Write a paragraph.

Energy Transfer in Living Things

FOCUS QUESTION
How do plants and animals get the energy they need?

CD 2
TR 41

1 consumer

2 producer

3 food chain

4 carnivore

5 food

6 herbivore

7 decomposer

8 food web

Snake
Consumer

3

Frog
Consumer

Grasshopper
Consumer

Grass
Producer

2
Plant

1
Deer

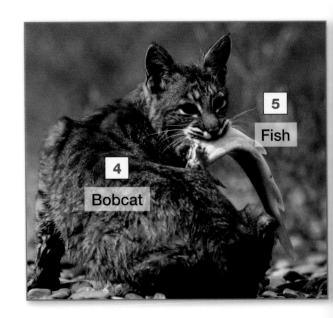

5
Fish

4
Bobcat

Word Study
Word Origins

Carnivore and **herbivore** come from Latin words.

- **Carno** means "flesh."
- **Herba** means "grass."
- **Vorare** means "to swallow" or "to eat."

A **carnivore** eats meat.

An **herbivore** eats plants.

7 Fungi

Vocabulary in Context 🎧 CD 2 TR 42

Green plants make, or produce, their own **food**. Plants are **producers.** During photosynthesis, plants change the energy in sunlight to energy in food. Animals are **consumers.** They eat plants and other animals to get energy. Bacteria and fungi are **decomposers.** They break down wastes and dead plants and animals to get the energy they use.

Energy moves from plants to animals in a **food chain.** Many different food chains in one area form a **food web.**

▶ For information on photosynthesis, see pages 42–45.

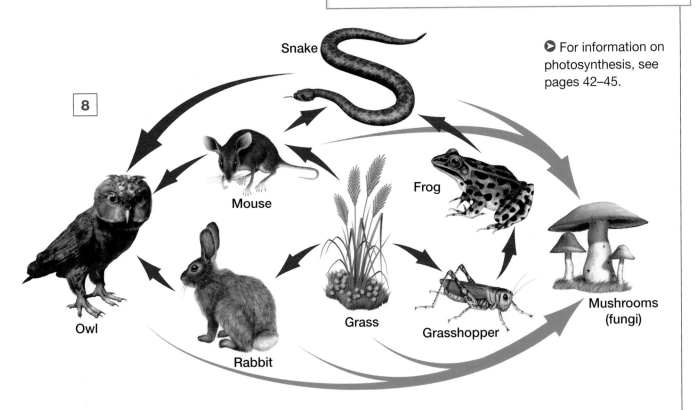

8

Snake

Mouse

Frog

Owl

Rabbit

Grass

Grasshopper

Mushrooms (fungi)

6 Rabbit

5 Plant

✓ Check Your Understanding

1. Look at the pictures. Name the herbivores.
2. What happens in a food chain?
3. How do plants and animals get the energy they need?

Critical Thinking Analyzing Evidence

4. Where does the energy in a food web come from?

📖 Workbook page 85

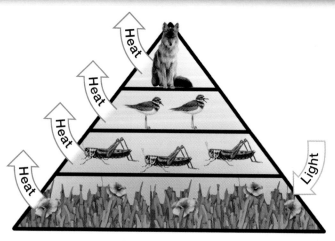

■ An Energy Pyramid

An Energy Pyramid CD 2 TR 43

Energy moves through a food chain as one organism eats another. But not all the energy moves to the next level in the chain. An **energy pyramid** shows how much energy transfers to the next level in a food chain. Each level uses some energy for growth. Each level gives off some energy as **heat.** Therefore, organisms transfer less energy than they receive. That is why each level is smaller than the one below it.

Science Skill Interpreting an Illustration

An illustration can help you understand something that you have read about. Look at the energy pyramid.

1. Which things in the pyramid are producers? Which ones are consumers?

2. How does the illustration show that heat is given off at each level?

3. How does the illustration show that less energy is passed on than was received?

> For more information on energy transformations, see pages 210–213.

Academic Vocabulary

| Not all energy | **moves** | to the next level in a pyramid. |
| | **transfers** | |

Symbiosis CD 2 TR 44

Symbiosis occurs when two different kinds of organisms live together in a close relationship. In **mutualism,** both organisms gain from the relationship. The oxpecker eats insects off the water buffalo. The water buffalo no longer has biting bugs.

In **commensalism,** one organism is helped. The other organism isn't helped or hurt. For example, some orchids (a kind of flowering plant) get more sunlight when they grow in trees. The tree isn't helped or hurt.

In **parasitism,** one organism is helped, but its **host** is harmed. Tapeworms are organisms that live in the **intestines** of other animals. They eat the animals' food. They cause the animals to become sick.

■ Mutualism: An Oxpecker and a Water Buffalo

■ A Predator and Its Prey

Predators and Their Prey CD 2 TR 45

A **predator** is an animal that hunts and eats other animals for food. The food that a predator hunts is its **prey.** Predators are carnivores. They kill and eat their prey. Owls are predators that **hunt** small animals, such as mice and rabbits.

Prey animals have ways to avoid predators. Some have great speed, and some have coloring that helps them hide.

✔ Check Your Understanding

1. What does an energy pyramid show?
2. What is the difference between mutualism and parasitism?
3. What are two ways that prey animals avoid predators?

Critical Thinking Applying Information

4. Cattle kick up dust and small insects in a field. Birds called cattle egrets eat the insects. What form of symbiosis is this? Explain your choice.

Research and Inquiry Use the internet, the library, or your science book to answer these questions.

1. What does a scavenger feed on? Name an example.
2. What are two examples of herbivores? What kinds of plants do they eat?
3. Why are brown-headed cowbirds sometimes described as parasites?

Writing Think about a pet such as a house cat. How does it meet its energy needs? Does it have any symbiotic relationships? Write a paragraph.

Cycles in Nature

FOCUS QUESTION
What is a cycle?

CD 2
TR 46

1 evaporation

2 condensation

3 precipitation

4 runoff

5 groundwater

6 cycle

7 water

8 cloud

9 rain

10 snow

Word Study

Suffixes

The suffix **ation** is used to form nouns from verbs. We use the new nouns for an action or process.

Evaporation comes from the verb **evaporate.**

> **Evaporation** is the process of evaporating.

Condensation comes from the verb **condense.**

> **Condensation** is the process of condensing.

Evaporation

Condensation

6

Runoff

Precipitation

Groundwater

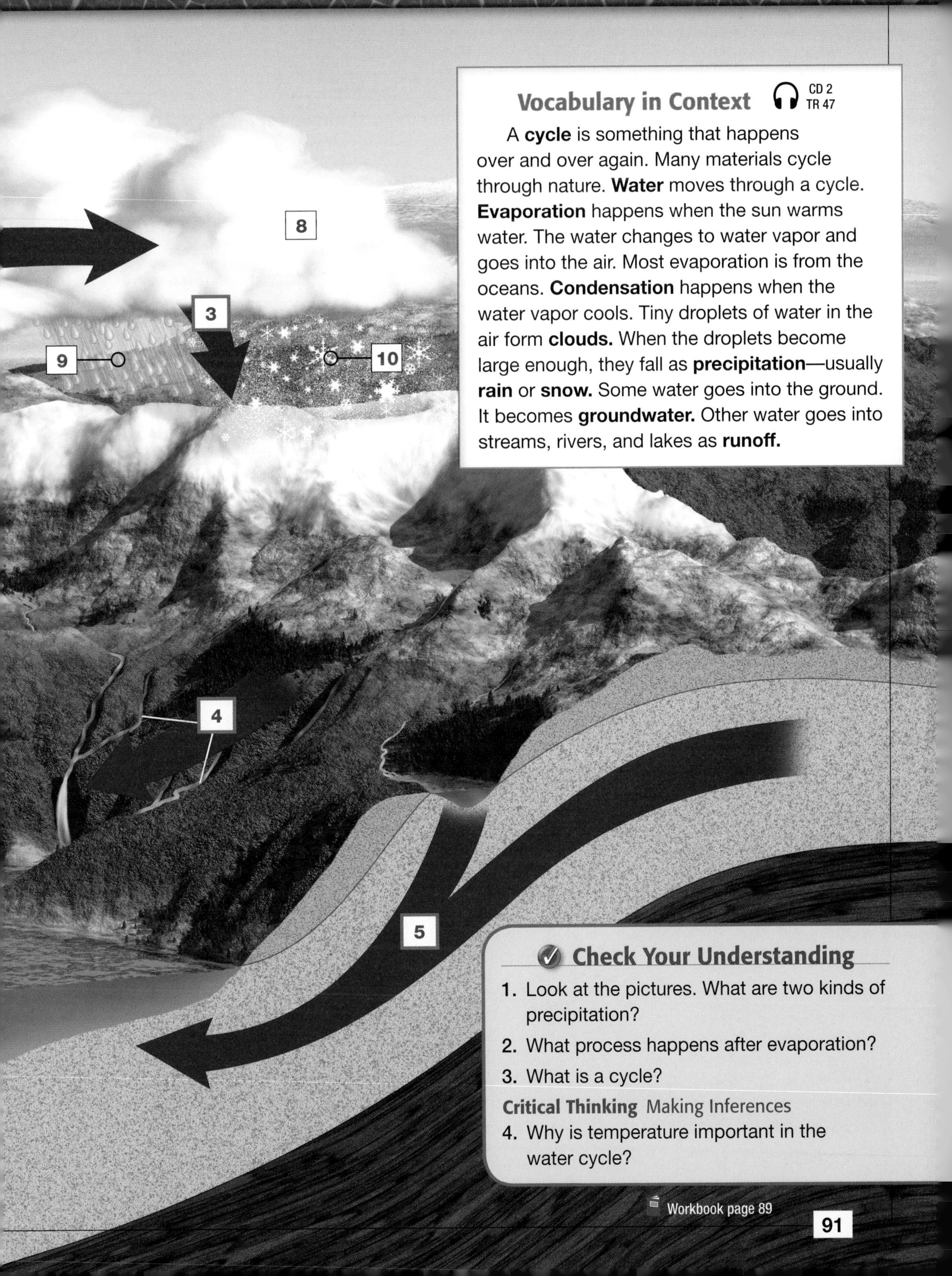

8

3

9 —○

○— 10

Vocabulary in Context 🎧 CD 2 TR 47

A **cycle** is something that happens over and over again. Many materials cycle through nature. **Water** moves through a cycle. **Evaporation** happens when the sun warms water. The water changes to water vapor and goes into the air. Most evaporation is from the oceans. **Condensation** happens when the water vapor cools. Tiny droplets of water in the air form **clouds.** When the droplets become large enough, they fall as **precipitation**—usually **rain** or **snow.** Some water goes into the ground. It becomes **groundwater.** Other water goes into streams, rivers, and lakes as **runoff.**

4

5

✅ Check Your Understanding

1. Look at the pictures. What are two kinds of precipitation?
2. What process happens after evaporation?
3. What is a cycle?

Critical Thinking Making Inferences

4. Why is temperature important in the water cycle?

📖 Workbook page 89

The Nitrogen Cycle

All living things need **nitrogen.** Air is 78% nitrogen gas. Most living things cannot take in nitrogen from the air. **Bacteria** in soil can use nitrogen gas. These bacteria change nitrogen gas into a form that plants can use. Then the plants can take in the nitrogen. Some animals take in nitrogen when they eat the plants. Other animals take in nitrogen when they eat the plant-eaters.

Animal wastes and dead plants and animals return nitrogen to the soil. Soil bacteria break down these wastes. They release nitrogen back into the air. This lets the cycle continue.

▶ For information on bacteria, see pages 26–29 and 78–79.

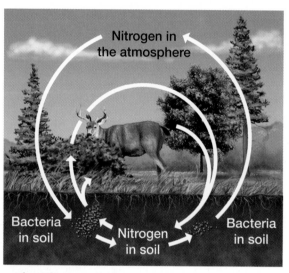

■ The Nitrogen Cycle

▶ For information on gases in the atmosphere, see pages 146–149.

| Science Skill | Reading a Model |

The nitrogen cycle model shows a cycle. The actions in a cycle repeat over and over again. Look at the diagram.

1. Where do plants get nitrogen?
2. How does the deer get nitrogen?

The Oxygen-Carbon Dioxide Cycle

Living things need different gases. Plants need carbon dioxide. Animals need oxygen. Plants and animals take in and give off these gases in a cycle. Animals breathe in oxygen. They give off carbon dioxide. Plants use carbon dioxide from the air. They release oxygen.

■ The Oxygen-Carbon Dioxide Cycle

Academic Vocabulary

Living things	give off	gases during the oxygen-carbon dioxide cycle.
	release	
	discharge	

Plants in the Water Cycle CD 2 TR 50

Plant roots take in water from the ground. This groundwater travels up from the roots, through the stem, to the leaves. Tiny openings in the leaves discharge water vapor. This process is called **transpiration.** The water vapor rises into the air and cools. It condenses to form clouds. Some rain that falls from the clouds goes into the ground.

Word Study
Nouns Used as Verbs
Cycle can be a noun or a verb.

In this sentence, **cycle** is a noun.

  The water **cycle** happens over and over again.

In this sentence, **cycle** is a verb.

  Water **cycles** through the ocean, air, and land.

■ Plants in the Water Cycle

✓ Check Your Understanding

1. What things return nitrogen to the soil?
2. What living things take in oxygen? What living things give off oxygen?
3. What is transpiration?

Critical Thinking Thinking About Systems
4. What are three things that cycle in nature?

 Research and Inquiry Use the internet, the library, or your science book to answer these questions.

  1. How do compost piles return nitrogen to the soil?
  2. Rain forests are being cut down at an increasing rate. How does this affect the oxygen-carbon dioxide cycle?
  3. What is acid rain? What causes it?

 Writing Imagine you are a drop of water in a river. Describe your trip through the water cycle. Write a paragraph.

Responding to the Environment

FOCUS QUESTION
How do living things respond to the environment?

CD 2
TR 51

1 migration

2 stimulus

3 response

4 estivation

5 hibernation

6 phototropism

1

Herd of caribou

Flock of birds

■ Birds fly south for the winter.

2

■ In spring, herds of caribou migrate north. They migrate south in winter.

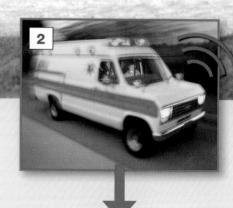

3

Word Study

Irregular Plurals

You make many words plural by adding the letter **s** to the end of the word. These are regular plurals.

The plural of the word **stimulus** is irregular.

The plural of **stimulus** is **stimuli**.

A loud noise is a **stimulus**.

Changes in light and temperature are **stimuli**.

94

▶ For information on animals, see pages 46–49.

Vocabulary in Context 🎧 CD 2 TR 52

Do you cover your ears when you hear a loud noise? The loud noise is a **stimulus.** Covering your ears is a **response.** All living things respond to stimuli from the environment. A change in seasons is a stimulus. **Migration** is one way animals respond to changing seasons. Migration is moving to a different place. For example, many birds fly south in winter to find warm weather. In spring, herds of caribou migrate north, where their babies are born. Some animals respond to cold in winter by hibernating. **Hibernation** is a very deep sleep. Other animals respond to heat in summer by estivating. **Estivation** is also a very deep sleep.

Even plants respond to stimuli. For example, plants grow toward light. This is called **phototropism.**

6

Summer

4

Frog

Winter

5

Chipmunk

✅ Check Your Understanding

1. Look at the pictures. What is the chipmunk doing? When is it doing this?

2. Why do many birds fly south in winter?

3. How do living things respond to the environment? Give two examples.

Critical Thinking Making Observations

4. What animals have you seen migrating? What time of year did you see them? Which direction were they going? Why?

📖 Workbook page 93

Stem

Root

■ The pull of gravity causes roots to grow down and stems to grow up.

▶ For information on gravity, see pages 186–189.

■ A Sundew Plant with Its Leaf Open

■ A Sundew Plant with an Insect in Its Leaf

Plant Responses CD 2 TR 53

Animals aren't the only living things that respond to stimuli. Plants also react to stimuli. Plant stems grow upward. Plant roots grow downward. These are both responses to gravity. They are called **gravitropism.** Plant leaves and flowers turn to face a source of light. This reaction is called phototropism.

Word Study
Word Parts

Phototropism has two word parts: **photo** and **tropism.**

- **Photo** means "light."
- **Tropism** means "move in a set direction."

Phototropism means "moving toward light."

Academic Vocabulary

Plants	respond	to a source of light.
	react	

Watching Plants Move CD 2 TR 54

Tropisms are movements living things make in one direction. Plants make other types of movements as well. Flower buds open slowly, over many days. Some flowers open only in the morning or only at night. Parts of certain plants, like the sundew, move to catch food. The sundew has sticky leaves that attract insects. The plant can sense when an insect touches its leaves. The leaves slowly close and trap the insect. The sundew uses the insect for food. Then the leaves open again.

Science Skill Interpreting Time-Lapse Photos

Sometimes people take a series of photos over time. Such photos are called time-lapse photos. They can show very quick changes. They can show very slow changes. Look at the photographs of the sundew plant.

1. Which part of the plant is moving? How is it moving?
2. What movement do you think the plant will make next?

Behaving by Instinct CD 2 TR 55

A **behavior** is any action an animal does. When a bright light shines in your eyes, you close your eyes slightly, or squint. Squinting is a **reflex.** You squint without thinking. A reflex is a simple action. You do the action without thinking in response to a stimulus. Then you put on sunglasses to keep the light out of your eyes. This is a **learned behavior.** You have learned how to protect your eyes.

Some behaviors are **instincts.** An instinct is a series of actions. The animal always does the actions in response to a certain stimulus. For example, a greylag goose's egg rolls out of the nest. The goose always responds the same way. It pulls the egg back with its beak. Even if someone takes the egg away, the goose makes the same motions with its beak. Many birds have the instinct to migrate when the weather changes in the fall or spring. They join together in large flocks and fly south for the winter or north for the summer.

■ Squinting is a reflex.

■ A goose always uses its beak to pull an egg back to the nest.

✅ Check Your Understanding

1. Plant stems and roots both show gravitropism. How are their responses different?

2. Gravitropism and phototropism are two ways plants move in response to their environment. What are two other ways?

3. What makes a behavior an instinct?

Critical Thinking Integrating Information

4. Squinting your eyes in response to a bright light is a reflex. What is another reflex you have? How does it help you?

 Research and Inquiry Use the internet, the library, or your science book to answer these questions.

1. What happens when scientists try to grow plants in space?

2. People learn from reacting to their environment. Many animals also learn. Find one or more examples of animals learning. What did the animals learn?

3. People respond to information from their senses. Two senses are taste and smell. Explain how responses to things you taste or smell protect your body.

 Writing Pretend you are a plant. It is a sunny day in the summer. Write a journal entry telling different ways that you respond to stimuli in your environment.

Conservation

CD 2
TR 56

1 extinct species

2 dodo

3 dinosaur

4 seed fern

5 mammoth

6 quagga

7 endangered species

8 humpback whale

9 black rhino

10 whooping crane

11 mountain gorilla

12 giant panda

13 Siberian tiger

14 hedgehog cactus

---

1 Extinct Species

(date of extinction)

Dodo
(about 1694 AD)

Dinosaur
(65 million years ago)

Seed Fern
(about 290 million years ago)

Mammoth
(8–10,000 years ago)

Quagga
(about 1883 AD)

▶ For information on different kinds of animals, see pages 46–57.

Word Study

Prefixes

The prefix **en** means "to cause to be."

The word **danger** means "a harmful situation."

Something that is **endangered** is "caused to be in a harmful situation."

An **endangered** species is a species that is in danger of becoming extinct.

▶ For information on species, see page 80.

Vocabulary in Context 🎧 CD 2 TR 57

Extinct species are species that have died out. **Dinosaurs, seed ferns,** and **mammoths** no longer live on Earth. Many plants and animals alive today are **endangered species.** They exist in small numbers and may die out.

Species become extinct or endangered for many reasons. Some extinct animals may have died out because of climate changes. Human actions threaten many species. People nearly hunted **rhinos** and **humpback whales** to extinction. People disturb places where animals like the **mountain gorilla** and **giant panda** live. These animals are endangered because they cannot find enough food or space to live. Some **cactus** plants and **tigers** are endangered because they live in only a small area.

7	Endangered Species

(number in the wild)

Humpback Whale
(about 15,000)

Black Rhino
(about 3,725)

Whooping Crane
(about 300)

Mountain Gorilla
(about 700)

Giant Panda
(fewer than 1,000)

Siberian Tiger
(about 400)

Hedgehog Cactus
(not known)

✅ Check Your Understanding

1. Look at the pictures. What are some extinct species? What are some endangered species?

2. Why are giant pandas endangered?

3. Why do living things become extinct?

Critical Thinking Recognizing Cause and Effect

4. People bring new plants to an area. The new plants spread very quickly. How can this cause problems for the plants already living in the area?

📖 Workbook page 97

Conservation

Word Study

Irregular Plurals

The word **species** does not form the plural by adding an *s*.

This word has the same form for the singular and the plural.

> The bald eagle was an endangered **species**.

> Thousands of **species** are endangered.

▶ For information on species and subspecies, see pages 74–77.

▶ For information on rain forests, see pages 82–83.

■ Two medicines from the rosy periwinkle plant are used to treat leukemia and Hodgkin's disease.

Tigers in Danger CD 2 TR 58

Tigers are big, striped wild cats. They all belong to the same **species.** Tigers come from Asia. Tigers in different parts of Asia belong to different **subspecies.** During the past century, there were eight subspecies of tigers. Today, there are only five subspecies. Three types of tigers are extinct. Hunting is the main reason these tigers are gone. Loss of **habitat,** or homes, is another cause. All tigers are endangered.

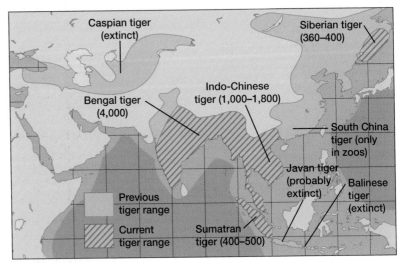

■ Tigers in Danger

Science Skill — Reading a Map

The map above shows where tigers lived in the past and where they live now. The key tells you how to read the information on the map. The orange color shows where tigers lived before. The red lines show where tigers live now. The numbers next to the names of tiger subspecies tell how many tigers are alive.

1. Look at where tigers lived before. How is the size of this area different from the size of the area where tigers live now?

2. Which subspecies of tigers are extinct?

3. One subspecies of tigers may become extinct soon. Which one do you think it is? Explain.

Saving Rain Forest Plants CD 2 TR 59

People have used plants for **medicines** for centuries. Many scientists believe we can find new medicines in plants. Scientists are studying plants from many places. They are studying plants from **rain forests.** But today, rain forests are endangered. So many of these plants may become extinct. Scientists hope to save the rain forests and the plants.

Bald Eagles Recover CD 2 TR 60

Bald eagles were once common in the United States. But hunters killed many bald eagles. This caused their numbers to go down. **Pollution** also caused problems. In the 1950s, a chemical called DDT polluted waterways. Fish had DDT in their bodies. The eagles ate the polluted fish. The chemical made their eggshells very weak. This resulted in their eggs breaking. Many baby eagles died.

The U.S. government wanted to save the bald eagle. In the 1970s, the government passed a law against DDT. Laws also protected the eagles' homes. As a result, the numbers of bald eagles started to go up. The bald eagle is no longer an endangered species. But it is still protected by the government.

■ A Bald Eagle Feeding Its Young

Academic Vocabulary

| Pollution | **caused** | weak eggshells. |
| Weak shells | **resulted in** | broken eggs. |

✓ Check Your Understanding

1. Why are tigers endangered?
2. Why are people interested in saving rain forest plants?
3. What caused bald eagles to become endangered in the past?

Critical Thinking Making Inferences

4. Think about reasons animals become endangered. Now think about plants. How can plants become endangered?

 Research and Inquiry Use the internet, the library, or your science book to answer these questions.

1. Choose an endangered species from the first two pages of this lesson. What has caused it to become endangered? How are people protecting it?
2. What did people use DDT for? What makes this chemical dangerous?
3. How do zoos help endangered species? What are some problems with zoos?

 Writing Think of an endangered species you learned about. Write a newspaper ad to get people to help protect the endangered species. Give ideas of how people can help.

Space

FOCUS QUESTION
What objects are found in space?

CD 3
TR 1

1 space

2 star

3 galaxy

4 solar system

5 planets

6 telescope

7 radio telescope

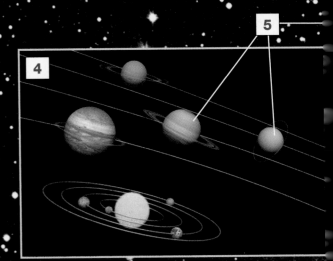

Word Study

Multiple-Meaning Words

The word **space** has different meanings.

Space can mean "an empty spot."

Plants need enough **space** to grow.

Space can also mean "the area beyond Earth." Planets, stars, and other objects are in **space.**

Rockets fly in **space.**

Vocabulary in Context CD 3 TR 2

Space is the area beyond Earth. Many kinds of objects are found in space. The largest objects are called **galaxies.** A galaxy is a huge system of dust, gas, and millions of **stars.**

There are billions of galaxies in the universe. Our sun is a star in the Milky Way galaxy. Eight **planets** circle our sun. They form a **solar system.** Earth is part of the solar system.

We can see many objects in space from Earth with just our eyes. But many are so far away that we need **telescopes.**

▶ For information on planets, see pages 110–111.

7

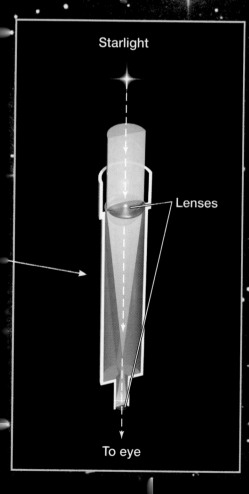

Starlight

Lenses

To eye

✅ Check Your Understanding

1. Look at the pictures. Which pictures show tools that we use to see objects in space?

2. What is a galaxy made of?

3. What objects are found in space?

Critical Thinking Comparing and Contrasting

4. How is a galaxy different from a solar system?

Distances in the Solar System	
Planet	Distance From the Sun (AU)
Mercury	0.39
Venus	0.72
Earth	1
Mars	1.5
Jupiter	5.2
Saturn	9.5
Uranus	19.2
Neptune	30.1

■ Distances in the Solar System

Distances in Space CD 3 TR 3

Distances in space are very big. Scientists measure distances in space in **astronomical units (AU)** and **light-years.** Earth is 1 AU from the sun. One AU equals 150 million kilometers.

After the sun, the star nearest Earth is Proxima Centauri. It is so far away that the distance is given in light-years. A light-year is how far light travels in one year. A light year is much larger than an AU. A light-year is 9.46 trillion kilometers. Proxima Centauri is 4.2 light-years from Earth.

Science Skill   Reading Numbers in a Table

When you read a table with numbers, find the unit of measure. For example, tables can include temperatures, distances, or masses. Make sure you know the measuring system used in the table. Look at the table of distances in the solar system.

1. What unit of measure is used in the table?
2. Which planet is farthest from the sun? How far away from the sun is it?
3. Which planet is closest to the sun? What is this planet's distance from the sun?

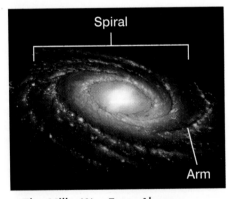

Spiral

Arm

■ The Milky Way From Above

The Milky Way Galaxy   CD 3 TR 4

The Milky Way is a **spiral** galaxy. There is a flat bulge in the center of the spiral. The arms contain stars, gases, and dust that circle the center. New stars form near this center. Our solar system is found in one of the arms. The Milky Way is about 100,000 light-years from end to end. It consists of about 100 billion stars.

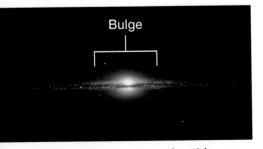

Bulge

■ The Milky Way From the Side

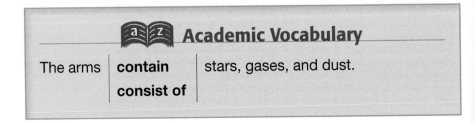

a-z Academic Vocabulary

The arms	contain	stars, gases, and dust.
	consist of	

Telescopes CD 3 TR 5

A telescope makes faraway objects seem larger. Telescopes help us see farther into space. Scientists use telescopes to study planets, stars, and galaxies.

Some telescopes collect light waves with lenses. Other telescopes collect light waves with lenses and mirrors. Radio telescopes collect **radio waves** with bowl-shaped dishes. Astronomers often build telescopes on mountaintops, away from city lights.

■ The South African Astronomical Observatory in Sutherland, South Africa

● For information on telescopes, see pages 6–7.

● For information on light waves and radio waves, see page 201.

Word Study
Word Parts

Telescope has two word parts: **tele** and **scope.**

- **Tele** means "distant" or "far."
- **Scope** means "view" or "see."

  A **telescope** helps us see objects in the distance.

✔ Check Your Understanding

1. What planet is almost 20 AU from the sun?
2. How big is the Milky Way galaxy?
3. How do telescopes help astronomers?

Critical Thinking Applying Information

4. Imagine you traveled to another galaxy. You want to send a letter to your school. How would you address the envelope? Include the planet and galaxy in your address.

 Research and Inquiry Use the internet, the library, or your science book to answer these questions.

1. What is the Hubble Space Telescope?
2. Earth is in the Milky Way galaxy. What is another galaxy that we can see from Earth?
3. What did astronomer Edwin Hubble find out about galaxies?

 Writing Describe Earth's place in our galaxy. Write a paragraph for a travel brochure.

Stars

CD 3
TR 6

1 nebula

2 star

3 main sequence star

4 red giant

5 supergiant

6 white dwarf

7 supernova

8 neutron star

9 black hole

10 constellations

11 sun

1

2

3

3

4

5

Word Study

Antonyms

Antonyms are words that mean the opposite. **Dwarf** and **giant** are antonyms.

Dwarf means "smaller than normal."

I grew a **dwarf** pumpkin.

Giant means "larger than normal."

The **giant** pumpkin weighed 300 kilograms.

5

Supergiant

Sun

11

▶ For more information on gravity, see pages 186–187.

Vocabulary in Context CD 3 TR 7

A **star** is a hot ball of glowing gases. Our **sun** is a medium-sized star. Stars are different colors. The sun is yellow. Red stars are cooler than the sun. Blue stars are hotter than the sun.

Stars are born in a **nebula.** A nebula is a cloud of dust and gas. Our sun is a **main sequence star.** A main sequence star burns hydrogen as fuel. As a smaller main sequence star uses up its fuel, it starts to burn out. First it swells up and becomes a **red giant.** Later it shrinks and becomes a **white dwarf.** As it shrinks, it leaves behind a new nebula. A white dwarf is about the same size as our sun.

A very large main sequence star can become a **supergiant.** A supergiant is many times larger than our sun. Then it might explode and become a **supernova.** Some supergiants end their lives as **neutron stars.** A neutron star is about the size of a small city. Other supergiants end their lives as **black holes.** A black hole has very strong gravity. Nothing can escape from a black hole.

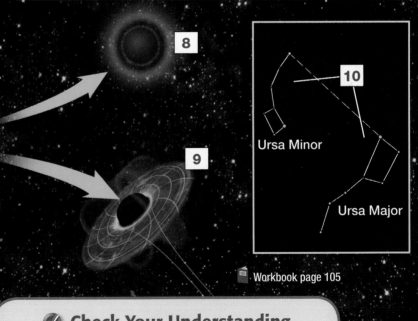

1

6

7

8

9

10

Ursa Minor

Ursa Major

6

White dwarf

Neutron star

8

📖 Workbook page 105

✅ Check Your Understanding

1. Look at the pictures. Where do stars start life?
2. What happens to a red giant at the end of its life?
3. What is a star?

Critical Thinking Comparing and Contrasting

4. How are stars like the living things you know? How are they different?

Stars

Word Study

Word Parts

Magnitude is made up of two word parts: **magni** and **tude.**

- **Magni** means "great" or "big."

- The word part **tude** means the "state or quality of being."

Magnitude means "the quality of being big."

Star Magnitude CD 3 TR 8

Some stars look brighter than others. Scientists group stars by brightness or **magnitude.** Each star has a magnitude number. A very bright star has a low magnitude number. A dim star has a higher magnitude number. The brightness of a star depends in part on its distance from Earth. A star appears brighter if it is close to Earth.

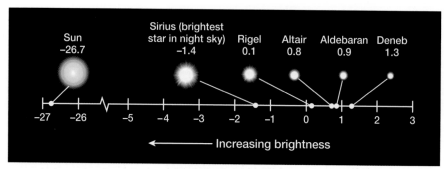

■ Star Magnitude

The Hertzsprung-Russell Diagram CD 3 TR 9

The Hertzsprung-Russell Diagram (H-R diagram) classifies the features of stars. The diagram arranges stars in groups. The side of the diagram shows how bright stars are. The numbers across the bottom show **temperature.**

Stars near the top of the diagram are big and bright. Stars near the bottom of the diagram are small and dim. Stars on the left side are blue and hot. Stars on the right side are yellow or red. They are cooler than blue stars.

Science Skill Reading a Diagram

A diagram is like a picture. A diagram helps you understand the written description. Look at the diagram.

1. Is a white dwarf bright or dim?

2. Where are the giant stars found on the diagram? Where are the blue stars?

3. Which is hotter, a supergiant or a red giant? How do these stars compare with the sun?

■ The Hertzsprung-Russell Diagram

The diagram described above shows:

- Supergiant
- Giant
- Main Sequence Stars
- White Dwarfs
- The Sun

Increasing Brightness (vertical axis)

Temperature (Kelvin): 30,000 15,000 10,000 6,000 4,500 3,000

Academic Vocabulary

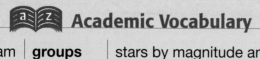

The H-R diagram	groups	stars by magnitude and temperature.
	classifies	
	arranges	

Pictures in the Sky: Constellations CD 3 TR 10

Have you ever noticed shapes in clouds? Sometimes you see a face or an animal. Long ago, people saw shapes made by groups of stars in the sky. They called these groups of stars constellations. They named the constellations for animals, objects, and people in stories. Knowing constellations helped people find certain stars in the sky.

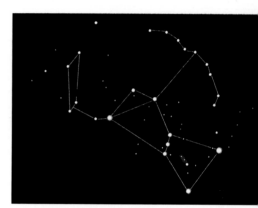

■ The Constellation Orion

✅ Check Your Understanding

1. From Earth, how bright is the sun compared to other stars?
2. Which is hotter, the sun or a white dwarf?
3. What is a constellation?

Critical Thinking Applying Information

4. As seen from Earth, the star Betelgeuse has a magnitude number of 0.5. Is it brighter or dimmer than Sirius? Is it brighter or dimmer than Altair?

 Research and Inquiry Use the internet, the library, or your science book to answer these questions.

1. How did early people use their knowledge of the constellations?
2. What are the dates of some historic supernovas? Which one caused the Crab Nebula to form?
3. What is a binary star?

 Writing Explain the difference between a red giant and a white dwarf. Include information on size, magnitude, temperature, and how the stars change. Write a paragraph.

Our Solar System

FOCUS QUESTION
What objects are found in our solar system?

CD 3
TR 11

1 dwarf planet
2 orbit
3 moon
4 comet
5 sun
6 asteroid
7 meteoroid

Planets

8 Neptune
9 Uranus
10 Saturn
11 Jupiter
12 Mars
13 Earth
14 Venus
15 Mercury

Word Study

Word Origins

The word **orbit** comes from a Latin word.
Orbita means "path" or "track."

The moon's **orbit** is its path around Earth.
The moon **orbits** Earth. It follows a path around Earth.

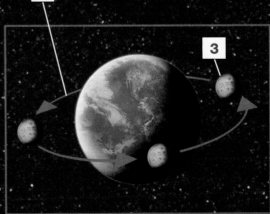

4

Vocabulary in Context 🎧 CD 3 TR 12

Our solar system is made up of the **sun,** eight **planets,** three **dwarf planets, moons,** and other objects that **orbit** the sun. These other objects include **comets, asteroids,** and **meteoroids.** Planets are round. They orbit the sun. Moons orbit planets. A dwarf planet is small and round. It orbits the sun. Comets are balls made of ice, rock, and gases. Asteroids are large chunks of rock and metal. Meteoroids are smaller chunks of rock and metal. They can be as small as dust or as large as boulders.

➤ For more information on space, see pages 102–103.

12

5

13

15   14

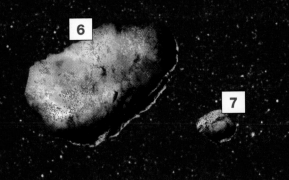

6

7

✅ Check Your Understanding

1. Look at the pictures. List the planets from nearest the sun to farthest from the sun.

2. How big are meteoroids?

3. What objects are found in our solar system?

Critical Thinking Comparing and Contrasting

4. How are asteroids and comets alike? How are they different?

■ Jupiter and Its Largest Moons

▶ For more information on Earth, the moon, and the sun, see pages 114–115.

Jupiter and Its Moons CD 3 TR 13

Jupiter is the fifth planet from the sun. It is the largest planet. It is made mostly of gases. The **Great Red Spot** is a large area on the surface of Jupiter. It is a giant storm three times larger than Earth.

About **60 moons** move around Jupiter. The four largest moons are Callisto, Europa, Ganymede, and Io.

Science Skill   Interpreting an Illustration

An illustration can show relationships. It can compare the sizes of objects. It can show where objects are located. Look at the illustration of Jupiter and its largest moons.

1. Which moon is closest to Jupiter?
2. Which moon is the smallest?
3. Which moon has the biggest orbit?

 Academic Vocabulary

| The moons | **move around** | Jupiter. |
| | **revolve around** | |

A Famous Comet CD 3 TR 14

Comets are made of ice, rock, and gases. They revolve around the sun in stretched-out orbits. A comet's orbit can take it close to the sun. The heat from the sun melts some of the comet's ice. The ice makes a glowing tail. This glowing object can sometimes be seen from Earth.

Halley's comet is probably the most famous comet. It is very bright. It appears about every 76 years. It is named for Sir Edmund Halley. Halley figured out that the comet seen in 1531 and the comet seen in 1607 were the same object.

Orbit of Halley's comet

■ A Comet's Stretched-Out Orbit

■ Halley's Comet

Dwarf Planets CD 3 TR 15

A dwarf planet is a round object that orbits the sun. A dwarf planet is too small to be a planet. The dwarf planet Ceres is between Mars and Jupiter. The dwarf planet Pluto was detected in 1930. Pluto is usually farther from the sun than the planet Neptune. The dwarf planet Eris was discovered in January 2005. Eris is more than two times farther from the sun than Pluto. It is about 30 percent larger than Pluto. Eris and Pluto appear to be made of rock and ice.

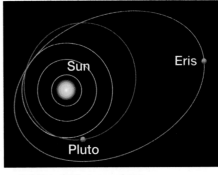

■ Orbits of Pluto and Eris

Word Study

Synonyms

A synonym is a word that means the same as another word. The words **detect** and **discover** are synonyms.

The scientist | **detected** | a new planet.
| **discovered** |

✓ Check Your Understanding

1. List Jupiter's four largest moons from closest to Jupiter to farthest from Jupiter.

2. Halley's comet last passed Earth in 1985–1986. When will it pass Earth again?

3. How does Eris compare in size with Pluto?

Critical Thinking Making a Prediction

4. Do you think scientists will find more dwarf planets? Explain.

 Research and Inquiry Use the internet, the library, or your science book to answer these questions.

1. Find out more about Jupiter's four largest moons. How big are they? What are they made of?

2. What happened to comet Shoemaker-Levy 9 in 1992?

3. What did the spacecraft NEAR Shoemaker do in February 2001?

Writing Imagine you are taking a trip around the solar system. What sights will you see? Tell about the planets, moons, and other objects in the solar system. Write a paragraph.

Earth, the Moon, and the Sun

FOCUS QUESTION

Why does the sun look like it moves across the sky during the day?

CD 3
TR 16

1 sun
2 seasons
3 day
4 night
5 revolve

6 tilt
7 Earth
8 rotation
9 spin

10 rotate
11 axis
12 moon
13 orbit

2

Spring   Summer   Fall   Winter

Word Study

Word Families

Rotate is a verb.	The wheels on a car **rotate.**
Rotation is a noun.	The brakes stop the wheels' **rotation.**

Both words come from the Latin word *rotare,* which means "to turn around."

➤ For information on the solar system, see pages 110–113.

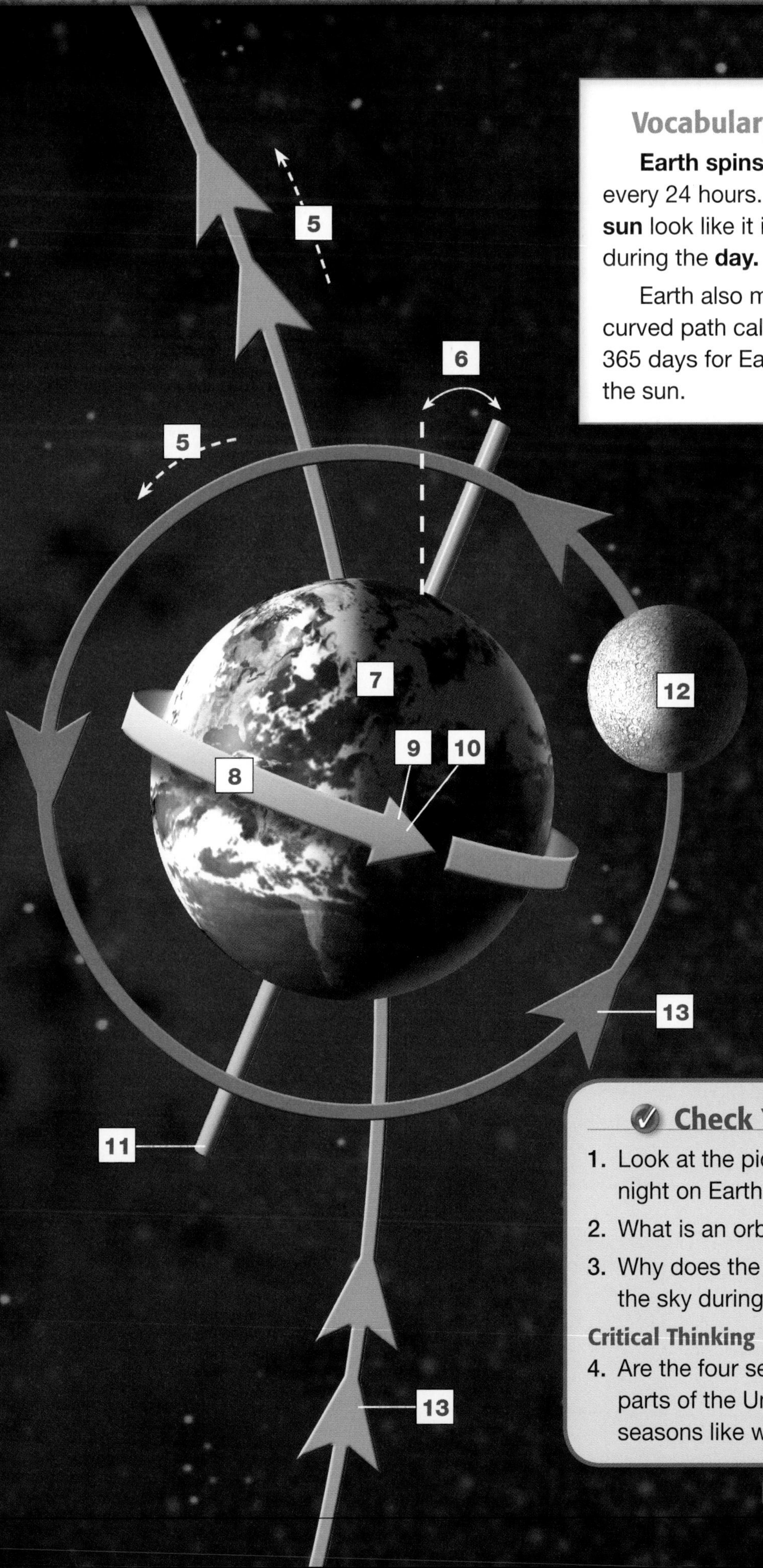

5

6

5

CD 3
TR 17

Vocabulary in Context

Earth spins, or **rotates,** on its **axis** once every 24 hours. Earth's **rotation** makes the **sun** look like it is moving across the sky during the **day.**

Earth also moves around the sun in a curved path called an **orbit.** It takes about 365 days for Earth to **revolve** once around the sun.

7

12

9 **10**

8

11

13

✅ Check Your Understanding

1. Look at the pictures. What causes day and night on Earth?

2. What is an orbit?

3. Why does the sun look like it moves across the sky during the day?

Critical Thinking Applying Information

4. Are the four seasons the same in all parts of the United States? What are the seasons like where you live?

13

📖 Workbook page 113

Length of Day and Night 🎧 CD 3 TR 18

One day and night is 24 hours long on Earth. The part of Earth facing the sun has day. The part facing away from the sun has night. In most places, the length of day and night changes with the seasons. Summers have longer days and winters have shorter days.

City	Length of day January 1	Length of day July 1
Nome, Alaska	4 hours, 12 minutes	21 hours, 9 minutes
Chicago, Illinois	9 hours, 13 minutes	15 hours, 11 minutes
Miami, Florida	10 hours, 34 minutes	13 hours, 43 minutes

■ Length of Day and Night

Science Skill   Making Observations

Good scientists carefully observe. Then they record the data. Then they use the data to answer questions. Look at the data in the table above.

1. On which date are days longer in all three cities?
2. In which city does the length of the day change the most?
3. In which city does the length of the day change the least?

Summer and Winter Seasons 🎧 CD 3 TR 19

For information on the sun's energy, see pages 106–109.

A year is divided into four seasons. The tilt of Earth's axis causes seasons. Summer is the warmest season. When the northern half of Earth tilts toward the sun, it is summer there. Meanwhile, the southern half of Earth tilts away from the sun. It is winter there. When it is winter in the United States, it is summer in South America.

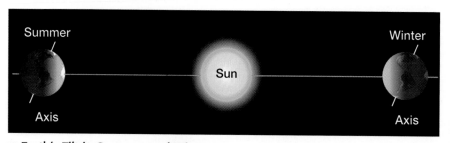

■ Earth's Tilt in Summer and Winter

Phases of the Moon CD 3 TR 20

The sun always lights half of the moon. The shape of the moon seems to change as it orbits Earth. Changes in the way the moon appears are called **phases.** The large moons in the drawing show what we see from Earth. The lines across the small moons show which half of the moon faces Earth.

■ Phases of the Moon

 Academic Vocabulary

| The sun | seems | to move across the sky during the day. |
| | appears | |

Word Study

Synonyms

Synonyms are words that mean the same thing.

Revolve and **orbit** are synonyms.

The moon **orbits,** or **revolves,** around Earth.

✓ Check Your Understanding

1. During which season are days the shortest?
2. What season is it in the United States when it is winter in South America?
3. How many phases does the moon have?

Critical Thinking Making Inferences

4. Why does the moon seem to change shape during each month?

 Research and Inquiry Use the internet, the library, or your science book to answer these questions.

1. When is the longest day of the year? How long is that day in your city or town?
2. What does the word *equinox* mean? When does an equinox happen?
3. Who first suggested that Earth moves around the sun? Why did he think this?

 Writing Imagine that Earth stops rotating and orbiting the sun. What happens? Write a paragraph.

Eclipses and Tides

CD 3
TR 21

1 tides
2 eclipse
3 high tide
4 low tide
5 solar eclipse

6 partial eclipse
7 lunar eclipse
8 shadow
9 total eclipse

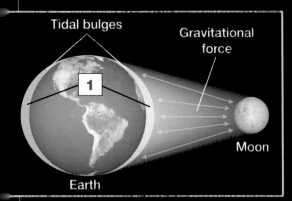

Tidal bulges
Gravitational force

1

Moon

Earth

2

3

4

Word Study
Word Families

Eclipse can be used as a noun or a verb.

As a noun, **eclipse** means "the blocking of the light on one object by another object."

We saw a partial **eclipse** of the moon.

As a verb, **eclipse** means "to block the light of the sun."

The moon **eclipsed** the sun's light.

➤ For information on light, see pages 202–205.

➤ For information on Earth, moon, and sun, see pages 114–117.

Vocabulary in Context 🎧 CD 3 TR 22

The moon is the closest object in space to Earth. The moon is much smaller than Earth, but it still affects Earth in different ways. The moon pulls on Earth's waters. This causes **tides.** A tide is the rise and fall of water along a shore.

When something blocks sunlight, it produces a **shadow.** A **solar eclipse** occurs when the moon passes between the sun and Earth. The moon casts a shadow on Earth. A **lunar eclipse** happens when Earth passes between the sun and the moon. Earth casts a shadow on the moon.

5

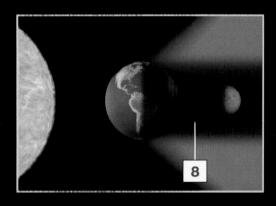

7

8

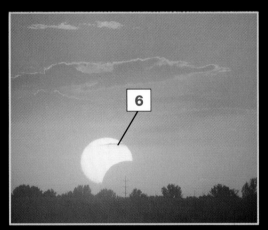

6

9

✓ Check Your Understanding

1. Look at the pictures. What blocks the sun's light from Earth during a solar eclipse?

2. What does Earth do that causes lunar eclipses?

3. How does the moon affect Earth?

Critical Thinking Comparing and Contrasting

4. Think about a lunar eclipse and a solar eclipse. How are they the same? How are they different?

📖 Workbook page 117

■ High Tide on June 3: 6:02 A.M.
and 6:36 P.M.

■ Low Tide on June 3: 12:41 P.M.

High and Low Tides CD 3 TR 23

Along many ocean shores, tides make sea level slowly rise and fall by a few meters twice each day. A **tidal range** is the difference between high tide and low tide. A few places on Earth have a very large tidal range. One of these places is the Bay of Fundy in New Brunswick, Canada. The tidal range there is 12 to 16 meters. The average tidal range around the world is 2 to 3 meters.

Science Skill   Contrasting Photos

The two photos show high tide and low tide at Hopewell Rocks in the Bay of Fundy. Look at the photos and the times listed on the photos.

1. You want to walk around Hopewell Rocks on June 3. What time will you visit?

2. You want to see Hopewell Rocks by boat on June 3. What time will you visit?

Total and Partial Eclipses CD 3 TR 24

An eclipse can be partial or total. In a total eclipse, all the sun's or moon's light is blocked. In a total solar eclipse, the moon blocks the sun. People on Earth see only a glow around the moon. In a total lunar eclipse, the moon is completely covered in shadow.

Sometimes only part of the light is blocked. This causes a partial eclipse. In a partial lunar eclipse, only a part of the moon passes through the darkest part of Earth's shadow. In a partial solar eclipse, part of the sun is blocked by the moon.

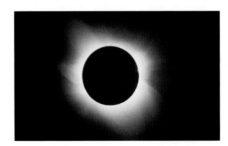

■ Total Solar Eclipse

■ Partial Lunar Eclipse

 Academic Vocabulary

Earth's shadow	causes	a lunar eclipse.
	results in	

For information on phases of the moon, see page 117.

Word Study
Word Origins

Solar and **lunar** come from Latin words.

The word **solaris** means "sun."

   Solar power uses energy from sunlight.

The word **lunaris** means "moon."

   Astronauts collected **lunar** rocks on the moon.

How the Sun Affects Tides CD 3 TR 25

The moon's **gravity** pulls on water in Earth's oceans and results in tides. The sun also pulls on Earth's water. The moon, sun, and Earth line up during a full moon or a new moon. The sun and the moon pull together. The tide is highest then. This is called a **spring tide.** The sun is at a right angle to the moon during its first- and third-quarter phases. The tide is lowest then. This is called a **neap tide.**

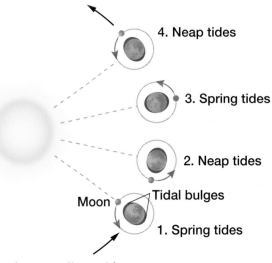

4. Neap tides

3. Spring tides

2. Neap tides

Tidal bulges

Moon

1. Spring tides

■ How the Sun Affects Tides

✔ Check Your Understanding

1. What is a tidal range?
2. What happens to the moon in a total lunar eclipse?
3. What is a spring tide?

Critical Thinking Recognizing Cause and Effect
4. Why are spring tides higher than neap tides?

 Research and Inquiry Use the internet, the library, or your science book to answer these questions.

1. What causes the unusually high tides in the Bay of Fundy?
2. It's not safe to look at a solar eclipse directly. You can badly hurt your eyes. How can you watch a solar eclipse safely?
3. Find out about eclipses in history. What did ancient people think was happening?

 Writing Your friend says the moon is much smaller than Earth. It cannot have much effect on Earth. Think about tides and eclipses. How would you answer your friend? Write a paragraph.

Space Exploration

CD 3
TR 26

1 space probe
2 satellite
3 space station
4 Space Shuttle
5 external fuel tank
6 booster rocket
7 spacecraft
8 launchpad
9 astronaut
10 space suit

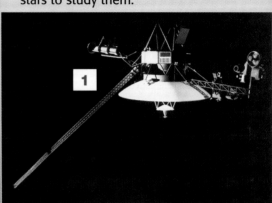

■ A space probe travels to other planets or stars to study them.

1

2

■ A satellite orbits a planet, moon, or star. Satellites can send radio and TV waves to and from Earth. They can also study stars, planets, and moons.

Word Study

Compound Words

Compound words are two or more words combined to make one word. The words below are open compounds. Each pair of words names one thing, but is written as two words. When you say these words, put the stress on the first word.

space shuttle	**space** suit
space station	**space** probe

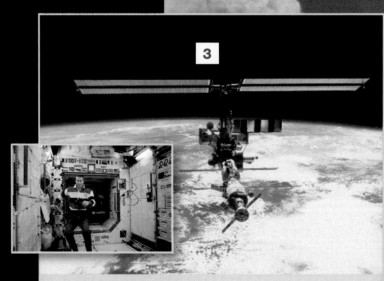

3

■ Scientists can live and work on a space station for weeks or months at a time.

■ Astronauts fly into space and return to Earth in the Space Shuttle.

5

4

6

7

8

Vocabulary in Context 🎧 CD 3 TR 27

People have always been curious about space. Ancient people recorded the movements of stars and planets. Scientists use telescopes to look into space. Scientists first built telescopes in the 17th century. Scientists still use telescopes today.

In the 20th century, scientists built rockets. They launched **satellites** that orbit Earth. Some **spacecraft** were powerful enough to break free from Earth's gravity. **Astronauts** traveled to the moon. Rockets and **booster rockets** lifted astronauts from **launchpads** into space in the **Space Shuttle.** Scientists launched **space probes** to study other planets. Now astronauts even live on a **space station!**

➤ For information on gravity, see pages 186–189.

9

10

✅ Check Your Understanding

1. Look at the pictures. What happens as the space shuttle launches?

2. Why does a rocket have to be powerful to launch people into space?

3. How do scientists study other planets?

Critical Thinking Comparing and Contrasting

4. How are space probes and telescopes similar? How are they different?

Early Space Exploration 🎧 CD 3 TR 28

Robert Goddard launched the first liquid-fueled rocket in 1926. Other scientists built on Goddard's work. By 1945, rockets reached outer space.

The USSR launched the first satellite, called *Sputnik,* in 1957. *Sputnik 2* carried the first space traveler. It was a dog named Laika.

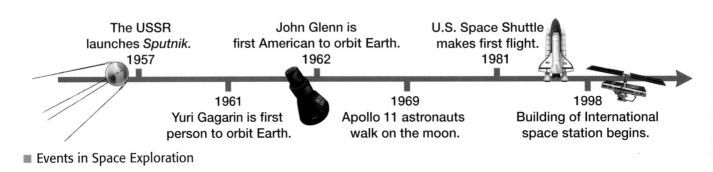

The USSR launches *Sputnik.*
1957

John Glenn is first American to orbit Earth.
1962

U.S. Space Shuttle makes first flight.
1981

1961
Yuri Gagarin is first person to orbit Earth.

1969
Apollo 11 astronauts walk on the moon.

1998
Building of International space station begins.

■ Events in Space Exploration

Science Skill Reading a Time Line

A time line puts a series of events in order. It tells when each event happened. Look at the time line of space exploration.

1. When did astronauts walk on the moon?

2. What important event happened in 1981?

3. When did John Glenn orbit Earth?

▶ For information on the moon, see pages 114–117.

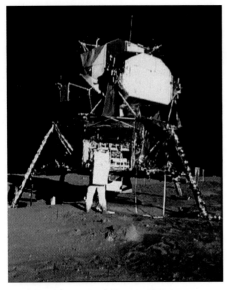

■ The Lunar Module on the Moon

Walking on the Moon 🎧 CD 3 TR 29

Neil Armstrong and Buzz Aldrin were the first people to land on the moon. "The *Eagle* has landed," Neil Armstrong said when their spacecraft arrived on the moon. The **lunar module** was named the *Eagle.* It was July 20, 1969. Armstrong and Aldrin spent hours walking on the moon. They collected rocks. They took many pictures. Another crew member named Michael Collins stayed above the moon's surface in another spacecraft. This **command module** transported the crew safely back to Earth.

Word Study

Word Origins

The word **astronaut** comes from Greek and Latin.

- The Latin word **astrum** means "star."
- The Greek word **nautes** means "sailor," a sea traveler.

International Space Station CD 3 TR 30

Many countries worked together to build the International Space Station (ISS). Astronauts from many countries take turns living and working on the ISS. Spacecraft, such as the Space Shuttle, transport astronauts to the space station. The astronauts stay on the station for months at a time. They eat, sleep, and exercise. They do experiments and make repairs. This helps scientists learn how humans can live and work in space for long periods of time.

■ Astronaut Jeff Williams from the United States (left) and ISS Commander Pavel Vinogradov from Russia in the International Space Station.

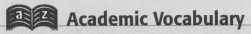 **Academic Vocabulary**

| The Space Shuttle | **carried** | scientists into space. |
| | **transported** | |

✓ Check Your Understanding

1. What was *Sputnik*?
2. What did Aldrin and Armstrong do while they were on the moon?
3. Who lives on the ISS?

Critical Thinking Integrating Information
4. Why is it important for scientists to learn how humans can live in space for a long time?

 Research and Inquiry Use the internet, the library, or your science book to answer these questions.

1. What kinds of information about our solar system have space probes provided?
2. Find out more about living on the ISS. Describe the effects of reduced gravity on life aboard the space station.
3. How does a space suit protect an astronaut?

 Writing Imagine you are an astronaut leaving for a two-month stay on the ISS. You can take three items with you. What would you take, and why? Write a paragraph.

Minerals and Rocks

CD 3
TR 31

1 minerals

2 feldspar

3 crystals

4 quartz

5 diamond

6 press together

7 rocks

8 igneous rocks

9 granite

10 basalt

11 sedimentary rocks

12 limestone

13 sandstone

14 layers

15 fossil

16 metamorphic rocks

17 marble

18 slate

| 1 | Minerals |

| 3 | Crystals |

4

2

5

| 8 | Igneous Rocks |

9

10

Word Study

Multiple-Meaning Words

The word **rock** can be a noun or a verb.

The noun **rock** can mean "any piece of stone from which Earth's crust is made."

The bottom of the hill was covered with many **rocks.**

The verb **rock** can mean "to move something back and forth gently."

The mother **rocks** her baby in her arms.

○ For information on chemical formulas, see pages 178–180.

○ For information on soil and sand, see page 36.

○ For information on shells, see pages 50–51.

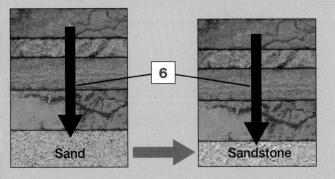

Sand → Sandstone

6

Vocabulary in Context

 CD 3 TR 32

Minerals are natural solids from inside Earth. Common minerals include **quartz** and **feldspar.** Some minerals, such as quartz, form **crystals.** A **diamond** is a crystal. Each mineral has its own chemical formula. For example, the chemical formula of quartz is SiO_2. This means that quartz is made of silicone and oxygen.

Rocks are made of minerals. Rocks are divided into three groups. **Sedimentary rocks,** such as **sandstone** and **limestone,** form when bits of sand, soil, and shells are **pressed together** in **layers. Fossils** are often in sedimentary rock. A fossil is a dead plant or animal. Over many years, it became part of the rock. **Igneous rocks,** such as **granite** and **basalt,** are made from melted rock. **Metamorphic rocks,** such as **marble** and **slate,** form when rocks get very hot and are pressed together deep in the ground.

7 Rocks

11 Sedimentary Rocks

12

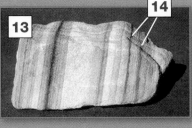

13 **14**

15

16 Metamorphic Rocks

17

18

✔ Check Your Understanding

1. Look at the pictures. Name the minerals. Name the rocks.

2. What is a mineral?

3. What are rocks made of?

Critical Thinking Making Observations

4. Think of the rocks near your house. What kinds of rocks are they?

📖 Workbook page 125

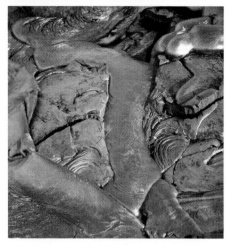

■ Basalt is an igneous rock. Basalt forms when lava from a volcano cools very quickly.

▶ For information on volcanoes, see pages 138–141.

▶ For information on weathering and erosion, see pages 138–141.

Classifying Rocks

Rocks are classified by how they form. Igneous rocks form when melted rock cools and gets hard. Igneous rocks are often found near **volcanoes.**

Sedimentary rocks form when tiny bits of rock, shells, and parts of dead plants and animals are pressed together in layers. Fossils are most often found in sedimentary rocks. Sedimentary rocks are often found near rivers and oceans.

Metamorphic rocks form when heat and pressure change one kind of rock into another kind of rock. Metamorphic rocks are often found deep inside Earth.

The Rock Cycle

The rock cycle diagram below shows how any rock can change into any other kind of rock. For example, **weathering** (the effects of weather) breaks down rocks into tiny pieces. These pieces are **sediment.** Rivers carry this sediment away. This is called **erosion.** Over time, layers of sediment are pressed together. The result is sedimentary rock. Heat and pressure can transform sedimentary rock to metamorphic rock. Metamorphic rock can later melt and harden to form igneous rock.

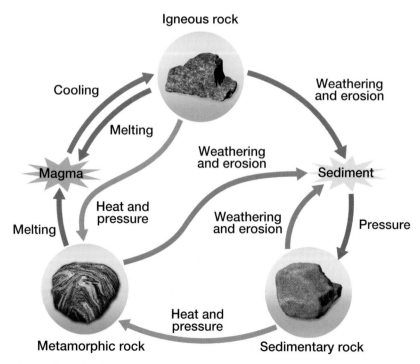

■ The rock cycle shows how any rock can change into any other kind of rock.

Science Skill — Interpreting a Rock Cycle Diagram

The rock cycle diagram on page 128 shows how rocks can change into different forms in the rock cycle. It also shows the different processes that form and change rocks. Look at the diagram.

1. How does sedimentary rock change into metamorphic rock?
2. What happens to metamorphic rock when it melts and then cools?
3. What changes an igneous rock into a sedimentary rock?

Academic Vocabulary

Heat and pressure can	change	rock.
	transform	

✅ Check Your Understanding

1. What type of rock is often found deep inside Earth?
2. What is sediment?
3. How can sedimentary rock become igneous rock?

Critical Thinking Hypothesizing

4. How do volcanoes help to form rock?

Research and Inquiry Use the internet, the library, or your science book to answer these questions.

1. What properties do scientists use to describe minerals?
2. How do diamonds form? Where are most diamonds found? Why are they so expensive?
3. What is the difference between extrusive and intrusive igneous rock?

Writing Imagine that you are an igneous rock. Describe what happens to you as you move through the rock cycle. You might end up deep inside Earth or on the surface. You might become a different kind of rock entirely. Write a paragraph describing your adventures.

Earth's Structure

FOCUS QUESTION
What are the layers of Earth?

CD 3
TR 35

1 plates

2 plate boundaries

3 continent

4 fossil

5 crust

6 upper mantle

7 lower mantle

8 outer core

9 inner core

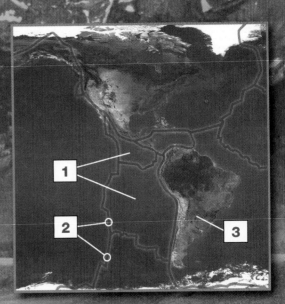

Word Study

Multiple-Meaning Words

The word **plate** has different meanings.

Plate can mean "a flat dish you put food on."

I filled my **plate** with vegetables and salad.

Plate can also mean "part of Earth's crust."

Earth's **plates** float on the mantle.

> For information on solids and liquids, see pages 162–165.

Vocabulary in Context
CD 3 TR 36

Earth is made of several layers. The main layers are the **crust,** the mantle, and the core. Both the core and mantle are divided into upper and lower parts.

The **continents** and the land under the oceans form Earth's crust. The crust is made of pieces of solid rock. The continents form the continental crust. The continental crust is thicker than the crust under the oceans. The crust floats in the **upper mantle.** The upper mantle is made of semisolid rock. It is harder and cooler than the **lower mantle.** The lower mantle is less solid than the upper mantle because it is hotter. The **outer core** is made of liquid metal. The **inner core** is solid metal.

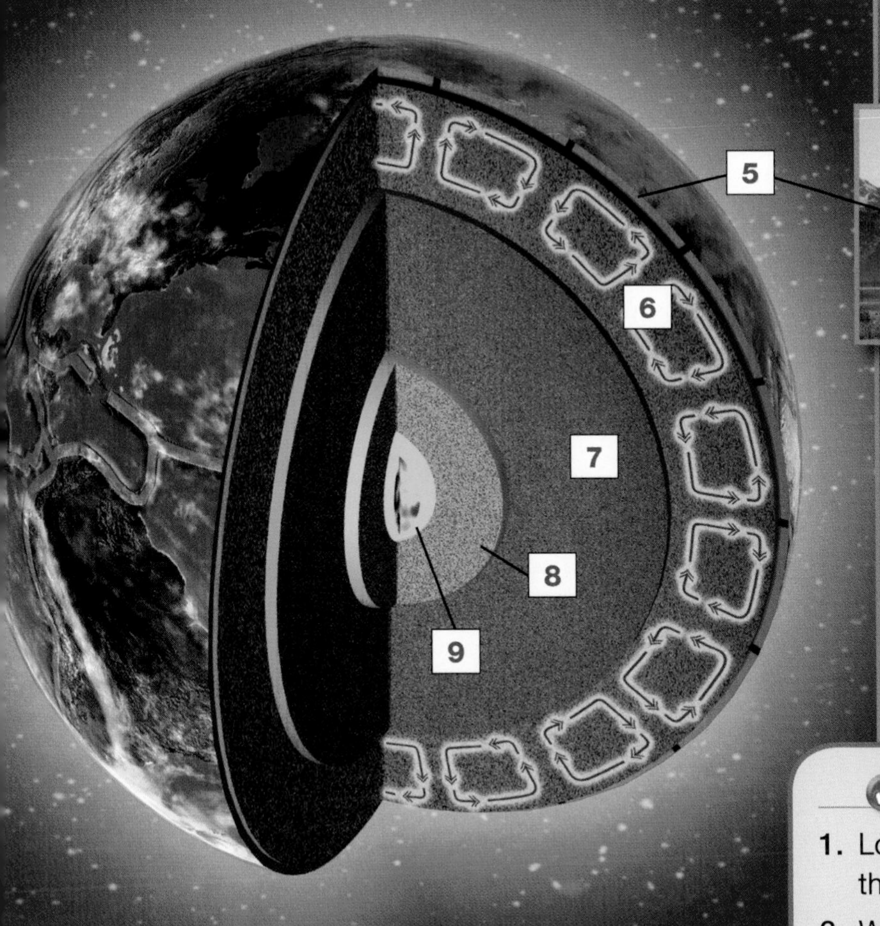

5

6

7

8

9

✓ Check Your Understanding

1. Look at the pictures. What part of Earth is the part you see every day?
2. What is the outer core of Earth made of?
3. What are the layers of Earth?

Critical Thinking Comparing and Contrasting

4. How are Earth's crust and its inner core similar? How are they different?

Workbook page 129

131

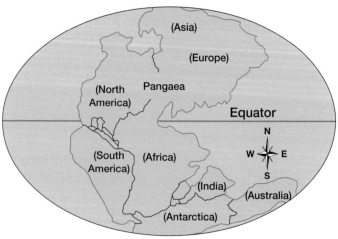

Long ago, all the land on Earth was one continent. Scientists call it Pangaea. Later, the pieces moved apart.

> For information on fossils, see page 127.

Continental Drift

Did you ever notice that if you put South America next to Africa they seem to fit together? Long ago, all the land on Earth was one big continent. Scientists call this continent **Pangaea.** Over time, pieces of Pangaea moved apart. This **continental drift** is still happening!

Fossils and rocks support this theory. Similar rocks in Africa and South America contain the same kind of fossils. This evidence tells us that these continents were once close together. The same kinds of plants and animals lived in both places.

Science Skill — Reading a Map

Look at the map of Pangaea. Remember that north, south, east, and west tell where places are on a map. For example, in this map part of North America is *south* of the equator.

1. Which continent is south of India? What continent is just west of India?
2. Which continent borders Australia?
3. What continents border North America?

Seafloor Spreading

Seafloor spreading helps cause continental drift. Two continental plates under the sea move apart, and a crack forms between them. **Magma** (molten rock) rises into the crack from Earth's mantle below. When the magma meets the water, it cools into rock. This rock spreads out on the ocean floor below the water. It pushes the plates farther apart. Then the rock piles up and forms a group of underwater mountains. These mountains are called an **oceanic ridge.**

Seafloor Spreading

> For information on how rock changes, see page 128.

Academic Vocabulary

The mantle is the layer of Earth just	under	the crust.
	below	
	beneath	

Plate Tectonics CD 3 TR 39

The motion of Earth's plates causes continental drift. Scientists call this motion **plate tectonics.** The plates move just a few centimeters each year. Since the plates are always moving, they can crash into each other, move apart, or rub against each other.

A **plate boundary** is where two plates meet. These boundaries can be on a continent or beneath the ocean.

Word Study
Word Origins
The word **tectonics** comes from Greek.

The word **tektonikos** means "builder."

Plate **tectonics** explains continental drift.

▶ For information on plates and plate boundaries, see pages 144–145.

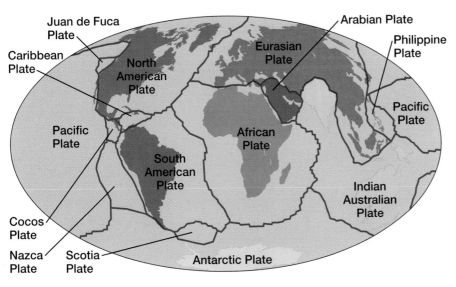

■ Plate Boundaries

✓ Check Your Understanding

1. What evidence supports the theory of continental drift?

2. How does magma affect seafloor spreading?

3. What causes continental drift?

Critical Thinking Applying Information

4. Two tectonic plates crash into each other. What will be the result? Why do you think so?

 Research and Inquiry Use the internet, the library, or your science book to answer these questions.

1. What do Earth's plate motions have to do with mountains such as the Himalayas in India?

2. What are ocean trenches? How do they help explain why crust added at ocean ridges doesn't make Earth any larger?

3. Why do Earth's plates move?

 Writing Based on what you know about plate tectonics, what do you think Earth might look like five million years from now? Write a paragraph.

Earth's Surface

CD 3
TR 40

1 plain

2 mesa

3 canyon

4 mountain

5 lake

6 oceans

7 delta

8 rivers

9 continents

1 Hungarian Great Plain, Europe

2 Canyonlands National Park, Utah

Grand Canyon, Arizona

3

Word Study

Superlative Adjectives

We use superlative adjectives to compare three or more things. They often have the ending **est**.

Mount Everest is the **highest** mountain in the world.

Some superlative adjectives are formed with **the most.**

Mount Everest is **the most famous** mountain in the world.

➤ For information on continents, see pages 130–133.

Vocabulary in Context
 CD 3 TR 41

From tall **mountains** to flat **plains,** Earth's surface has extremes. The deepest part of the **ocean** is the Marianas Trench. It is in the South Pacific and is 10,923 meters deep. The highest mountain is Mount Everest, in Nepal. It is 8,850 meters high. The longest **river** is the Nile, which flows through northeastern Africa. It is more than 6,500 km long. The largest **lake** of fresh water is Lake Superior, in North America. The largest **continent** is Asia. The largest **canyon** is the Yarlung Zangbo Canyon, in Tibet.

Mount Everest, Nepal

4

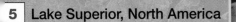

5 Lake Superior, North America

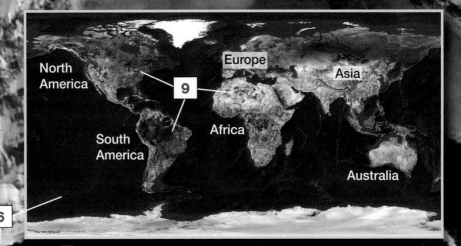

North America

Europe

Asia

9

South America

Africa

Australia

6

Nile River Delta, Egypt

7

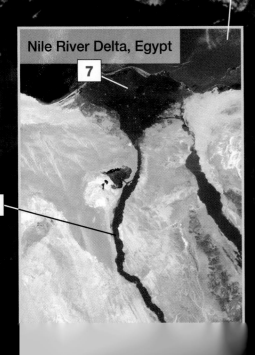

8

✔ Check Your Understanding

1. Look at the pictures. How can a river change Earth's surface?

2. What is the Marianas Trench?

3. What types of land and water make up Earth's surface?

Critical Thinking Interpreting Information

4. Which is greater: the height of the highest mountain or the depth of the deepest ocean?

■ A Glacier

❯ For more information on states of matter, see pages 162–165.

❯ For information on water on Earth, see pages 90–91.

Water on Earth CD 3 TR 42

More than two-thirds of Earth's surface is covered by water. There is **salt water** in the oceans. There is **fresh water** in rivers, ponds, lakes, and streams. Water is also located underground. This **groundwater** makes up a large part of our fresh water supply.

We can find water in other forms, too. Water vapor is found in the **atmosphere. Glaciers** are large, slowly moving masses of ice. Many areas of Earth's surface are often covered in snow.

Earth's Landforms CD 3 TR 43

Mountains, valleys, hills, canyons, and mesas are some of the features of Earth's surface. They are called **landforms.** They can be large, like mountains, or smaller, like **hills.**

Some landforms, such as many mountains, are caused by volcanoes. Some landforms, such as mesas and canyons, are made by wind and moving water. Some landforms are made when glaciers move slowly across Earth's surface.

■ A Topographic Map of Sailboat Island

■ A Picture of Sailboat Island

❯ For information on volcanoes, see pages 138–141.

Science Skill   Reading a Topographic Map

The **topography** of Earth is the shape of its surface. In some places, the topography is flat. In other places, it is hilly. A **topographic map** shows the topography of an area. Topographic maps always have lines called "contour lines." These lines show the elevation—the height—of the land. Look at the topographic map above. Imagine you are looking down on an island.

1. Where is the highest point on the island?

2. How would you describe the topography of this island?

Fresh Water Meets Salt Water

CD 3
TR 44

What happens when rivers and oceans meet?

As a river flows toward the ocean, it carries soil and small pieces of rock along with it. When the river reaches the ocean, the water slows down. The soil and gravel drop to the bottom. Over time, this soil and gravel accumulate, and the area builds up above the level of the water. This buildup of land is called a delta.

■ The Nile River Delta

Word Study

Word History

A delta often has a triangular shape. The historian Herodotus (484–425 BCE) first used the term "delta" to name a landform. He thought the mouth of the Nile looked like the Greek letter *delta*, which is written as a triangle: Δ.

🔤 Academic Vocabulary

| Soil and gravel | **accumulate** | to form a delta. |
| | **build up** | |

✔ Check Your Understanding

1. Where is water vapor found on Earth?
2. What are some ways that landforms are made?
3. Where does a delta form?

Critical Thinking Hypothesizing
4. Water in a river slows down when it reaches the ocean. Why do you think this happens?

 Research and Inquiry Use the internet, the library, or your science book to answer these questions.

1. Do all lakes contain fresh water? Explain.
2. How are glaciers formed? What landforms are caused by glaciers?
3. Why is the water in oceans salty?

 Writing You are a guide at one of the landforms in this lesson. What do you tell your visitors about the landform? Write a paragraph.

Earthquakes and Volcanoes

FOCUS QUESTION
When do earthquakes happen?

CD 3
TR 45

1 plates
2 earthquake
3 seismic waves
4 epicenter
5 focus
6 fault
7 tsunami
8 volcano
9 lava
10 eruption
11 magma
12 vent
13 crater

7

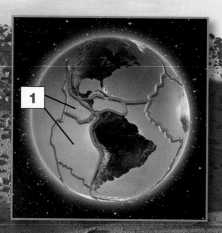

1

3

4

2

6

5

Word Study

Multiple-Meaning Words

The word **fault** has different meanings.

Fault can mean "an error or a defect."

Joe has some **faults,** such as turning in his assignments late and talking in class.

Fault can also mean "a crack or split in Earth's surface."

Most earthquakes occur along **faults.**

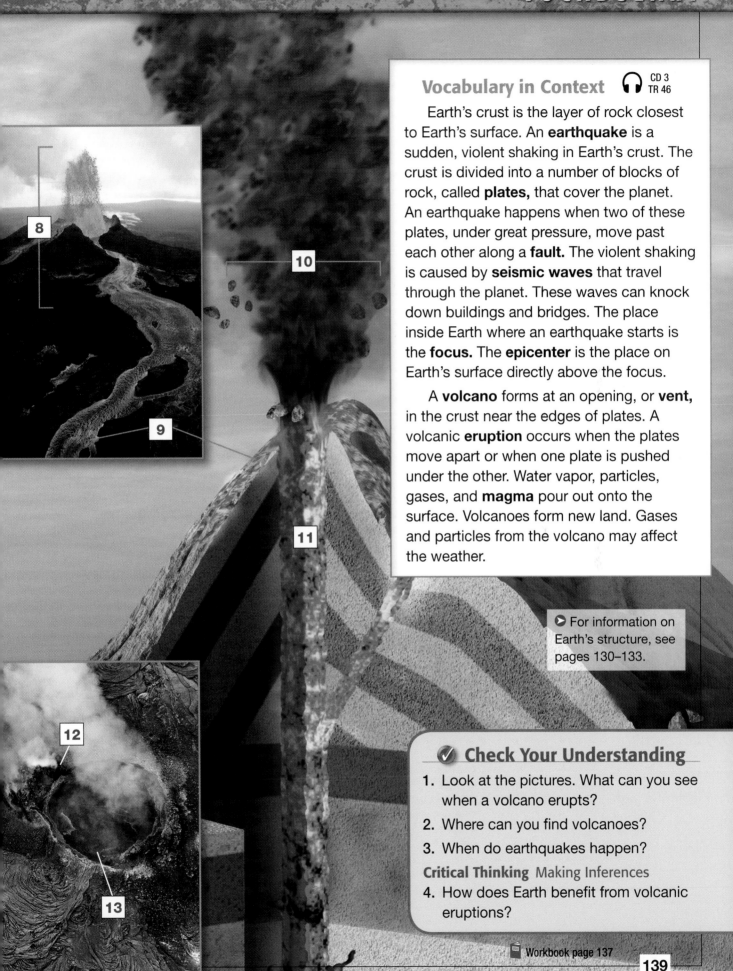

Vocabulary in Context 🎧 CD 3 TR 46

Earth's crust is the layer of rock closest to Earth's surface. An **earthquake** is a sudden, violent shaking in Earth's crust. The crust is divided into a number of blocks of rock, called **plates,** that cover the planet. An earthquake happens when two of these plates, under great pressure, move past each other along a **fault.** The violent shaking is caused by **seismic waves** that travel through the planet. These waves can knock down buildings and bridges. The place inside Earth where an earthquake starts is the **focus.** The **epicenter** is the place on Earth's surface directly above the focus.

A **volcano** forms at an opening, or **vent,** in the crust near the edges of plates. A volcanic **eruption** occurs when the plates move apart or when one plate is pushed under the other. Water vapor, particles, gases, and **magma** pour out onto the surface. Volcanoes form new land. Gases and particles from the volcano may affect the weather.

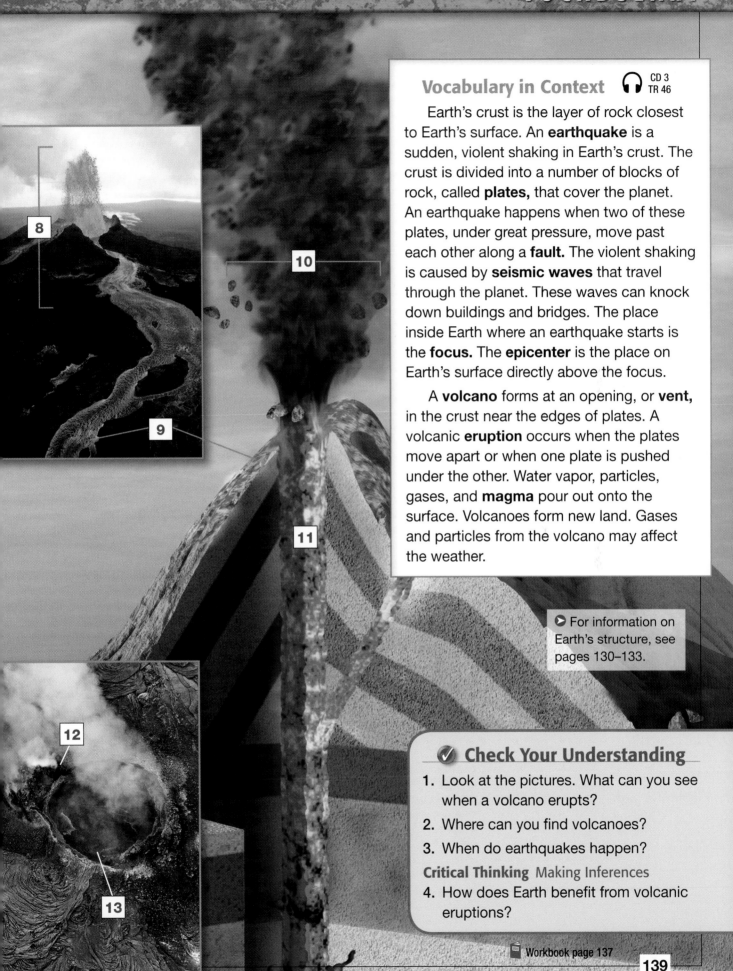

▶ For information on Earth's structure, see pages 130–133.

✓ Check Your Understanding

1. Look at the pictures. What can you see when a volcano erupts?
2. Where can you find volcanoes?
3. When do earthquakes happen?

Critical Thinking Making Inferences

4. How does Earth benefit from volcanic eruptions?

📖 Workbook page 137

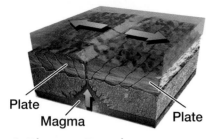

Plate
Magma
Plate

■ A. Divergent Boundary

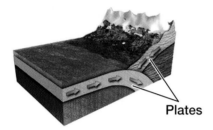

Plates

■ B. Convergent Boundary

Plates

■ C. Transform Boundary

▶ For information on layers of the Earth and plate tectonics, see pages 130–133.

▶ For information on waves, see page 198.

Where Do Earthquakes Happen? CD 3 TR 47

Most earthquakes result when plates move over, under, or past each other. **Plate boundaries** are places where two plates meet. Earthquakes happen when the pressure on the rocks at plate boundaries builds up.

This happens in different ways. Plates can move apart, or **diverge.** As the rocks pull apart, magma rises from below. Plates can come together, or **converge.** The rocks are pushed from two different directions. This makes them bend and break. Earthquakes can also happen when plates move past one another without much motion up or down.

Science Skill Interpreting a Drawing

Look at each drawing. Study the drawings for differences. Read the labels on each drawing.

1. What material flows up as the plates move apart in drawing A?
2. What direction do the plates move in drawing B?
3. What tells you the direction the plates are moving in drawing C?

🅰🅉📖 Academic Vocabulary

| Earthquakes form where plates | **diverge** (pull apart). |
| | **converge** (come together). |

Surface Waves and Tsunamis CD 3 TR 48

Most **waves** on a lake or an ocean occur when wind energy moves over the surface. The energy that causes a **tsunami** comes from an earthquake on the seafloor. All of the water above the epicenter is affected. A wave forms. It does not seem large at first, but the energy is great. When the water hits the shore, it crashes over the land.

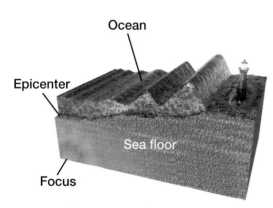

Ocean

Epicenter

Sea floor

Focus

■ Tsunami Waves

Where Do Volcanoes Form? CD 3 TR 49

Volcanoes often form at the boundaries between plates. They occur when the plates pull apart and magma flows up from below through cracks. Volcanoes can also form when plates come together. One plate moves under the other. The rock gets very hot and becomes magma. The magma rises, forming a volcano.

The mantle is the layer of Earth under the crust. Some areas of mantle are hotter than others. Volcanoes can form at these hot spots. As the plates move, the volcanoes form an island chain. The Hawaiian Islands are on a hot spot.

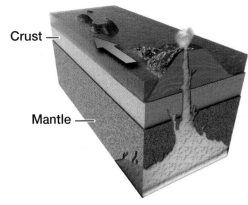

Crust —

Mantle —

■ Hot Spot Forming Islands

Word Study
Word Origins

Tsunami comes from two Japanese words.

The word **tsu** means "harbor."

The word **nami** means "wave."

A **tsunami** is a huge wave that is most damaging when it reaches a harbor or shore.

✓ Check Your Understanding

1. Where do earthquakes happen?
2. What provides the energy for most ocean waves? What provides the energy for a tsunami?
3. What are hot spots?

Critical Thinking Making Observations

4. The Mid-Atlantic Ridge is an underwater mountain range where the plates are moving apart. What can you expect to happen at this ridge?

 Research and Inquiry Use the internet, the library, or your science book to answer these questions.

1. What is a seismograph?
2. What safety precautions should you follow during an earthquake?
3. What is the Ring of Fire?

 Writing Imagine that you are visiting California. A small earthquake occurs near where you are staying. Write an email to a friend. Describe what happened.

Our Changing Earth

FOCUS QUESTION

What changes the shape of Earth's surface?

 CD 3 TR 50

1 erosion	5 weathering	9 sand dune
2 soil	6 abrasion	10 moraine
3 glacier	7 ice wedging	11 delta
4 sand	8 deposition	

1 | Erosion

■ Wind or water can carry soil away.

■ A glacier is a slowly moving mass of ice. A glacier can cut into rock and carry the pieces away.

4

5 | Weathering

Word Study

Suffixes

A suffix is a word part that is added to the end of a word. Adding the suffix **tion** or **sion** to a verb changes it to a noun.

erode + **sion** = **erosion**

   Erosion can wear down a hillside.

deposit + **tion** = **deposition**

   Deposition builds new landforms.

■ Tiny bits of rocks moved by air, water, or a glacier can cause abrasion.

142

8	Deposition

Wind can cause a sand dune to build up.

A moraine forms when a glacier moves rocks to a new place. The pieces of rock form a hill.

Vocabulary in Context

 CD 3 TR 51

Earthquakes and volcanoes can change Earth's surface. These changes happen quickly.

Earth's surface can change slowly, too. **Weathering,** such as **abrasion** and **ice wedging,** breaks rock into tiny pieces. Abrasion happens when tiny pieces of rock wear down larger pieces of rock. **Erosion** happens when water, **glaciers,** or wind carries sediment to new places. Sediment is tiny pieces of rock and soil. **Deposition** happens when sediment builds up in a place. Deposition builds new landforms such as **deltas, moraines,** and **sand dunes.** Glaciers, water, and wind can all cause deposition.

▶ For information on earthquakes and volcanoes, see pages 138–141.

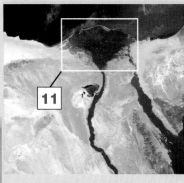

A delta forms when a river carries sediment to its mouth.

Ice wedging is the result of ice forming in small spaces in rocks. The ice breaks up the rock.

✅ Check Your Understanding

1. Look at the pictures. What kinds of changes are caused by ice?

2. What are three causes of deposition?

3. What changes the shape of Earth's surface?

Critical Thinking Analyzing Evidence

4. Younger mountains have pointed peaks. What causes some older mountains to have rounded peaks?

Workbook page 141

■ Plant roots push apart rock and cause mechanical weathering.

Weathering CD 3 TR 52

Mechanical weathering happens when rocks are broken into small pieces. Abrasion occurs when pieces of rock are rubbed off by tiny bits of rock moved by water, wind, or ice. Ice and plants also cause weathering. A seed may fall into a crack in a rock. When the seed sprouts and grows, the plant's roots make the crack bigger. Ice wedging also affects cracks in rock. Water gets into a crack. When the water freezes, it expands, and the crack gets bigger. The cracked rock finally breaks in two.

In **chemical weathering,** chemicals in water, such as oxygen and carbon dioxide, **react** with chemicals in rock. This breaks down the rock over time.

Science Skill   Recognizing Cause and Effect

The cause of something is the reason it happens. The results are called effects.

1. What causes abrasion?
2. What effect can a seed have on rock?
3. What is the effect of reactions between chemicals in water and chemicals in rock?

🔤 Academic Vocabulary

| Weathering | **happens** | when rock is broken down. |
| | **occurs** | |

■ A glacier can change the shape of a mountain.

Glaciers CD 3 TR 53

Over thousands of years, ice and snow can build up on mountains. They form glaciers. As a glacier moves, sand and rock inside the glacier wear down mountains and change their shape. A mountain's shape can tell us where glaciers formed in the past.

Erosion and Deposition

CD 3
TR 54

Weathering breaks rock into smaller pieces. Wind, water, or ice move these small pieces, called sediment, to new places. This process is erosion. The Grand Canyon was formed by water erosion. Over millions of years, water cut into the rock and carried pieces away. Sand is eroded from beaches by waves. Glaciers carry rocks and soil as they move. Wind carries dust and sand for miles.

When the wind or water slows down, the sediment drops out. This is deposition. Deposition forms river deltas and sand dunes. When a glacier deposits sediment, it can form a moraine, a type of hill.

■ Water erosion formed this canyon.

▶ For information on river deltas, see pages 134–137.

Word Study

Multiple-Meaning Words

The word **deposit** has different meanings.

Deposit can mean "put money in the bank."

I will **deposit** $300 tomorrow.

Deposit can also mean "leave something or put something down."

The river **deposits** sand and soil in the delta.

✓ Check Your Understanding

1. What can happen when water freezes in cracks in rock?
2. How can you tell where glaciers existed in the past?
3. What are three landforms built by deposition?

Critical Thinking Looking for Patterns

4. How do glaciers, wind, and water wear down landforms? How do they build up landforms?

Research and Inquiry Use the internet, the library, or your science book to answer these questions.

1. What is soil made of?
2. How can soil erosion become a problem?
3. What is a landform in your area that has been affected by erosion or deposition?

Writing Imagine an area that is full of steep hills. How do you think weathering and erosion will change this landscape? Write a paragraph.

The Atmosphere

1

FOCUS QUESTION
What is the atmosphere made of?

CD 3
TR 55

1 cloud
2 air
3 atmosphere
4 fog
5 pollution

6 water vapor
7 gas
8 particles
9 rain
10 wind

2

3

4

5

Word Study

Multiple-Meaning Words

The word **gas** has different meanings.

Cars use **gas**.

Gas is short for **gasoline**.

Gasoline is a liquid, not a **gas**.

Earth's atmosphere is made of several **gases**.

Oxygen and nitrogen are **gases**.

▶ For information on solids, liquids, and gases, see pages 162–165.

Vocabulary in Context CD 3 TR 56

The **atmosphere** is the **air** around Earth. We find **rain, fog, clouds,** and **wind** in the atmosphere. Earth's atmosphere makes life possible.

Air is made of several **gases.** The atmosphere also contains **pollution, water vapor,** and **particles.**

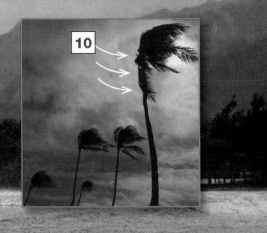

✔ Check Your Understanding

1. Look at the pictures. What kind of weather do you see?

2. What do we find in the atmosphere?

3. What is the atmosphere made of?

Critical Thinking Applying Information

4. What causes air pollution? Think about your city or town. Is there much air pollution? Why?

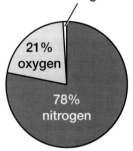

1% carbon dioxide, water vapor, and other trace gases

21% oxygen

78% nitrogen

■ Gases in the Atmosphere

❯ For information on gases, see pages 162–165.

Gases in the Atmosphere CD 3 TR 57

Air is made of several gases. The most common gases are **oxygen** and **nitrogen.** There are small amounts of other gases in Earth's atmosphere. These gases are called **trace gases.**

Science Skill Reading a Pie Chart

A pie chart shows the parts of something. The pie is cut into several slices. The size of the slice shows the amount. A large slice shows a large amount. A small slice shows a small amount. Look at the pie chart to the left. It shows that the atmosphere is composed of several gases.

1. What is the most common gas?
2. What percent of the atmosphere is oxygen?
3. What is one trace gas?

The Oxygen-Carbon Dioxide Cycle CD 3 TR 58

Animals and plants need gases to live. Plants need **carbon dioxide.** They get it from the air or the water. Plants make oxygen as waste.

Animals need oxygen. They get it from the air or the water. Animals make carbon dioxide as waste.

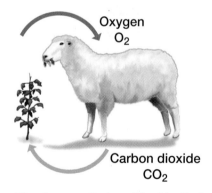

Oxygen O_2

Carbon dioxide CO_2

■ The Oxygen-Carbon Dioxide Cycle

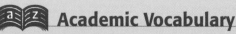 **Academic Vocabulary**

The atmosphere	is made	of several gases.
	is composed	
	consists	

Layers of the Atmosphere

 CD 3
TR 59

The atmosphere consists of several **layers.** The **troposphere** is closest to Earth. The troposphere is warm. The other layers of the atmosphere are very cold and the air is thin. Plants and animals can only live in the troposphere. Satellites fly in the **exosphere.** We often call the exosphere "space."

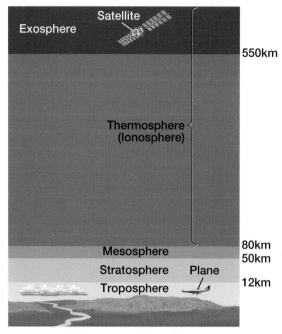

■ Layers of the Atmosphere

Word Study

Word Origins

Atmosphere is from two Greek words.

- **Atmos** means "gases."
- **Sphere** means "round" or "a ball."

    The **atmosphere** is the layer of gases around Earth.

✓ Check Your Understanding

1. What are the two most common gases in the atmosphere? Which one is more common?
2. What gas do people need? What gas do plants need?
3. Describe the troposphere. Describe the exosphere.

Critical Thinking Making Inferences

4. Can people live in the stratosphere? Why or why not?

 Research and Inquiry Use the internet, the library, or your science book to answer these questions.

1. What are the effects of pollution on the atmosphere?
2. What will happen if the carbon dioxide in the atmosphere increases?
3. Who discovered oxygen? How did he discover it?

 Writing Imagine that there are no plants on Earth. Explain what would happen. Write a paragraph.

Weather and Climate

FOCUS QUESTION
What does a weather report tell you?

CD 3
TR 60

1 clouds

2 precipitation

3 rain

4 snow

5 hail

6 wind

7 fog

8 water vapor

9 air mass

10 cold front

11 warm front

12 weather map

13 temperature

1

2 | Precipitation

3

4

5

Word Study

Multiple-Meaning Words

The word **weather** has different meanings.

Weather can mean "the current conditions of the atmosphere in a particular place."

> The **weather** will be partly cloudy today.

Weather can mean "the wearing away of rock by wind and rain."

> Years of rain, ice, and wind **weathered** the statue.

6

7

8

■ Moist air has a lot of water vapor in it.

Vocabulary in Context 🎧 CD 3 TR 61

A weather report gives information on the weather for the next few days. You can get a weather report on TV, on the internet, on the radio, or in the newspaper. On the radio, you might hear a weather report like this: "We will have sunny skies this morning. Around noon, a **cold front** will move through. Behind it is a cold, low-pressure **air mass. Clouds** will build up. We can expect **rain** and **hail. Winds** will be at about 8 mph. **Temperatures** will be in the 50s. Some **fog** will develop in low-lying areas by the morning. There is a 30% chance of **precipitation** again tonight."

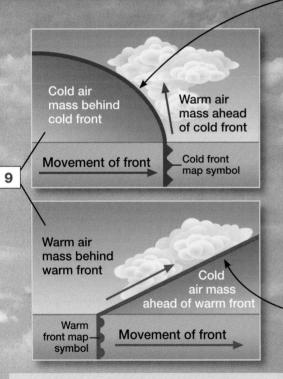

9

Cold air mass behind cold front

Warm air mass ahead of cold front

Movement of front

Cold front map symbol

Warm air mass behind warm front

Cold air mass ahead of warm front

Warm front map symbol

Movement of front

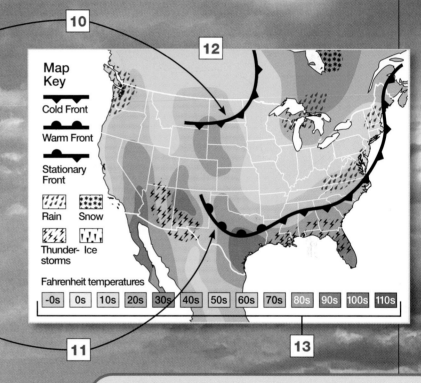

10

12

11

13

Map Key

Cold Front

Warm Front

Stationary Front

Rain   Snow

Thunder- Ice storms

Fahrenheit temperatures

| -0s | 0s | 10s | 20s | 30s | 40s | 50s | 60s | 70s | 80s | 90s | 100s | 110s |

■ A warm air mass is an area of air that is warmer than nearby air. A cold air mass is an area of air that is colder than nearby air. A cold front is a cold air mass pushing into a warm air mass. A warm front is a warm air mass pushing into a cold air mass.

▶ For information on the water cycle, see pages 90–91.

✅ Check Your Understanding

1. Look at the pictures. What are three forms of precipitation?

2. Read the weather report. What is bringing rain and hail into the area?

3. What does a weather report tell you?

Critical Thinking Looking for Patterns

4. Read the weather report. What do you think the weather will be like in the afternoon if the front does **not** move in?

📗 Workbook page 149

▶ For information on gases, see pages 162–165.

▶ For information on gravity, see pages 187–189.

Weather Maps   CD 3 TR 62

Some weather maps show temperatures across a region. Some display fronts. Others display areas of high and low pressure. **Atmospheric pressure** is the pressure, or weight, of the air over a certain place at that moment. **Isobars** are lines that connect areas with the same pressure. Areas of high pressure (**H**) usually block masses of low pressure (**L**). Low-pressure masses must go around masses of high pressure. Low-pressure masses often bring storms.

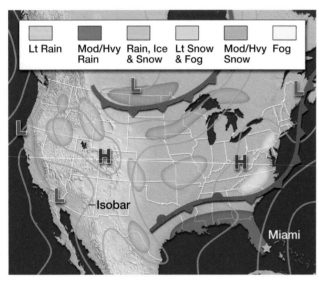

■ A Weather Map

Science Skill   Reading a Weather Map

People read weather maps to find out the weather conditions for that day and the next days. They usually want to know how the weather can affect plans. Look at the weather map.

1. How many areas have high pressure? How many have low pressure?

2. You live in Miami, Florida. It's marked with a star. Will you be able to go on a picnic today?

Word Study
Word Origins

Isobar comes from two Greek words.

• **Isos** means "equal."

• **Baros** means "weight."

Academic Vocabulary

Some maps	show	temperatures.
	display	

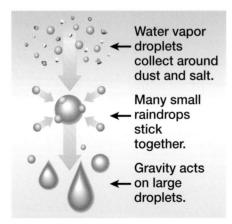

■ Raindrops Forming

Water vapor droplets collect around dust and salt.

Many small raindrops stick together.

Gravity acts on large droplets.

How Do Clouds and Rain Form?   CD 3 TR 63

When warm, moist air rises, it expands and becomes colder. Droplets of water vapor in the cold air collect around particles of **dust** or **salt.** A cloud forms when millions of these particles come together. Inside the cloud, droplets bump into each other. They stick together. A large droplet can form. If it becomes heavy enough, **gravity** acts on it. It falls to Earth as rain.

Weather and Climate CD 3 TR 64

Weather can change from hour to hour. **Climate** changes more slowly. Climate is the average weather for an area over many years. An area's climate includes its average **temperature** and its average amount of rain and snow. The United States has more than one climate. It has dry, mild, **tropical,** and **subtropical** regions. Alaska is a state with **polar** climate conditions.

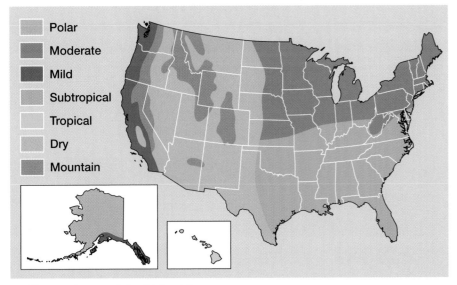

| Polar |
| Moderate |
| Mild |
| Subtropical |
| Tropical |
| Dry |
| Mountain |

■ Climate Areas of the United States

✅ Check Your Understanding

1. What do isobars on a weather map represent?

2. When does a raindrop fall to Earth?

3. How is climate different from weather?

Critical Thinking Interpreting Information
4. What kind of climate do you live in?

 Research and Inquiry Use the internet, the library, or your science book to answer these questions.

1. What is meteorology? What is NOAA?

2. Who was Wladimir Köppen? How did he describe climates?

3. Choose a climate. Find its location, its temperature range, its annual precipitation, and the kinds of plants that grow there.

Writing Suppose that a dust particle moves up into the air in Illinois. Describe what happens to it by the time it falls back to Earth again in a raindrop. Write a paragraph.

Extreme Weather

CD 3
TR 65

1 thunderstorm	7 waterspout
2 lightning	8 flood
3 updraft	9 tornado
4 water vapor	10 rotation
5 downdraft	11 hurricane
6 hail	12 eye

Icy cold air

1

2

3

Warm, moist air

4

Word Study

Synonyms

Synonyms are words that have the same meaning.

The wind speeds in some tropical storms reach 117 km/h and higher. These storms have different names in different parts of the world.

A **hurricane** is a tropical storm that forms in the North Atlantic Ocean or the East Pacific Ocean.

A **cyclone** is a tropical storm that forms in the South Pacific Ocean or parts of the Indian Ocean.

A **typhoon** is a tropical storm that forms in the western North Pacific Ocean or the South China Sea.

▶ For information on oceans, see pages 134–137.

▶ For information on the atmosphere, see pages 146–149.

Vocabulary in Context CD 3 TR 66

Thunderstorms form when warm, moist air rises into the atmosphere in an **updraft.** There it meets icy cold air. Moist air has a lot of **water vapor** in it. The warm air cools, and the moisture turns to rain or **hail.** The rain and hail fall in a **downdraft.** Many storms form in less than an hour. Most also go away quickly. Their heavy rains can cause **floods.** Their hail, winds, and **lightning** can damage property. **Tornadoes** form in strong thunderstorms. Tornadoes are rotating columns of moist air that touch the ground. Tornadoes can have wind speeds of up to 500 km/h. Usually they form over land. When a tornado forms over water, it is called a **waterspout. Hurricanes** are much larger than tornadoes. They form over warm ocean water. They can cause great damage.

5

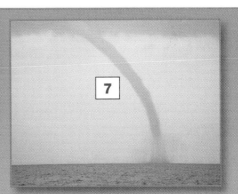

✔ Check Your Understanding

1. Look at the pictures. What is the name for the center of a hurricane?

2. Where do tornadoes form?

3. How does a thunderstorm form?

Critical Thinking Comparing and Contrasting

4. How are tornadoes and hurricanes similar? How are they different?

📖 Workbook page 153

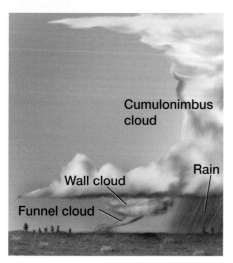

■ A Tornado in a Thunderstorm

❯ For information on the atmosphere, see pages 146–149.

How Tornadoes Form CD 3 TR 67

A tornado is a spinning column of moist air that touches the ground. Tornadoes often form in huge thunderstorms with strong rotating winds. Part of the storm hangs below the main cloud and stretches toward the ground. This is called a **wall cloud.** A **funnel cloud** sometimes forms from this wall cloud. When the funnel cloud touches the ground, it is called a tornado. Tornadoes have high wind speeds and strong updrafts. They can cause terrible damage.

Science Skill   Interpreting a Model

A diagram can show something you may never experience. This kind of diagram is called a model. Look at the model on the left of the tornado in the thunderstorm.

1. What kind of cloud is the funnel cloud a part of?
2. Is the funnel cloud in the model a tornado? How do you know?

Stages of a Hurricane CD 3 TR 68

A hurricane begins as a **tropical disturbance,** a storm over warm ocean water. When the storm shows some rotation, but its winds are below 62 km/h, it is called a **tropical depression.** When winds are 62 km/h to 117 km/h, it is called a **tropical storm.** Scientists give it a name. When its winds reach 117 km/h, it is a hurricane. The storm rotates, and an eye forms. Hurricanes have high winds, huge amounts of rain, and **storm surges.** A storm surge is water rushing over the land. Storm surges can cause great damage.

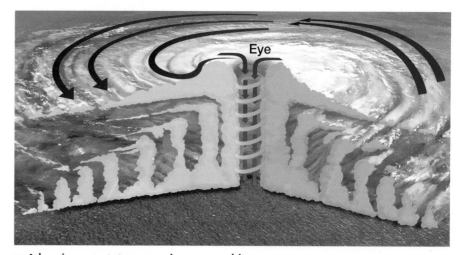

■ A hurricane rotates, or spins, around its eye.

Watches and Warnings CD 3 TR 69

Watches and **warnings** are given for severe weather. They are announced on television, radio, and the internet. A watch means that severe weather is possible. People should listen for more information. A warning indicates that severe weather has been seen. People should take cover. There may be danger. A hurricane warning might tell people to leave the area and move to a safer place. It might tell what roads have closed due to flooding. Most places use sirens to warn people of severe weather.

■ Tornado warning sirens warn people of severe weather.

Word Study
Modal Verbs

Might is used with another verb. It means "can possibly."

Hail or a tornado **might** form during a severe thunderstorm.

 Academic Vocabulary

A watch	**means**	that severe weather is possible.
	indicates	

✅ Check Your Understanding

1. What is a tornado?
2. What are the four stages of hurricane development?
3. What is the difference between a watch and a warning during severe weather conditions?

Critical Thinking Analyzing Information
4. Is a funnel cloud dangerous? Why do you think so?

 Research and Inquiry Use the internet, the library, or your science book to answer these questions.

1. What are the Fujita Scale and the Saffir-Simpson Scale?
2. Where is Tornado Alley? Why is it called that?
3. What are storm spotters? What do they do?

 Writing Imagine that you are a weather reporter. Describe what happens as a tornado forms. How might you report your sightings? Write a paragraph.

Natural Resources

CD 3
TR 70

1. water energy
2. wind energy
3. geothermal energy
4. nuclear energy
5. solar energy
6. recycle
7. fossil fuels
8. natural gas
9. coal
10. petroleum
11. minerals

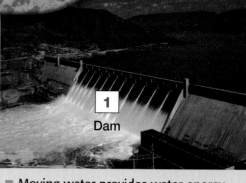

1 Dam

■ Moving water provides water energy.

Solar panel

3 Geyser

■ Geysers can create geothermal energy.

4 Atomic energy plant

■ Nuclear energy is made in an atomic energy plant.

5

■ We can use sunlight to create solar energy.

6

Recycle bin

■ When we recycle we use things again.

Word Study
Word Origins

The word **geothermal** is made up of two parts: the prefix **geo** and the word **thermal.**

Geo means "Earth" or "of the earth." **Thermal** comes from the Greek word **therme,** which means "heat." A **geothermal** energy source comes from heat inside Earth.

A geyser or natural hot spring is heated by **geothermal energy.**

2

Wind machines

Blade

■ We can use wind energy to make electricity.

Vocabulary in Context CD 3 TR 71

Natural resources are useful materials found in nature. Plants, animals, and water are natural resources. Natural resources provide us with food, clothing, shelter, and energy. **Minerals** and **fossil fuels** are also natural resources. They are found in Earth's crust. Minerals are natural solids from inside Earth. Gold and copper are minerals. **Coal, petroleum,** and **natural gas** are fossil fuels. Fossil fuels are formed over millions of years from dead plants and animals. They are used for energy.

Not all energy sources are fossil fuels. **Solar energy** and **geothermal energy** come from sunlight and Earth. **Wind energy** and **water energy** can also supply electricity. The wind turns the blades of wind machines. A dam traps the power from moving water.

7 | **Fossil Fuels**

❯ For information on electricity, see pages 218–221.

❯ For information on minerals, see pages 126–129.

❯ For information on Earth's crust, see pages 130–133.

8

9

10

11

Copper

Gold

✔ Check Your Understanding

1. Look at the pictures. What are three fossil fuels?
2. Where does solar energy come from?
3. What are natural resources used for?

Critical Thinking Analyzing Information
4. Which source of energy is found in Earth's crust?

📖 Workbook page 157

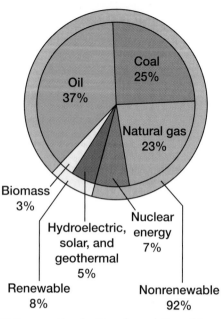

■ Energy Use in Developed Countries

Coal 25%
Oil 37%
Natural gas 23%
Biomass 3%
Nuclear energy 7%
Hydroelectric, solar, and geothermal 5%
Renewable 8%
Nonrenewable 92%

Renewable and Nonrenewable Resources CD 3 TR 72

Renewable resources are resources that can be replaced or reused. Trees, air, and water are renewable resources. Geothermal and solar energy will always be available. **Biomass** is dead plants and waste. Biomass is used to make fuel. Biomass is renewable because people can always grow new plants. Most **nonrenewable resources** come from fossil fuels. They cannot be replaced within our lifetimes. Oil, coal, and natural gas are nonrenewable. They take hundreds of millions of years to form.

Science Skill   Using Percentages

Percent means "parts of a hundred." A pie chart gives information about percentages. Look at the pie chart of energy use in developed countries (countries where people have a high income).

1. What percent of energy is supplied by coal?

2. What percent of energy is supplied by biomass? Is this a renewable or a nonrenewable energy source?

3. What percent of energy is supplied by oil, coal, natural gas, and nuclear energy together?

Word Study

The Prefix **Re**

When the prefix **re** is added to a word, it means "again."

To **reuse** materials is to use them again so there will be less waste.

🅰🅩 Academic Vocabulary

People	use	natural resources.
	consume	

■ Newspaper Ready to Be Recycled

Recycle, Reduce, and Reuse   CD 3 TR 73

It is important to conserve natural resources. We can conserve natural resources in three ways. To recycle means "to use old or used things to make new products." We can recycle glass, plastic, metal, and paper. To **reduce** means "to use fewer natural resources by consuming only what we need." To **reuse** means "to give old things new life." We can find new ways to use them again. For example, we can reuse empty jars for food storage. We can also give used books, toys, games, or outgrown clothing to charities.

Wind Farms CD 3 TR 74

Wind is a clean energy source. It is renewable, because the wind will always be there. A wind farm often has hundreds of wind machines. When the wind blows, the blades on the wind machines turn. Electricity is produced. Not every place has the strong, steady winds needed for wind farms. California and Texas have the most wind farms in the United States.

Blade

■ A Wind Machine

> For information on pollution, see page 148.

✓ Check Your Understanding

1. Why are fossil fuels nonrenewable resources?

2. What are the three ways we can conserve natural resources?

3. Why is wind-powered electricity renewable?

Critical Thinking Comparing and Contrasting

4. What are the differences between renewable and nonrenewable energy resources?

 Research and Inquiry Use the internet, the library, or your science book to answer these questions.

1. What is the greenhouse effect? What are its signs? Is it helpful or harmful?

2. How is electricity made from fossil fuels such as coal?

3. What are open pit mines? Why are they often harmful to the environment?

 Writing Imagine your community plans a new recycling program. Why is the program important? Write a letter to a newspaper. Give reasons to recycle.

Nature of Matter

FOCUS QUESTION
What can your senses tell you about matter?

CD 4
TR 1

1 senses	4 taste	7 burn	10 gas
2 color	5 texture	8 rust	11 liquid
3 odor	6 chemical changes	9 states	12 solid

1 Senses

- You can see colors in a rainbow.

- You can smell the odor of a flower.

- The taste of ice cream is sweet.

- You can feel the smooth texture of a cat's fur.

Word Study

Multiple-Meaning Words

The word **property** has different meanings.

Property can mean "an object owned by someone."

If you own a bike, it is your **property.**

Property can also mean "a characteristic or trait."

One **property** of this apple is that it is red.

► For information on measuring matter, see pages 166–169.

Vocabulary in Context CD 4 TR 2

Matter is made up of tiny bits too small to see. Matter can be a **solid,** such as ice, or a **liquid,** such as water. Matter can also be a **gas,** such as water vapor.

Your **senses** give you information about the properties of matter. You can see the **color** of a lemon and **taste** how sour it is. The **odor** of lemons can tell you that someone is making fresh lemonade.

Matter can change. Matter can change to become a solid, a liquid, or a gas. Some kinds of matter can burn or rust. Burning and rusting are examples of **chemical changes.**

| 6 | Chemical Changes |

7

8

| 9 | States |

Water vapor
10

Ice
12

Water
11

✔ Check Your Understanding

1. Look at the pictures of the senses. What words can you use to describe the color, odor, taste, or texture of what you see?

2. You see a glass of apple juice. Is the juice a solid, a liquid, or a gas?

3. What can your senses tell you about matter?

Critical Thinking Analyzing Information

4. What property of matter lets you tell the difference between salt and sugar?

📖 Workbook page 161

States of Matter CD 4 TR 3

Matter has three **states:** solid, liquid, and gas. The **particles** that make up matter are packed tightly together in a solid. A solid has a definite shape and **volume.** The particles in a liquid are farther apart. A liquid has a definite volume. But a liquid takes the shape of its container. The particles in a gas are very far apart. A gas fills its container.

Solid   Liquid   Gas

■ States of Matter

Science Skill   Interpreting an Illustration

The illustrations show how particles are arranged in each state of matter. Look at the illustrations.

1. In which state are the particles closest together?
2. In which state are the particles farthest apart?
3. Which states would change shape if you put them into a bottle?

Observing Matter CD 4 TR 4

A property is something that can help you recognize an object. When you use words to describe an object, you are talking about the object's physical properties.

You can use your senses to observe the properties of matter. Your senses can tell you the size, shape, color, taste, odor, and texture of an object. Small, round, red, sweet, fruity smelling, and smooth are properties of an object. You probably know the object is an apple.

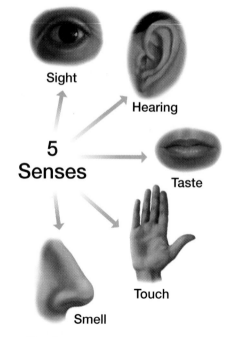

Sight

Hearing

5 Senses

Taste

Touch

Smell

■ The Senses

Academic Vocabulary

| You can | **recognize** | an object by its properties. |
| | **identify** | |

Physical and Chemical Properties CD 4 TR 5

You can identify matter by its properties. All matter has **physical properties.** You can recognize physical properties by observing the matter. Color, odor, taste, and state are some physical properties.

Matter also has **chemical properties.** You can observe these during a chemical change. For example, some kinds of matter can burn or rust. Those are chemical properties.

■ A Physical Property

■ A Chemical Property

Word Study
Word Families
The word **taste** can be used as a noun and as a verb.

I love the **taste** of chocolate. (noun)
You can **taste** the chocolate in the cake. (verb)

▶ For information on chemical changes, see pages 178–181.

✓ Check Your Understanding

1. What are the three states of matter?
2. What are physical properties? Give three examples.
3. What is a chemical property? Give an example.

Critical Thinking Interpreting Information
4. You change the shape of a lump of clay. Is it still a solid? Explain.

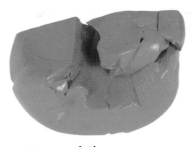
■ A Lump of Clay

 Research and Inquiry Use the internet, the library, or your science book to answer these questions.

1. How do scientists study particles that are too small to see?
2. How do the particles in matter move? How is the motion of particles in a solid different from the motion of particles in a liquid or a gas?
3. How is a plasma different from a gas? Where are plasmas found?

 Writing Find a picture of a common object. What are the properties of the object? Which senses can you use to observe those properties? Write a paragraph. Attach the picture to your paper.

Measuring Matter

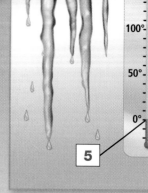

FOCUS QUESTION
How can we measure matter?

CD 4
TR 6

1 balance
2 mass
3 graduated cylinder
4 volume
5 melting point
6 freezing point
7 gas

8 thermometer
9 boiling point
10 liquid

11 solid
12 sink
13 float

5

150 g

100g

50g

2

3

4 — 80 mL

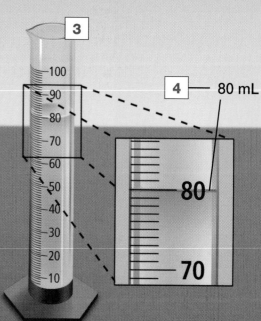

100g

50g

—100
—90
—80
—70
—60
—50
—40
—30
—20
—10

80

70

1

Word Study

Multiple-Meaning Words

The word **volume** has different meanings.

Volume can mean "loudness."

I can't hear the radio. Please turn up the **volume.**

Volume can mean "the amount of space something occupies."

The **volume** of lemonade in the pitcher is 2 liters (about 0.5 gallons).

▶ For information on measurements, see pages 10–13.

▶ For information on measuring tools, see pages 14–17.

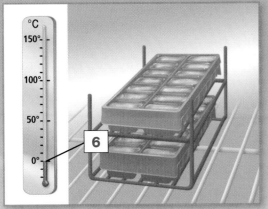

Vocabulary in Context 🎧 CD 4 TR 7

We can measure many properties of matter. **Mass** is the amount of matter in an object. We measure mass with a **balance. Volume** is the amount of space something occupies. We measure the volume of a **liquid** or a **solid** with a **graduated cylinder.** Matter also has **boiling points, melting points,** and **freezing points.** We measure these with a **thermometer.**

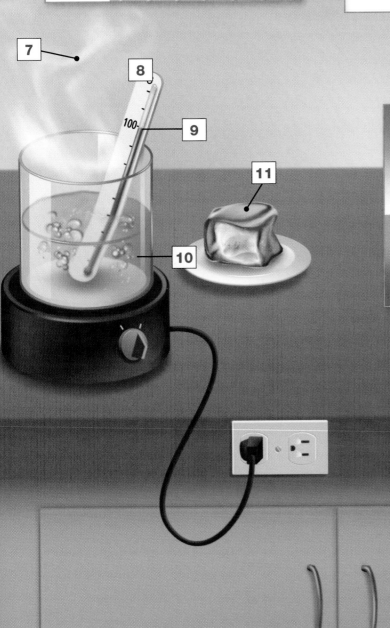

✓ Check Your Understanding

1. Look at the pictures. What do you notice about the freezing point and melting point of water?

2. What properties of matter can we measure?

3. How can we measure matter?

Critical Thinking Applying Information

4. What kinds of matter have you seen melt, freeze, or boil? Where did you see them?

Changes of State CD 4 TR 8

An ice cube is a **solid.** If you heat an ice cube, it melts and changes to water. Water is a liquid. The melting point of ice is 0°C. If you heat the water, it boils and becomes steam. Steam is a gas. The boiling point of water is 100°C.

Substance	Melting point	Boiling point
water	0°C	100°C
salt	801°C	1,413°C
oxygen	–218°C	–189°C

■ Melting Points and Boiling Points

| **Science Skill** | Using Numbers to Compare |

We can use math to compare the numbers in the table. Look at the Melting Points and Boiling Points table. Find the largest number and the smallest number.

1. Which substance has a higher melting point than water?

2. Which substance has a lower boiling point than water?

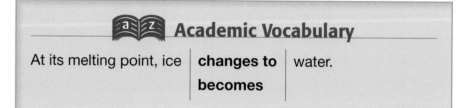

	Academic Vocabulary
At its melting point, ice	**changes to**	water.
	becomes	

● For information on gravity, see pages 186–189.

Force of gravity

Buoyant force

■ An object floats when the buoyant force is greater than the force of gravity.

Buoyancy CD 4 TR 9

When you put a solid in a liquid, a **buoyant force** pushes upward on the solid. The **force of gravity** pushes down on the solid. If the upward force is greater than the downward force, the solid floats. If the downward force is greater than the upward force, the solid sinks.

Mass, Volume, and Density CD 4 TR 10

All objects have mass and volume. The comparison of an object's mass to its volume is **density.** Density is the mass ÷ (divided by) the volume. We express density in grams per cubic centimeter (g/cc or g/cm³). Different materials have different masses for the same volume. The density of gold is 19.3 g/cc (grams per cubic centimeter).

$$D = \frac{M}{V}$$

1 cm
1 cm
1 cm

1 cubic centimeter

■ Finding Density

❯ For more information on metric units of measurement, see pages 10–13.

Word Study
Frequently Misused Words

Mass is the amount of matter in an object.

Weight is the force on an object caused by gravity.

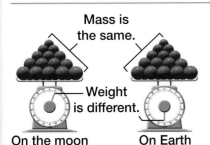

Mass is the same.

Weight is different.

On the moon   On Earth

An object's **mass** is the same on the moon as it is on Earth.

The object's **weight** is less on the moon because the moon's gravity is weaker.

✓ Check Your Understanding

1. What happens when you heat ice? What happens when you heat water?

2. A rock sinks in water. Why?

3. A rock has a mass of 84 g and a volume of 12 cc. What is its density?

Critical Thinking Analyzing Evidence

4. You have two objects. One sinks in water. The other one floats. Which one has a greater density?

 Research and Inquiry Use the internet, the library, or your science book to answer these questions.

1. A robot used to explore the moon weighs 80 pounds on Earth. How much does it weigh on the moon?

2. Why does a helium-filled balloon float in the air?

3. What is the density of aluminum? How is this related to its use in building airplanes?

 Writing You start to heat an ice cube. You continue heating until the temperature reaches 100°C. What happens? Write a paragraph.

Atoms and Molecules

FOCUS QUESTION
What is matter made of?

CD 4
TR 11

1 atom
2 electron
3 nucleus
4 proton
5 neutron
6 molecule
7 elements
8 metals
9 gold
10 silver
11 nonmetals
12 oxygen
13 carbon

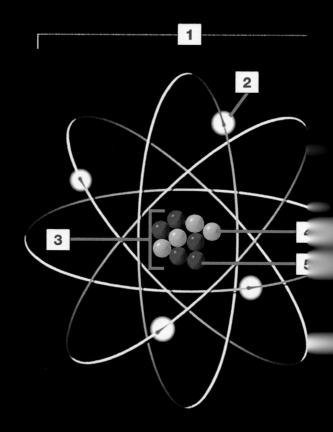

Word Study

Word History

Some elements are named for places. *Americium* is named after North America.

Element	Named for
polonium	Poland
germanium	Germany
europium	Europe
francium	France
californium	California

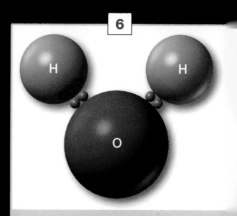

■ A water molecule is formed from two atoms of hydrogen (H) and one atom of oxygen (O).

➤ For information on how elements combine, see pages 178–179.

Vocabulary in Context CD 4 TR 12

Matter is all around you. **Metals** such as **gold** and **silver** are matter. **Nonmetals,** such as **oxygen** and **carbon,** are matter. The food you eat is matter. Your body is matter. Even the air you breathe is matter. Everything you can see, touch, taste, or smell is matter.

All matter is made up of tiny particles called **atoms.** These atoms are made up of even smaller particles called **protons, neutrons,** and **electrons.** An **element** is a pure substance that is made of only one kind of atom. Molecules form when two or more atoms join together. A water molecule is formed from two atoms of hydrogen and one atom of oxygen.

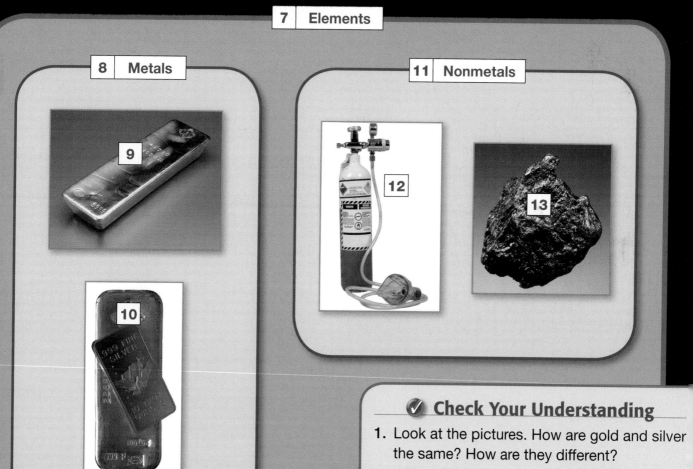

7 Elements

8 Metals

9

10

11 Nonmetals

12

13

✅ Check Your Understanding

1. Look at the pictures. How are gold and silver the same? How are they different?
2. Look around you. Write the names of three kinds of matter you can easily see.
3. What is matter made of?

Critical Thinking Visualizing

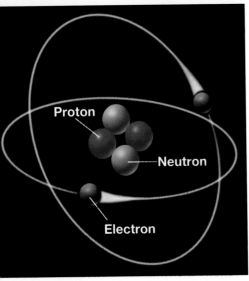

■ Structure of an Atom

Structure of an Atom CD 4 TR 13

Atoms are made up of three types of particles. Protons and neutrons are found in the center of the atom. This area is called the **nucleus.** Electrons are smaller particles that circle around the nucleus.

Some particles have an electrical charge. Protons have a positive charge. Electrons have a negative charge. Neutrons have no charge.

Science Skill Interpreting a Diagram

A diagram is a drawing. It shows how something is put together. Usually, the parts are labeled. Look at the diagram of the atom.

1. What do the labels tell you?
2. What are the parts of an atom?
3. How many electrons does the atom have?

Molecules CD 4 TR 14

A molecule forms when two or more atoms join together. Three atoms combine to form a water molecule. Water has two hydrogen atoms and one oxygen atom. But water has different **properties** than hydrogen or oxygen. For example, at room temperature water is a **liquid.** Hydrogen and oxygen are **gases** at room temperature.

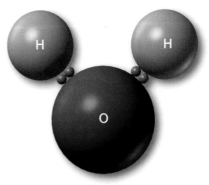

H = hydrogen
O = oxygen

■ A Water Molecule

● For information on properties of matter, see pages 162–163.

 Academic Vocabulary

| When two atoms | join together | they form a molecule. |
| | combine | |

The Periodic Table of Elements CD 4 TR 15

An element is matter that is made of only one kind of atom. Every atom in an element has the same number of protons in the nucleus.

The **periodic table** of elements organizes the elements. Each element has its own box in the table. The box shows the element's **symbol.** It also shows the element's **atomic number.** This is the number of protons in the nucleus. Elements are listed in order by atomic number. The elements are organized into different groups in the table. Two of the groups are metals and nonmetals. Aluminum is a metal. Oxygen is a nonmetal.

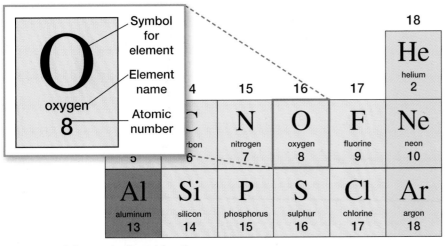

■ A Part of the Periodic Table: Oxygen

Word Study

Word History

Each element has a symbol. The symbol is often the first letter or first two letters of the name. The symbol for gold is Au, from the Latin word for gold, *aurum.*

Element	Symbol
carbon	C
nitrogen	N
gold	Au
hydrogen	H
aluminum	Al

❯ For the complete periodic table, see page 222.

✓ Check Your Understanding

1. What electrical charge does a proton have?
2. What elements combine to form a water molecule?
3. What does the periodic table do?

Critical Thinking Looking for Patterns
4. The atomic number of silver is 47. What does that tell you about silver?

 Research and Inquiry Use the internet, the library, or your science book to answer these questions.

1. What are isotopes?
2. How does the mass of a proton compare to the mass of an electron?
3. How many particles are in the nucleus of a hydrogen atom?

 Writing Imagine that you discovered a new element. As the discoverer, you can name the element. What will you name it? Why? Write a paragraph.

CD 4
TR 16

1 pure substances

2 elements

3 oxygen

4 aluminum

5 compounds

6 water

7 sugar

8 mixtures

9 heterogeneous mixture

10 granite

11 homogeneous mixture

12 air

1	Pure Substances

2	Elements

3

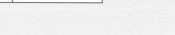

4

5	Compounds

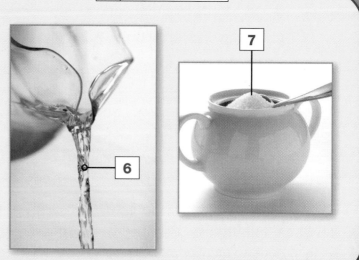
7

6

Word Study

Multiple-Meaning Words

The word **solution** has different meanings.

`5 x 8 = ?`

Solution can mean "the answer to a problem."

It was easy to find the **solution** to the math problem.

Solution can also mean "a type of mixture."

He mixed a **solution** of salt and water.

8 Mixtures

9 Heterogeneous Mixture

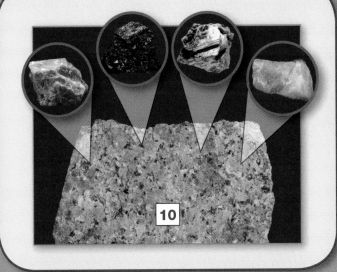

10

11 Homogeneous Mixture

12

Vocabulary in Context

CD 4
TR 17

A **pure substance** is matter that is made of only one kind of particle. An **element** is a pure substance that is made of only one type of atom. **Aluminum** is an element. A **compound** is a pure substance made of two or more elements that join chemically. **Water** is a compound of hydrogen and oxygen.

A **mixture** contains two or more pure substances. The substances are mixed together. They do not join chemically. **Air** is a mixture of gases. **Granite** rock is a mixture of compounds.

▶ For information on air, see pages 146–148.

▶ For information on how atoms join together chemically, see pages 178–181.

📖 Workbook page 173

✅ Check Your Understanding

1. Look at the pictures. What tells you that granite is a mixture?
2. You're eating cereal and milk. Are you eating a pure substance or a mixture?
3. How is a compound different from a mixture?

Critical Thinking Applying Information

4. You're drinking a glass of lemonade. Is it an element, a compound, or a mixture?

Compounds and Mixtures

Compound	Elements Joined in the Compound
water	hydrogen and oxygen
table salt (sodium chloride)	sodium and chlorine
sugar	carbon, hydrogen, and oxygen
baking soda	sodium, hydrogen, carbon, and oxygen
chalk	calcium, carbon, and oxygen

■ Common Compounds

▶ For information on atoms, see pages 170–173.

■ A Suspension: Salad Dressing

■ A Solution: Tea with Sugar

Common Compounds CD 4 TR 18

Atoms of two or more elements often combine to form a new pure substance. This new substance is a compound. **Carbon dioxide** is a compound. It is made up of the elements **carbon** and oxygen. Each molecule of carbon dioxide consists of one atom of carbon and two atoms of oxygen.

Table salt is another compound. The elements **sodium** and **chlorine** join to make salt.

Science Skill   Comparing and Contrasting

When we compare, we say how things are the same. When we contrast, we say how things are different. When data is in a table you can easily compare and contrast the information. Look at the table.

1. Which compound is made from the most elements?
2. Which compounds contain oxygen?
3. Which compounds contain carbon?

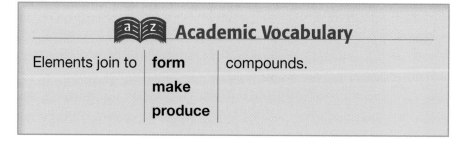

Academic Vocabulary

Elements join to	form	compounds.
	make	
	produce	

Types of Mixtures CD 4 TR 19

A mixture is not a pure substance. In a mixture, two or more substances come together. But they do not join chemically.

Mixtures can be grouped as heterogeneous or homogeneous. A **suspension** is one kind of heterogeneous mixture. When you shake salad dressing, drops of oil and drops of vinegar are scattered evenly in the bottle. But you can still see the different parts. This is a suspension.

A **solution** is a homogeneous mixture. In a solution, one material, such as sugar, **dissolves** in another material, tea. You cannot see the different parts in this kind of mixture.

Word Study
Prefixes

The prefix **hetero** means "not the same."

A **heterogeneous** mixture is not the same throughout.

The prefix **homo** means "the same."

A **homogeneous** mixture is the same throughout because the substances mix evenly.

Physical and Chemical Changes

 CD 4 TR 20

Matter can change shape and state. These are **physical changes.** During a physical change, the identity of the substance is not changed. When ice melts, it is a physical change. When glass breaks, it is a physical change.

During a **chemical change,** new substances form. The new substances may be elements or compounds. They have different properties from the original substance. When wood burns, it produces ashes and gases. They have different properties from wood.

■ A Physical Change

■ A Chemical Change

✔ Check Your Understanding

1. What elements join to form carbon dioxide?
2. What are the two kinds of mixtures? Give an example of each.
3. What are examples of two kinds of physical changes?

Critical Thinking Making Inferences

4. Is seawater a heterogeneous or homogeneous mixture? How do you know?

● For information on chemical changes, see pages 178–181.

 Research and Inquiry Use the internet, the library, or your science book to answer these questions.

1. What is a saturated solution?
2. What are some ways that you can separate the parts of a mixture?
3. What are some ways you can tell a chemical change has taken place?

 Writing What did you eat for lunch? Were any parts of your meal compounds? Which parts were homogeneous mixtures? Which parts were heterogeneous mixtures? Write a paragraph describing your lunch.

Chemical Reactions

FOCUS QUESTION
What happens during a chemical reaction?

CD 4
TR 21

1 equation
2 symbol
3 formula
4 element
5 burn
6 rust

7 compound
8 molecule
9 bond
10 atom
11 electron

Sodium (Na)

4

Chlorine (Cl)

1

$$2H_2 + O_2 \rightarrow 2H_2O$$

2   3

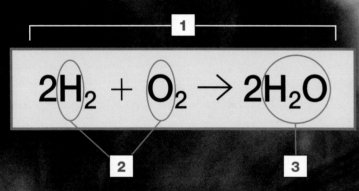

5

6

Word Study

Multiple-Meaning Words

The word **equation** is used in both mathematics and science.

In math, an **equation** is a statement that two amounts are equal. It uses an equal sign.

A simple math **equation** is $2 + 2 = 4$.

In science, an **equation** tells you what happens in a chemical reaction. It uses an arrow.

A simple chemical **equation** is $2Na + Cl_2 \rightarrow 2NaCl$.

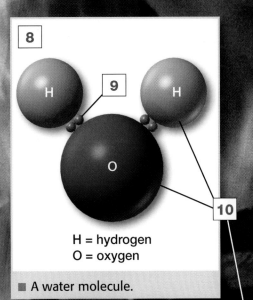

$2H_2 + O_2 \rightarrow 2H_2O$

7

■ Water is a compound.

8

H = hydrogen
O = oxygen

9

H

H

O

10

■ A water molecule.

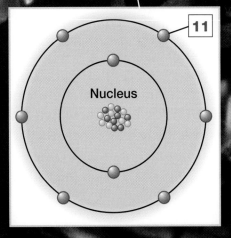

11

Nucleus

> For information on parts of an atom, see page 172.

Vocabulary in Context

CD 4
TR 22

All matter is made of tiny particles called **atoms.** An **element** is a pure substance made of only one kind of atom. Oxygen is an element. Atoms can join together and form **molecules.** A molecule is formed by two or more atoms. For example, oxygen usually occurs in molecules of two atoms. When two or more different atoms join together into a molecule, they form a **compound.** Water is a compound. It is formed from atoms of hydrogen and oxygen.

Every element has a **symbol.** The symbol for oxygen is O. The symbol for hydrogen is H. Every compound has a **formula.** The formula shows the atoms in a compound. A formula is made of numbers and symbols for the elements. The formula for an oxygen molecule is O_2. The formula for a water molecule is H_2O.

Molecules can also break apart. Then their atoms can join together in new ways and form different compounds. Atoms and molecules join together and break up in chemical reactions. Iron and oxygen join to make **rust.** Rusting is a chemical reaction. Some things can **burn.** Burning is a chemical reaction too. When something burns, it combines with oxygen and produces compounds. For example, when gas burns it produces compounds such as carbon dioxide and water.

> For information on element names and symbols, see pages 170–171.

✅ Check Your Understanding

1. Look at the pictures. What elements do you see? What compounds do you see?

2. What forms when two or more different atoms join together?

3. What happens during a chemical reaction?

Critical Thinking Looking for Patterns

4. Look at the equation for water. What does the arrow mean?

Workbook page 177

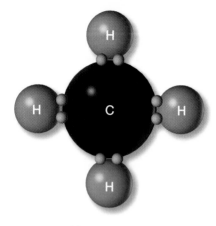

H = hydrogen
C = carbon

■ Chemical Bonds

Chemical Bonds CD 4 TR 23

When atoms join to form molecules, they can lose, gain, or share electrons. This forms a chemical bond between the atoms.

Chemical reactions break these bonds and form new ones. Some of these reactions give off energy. This kind of reaction is an **exothermic** reaction. Other reactions take in energy. This kind of reaction is an **endothermic** reaction.

Word Study
Word Origins

The words **endothermic** and **exothermic** consist of prefixes added to **thermic. Thermic** is from the Greek **therme,** which refers to heat.

- **Endo + thermic** means "taking in heat."
- **Exo + thermic** means "putting out heat."

Chemical Equations 🎧 CD 4 TR 24

A chemical equation tells what happens in a chemical reaction. The chemical equation $2H_2 + O_2 \rightarrow 2H_2O$ communicates what happens when hydrogen and oxygen join to form water. There are four atoms of hydrogen and two atoms of oxygen before the reaction. There are still four atoms of hydrogen and two atoms of oxygen after the reaction. Atoms are not lost. They are not made. They are just rearranged.

$$2H_2 + O_2 \rightarrow 2H_2O$$

■ A chemical equation shows the atoms and molecules in a reaction.

Science Skill Reading an Equation

Look at the chemical equation. The elements shown on the left of the yields sign ($\rightarrow$) are called the **reactants.** These are the substances that **react** to form the new compound. The substance on the right is water. It is called the **product.** The yields sign expresses the direction the reaction goes. The large numbers in the equation tell the number of each kind of atom or molecule in the reaction. The small numbers in the equation tell you how many atoms of each element are involved in the reaction. If an atom or a molecule does not have a number, there's only one atom or molecule.

1. What are the reactants in this equation?
2. What elements are combined in the product?

● For information on compounds, see pages 174–175.

Academic Vocabulary

Chemical equations	tell	what happens during a chemical reaction.
	communicate	
	express	

Conservation of Mass CD 4 TR 25

Think about how the atoms of hydrogen and the atoms of oxygen rearrange to form water.

You can measure the mass of the hydrogen and oxygen before they combine. Then you can measure the mass of the water. The mass of the reactants is the same as the mass of the product. Matter cannot be created. It cannot be destroyed. This is called the **law of conservation of mass.**

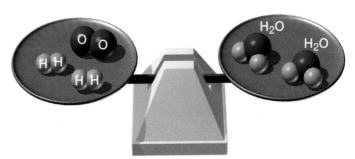

■ The mass of hydrogen and oxygen before the reaction is the same as the mass of the water after the reaction.

✔ Check Your Understanding

1. What type of particle can be shared by atoms in a chemical bond?
2. What does a chemical equation tell you?
3. What is the law of conservation of mass?

Critical Thinking Applying Information
4. A group of atoms of sodium and chlorine have a total mass of 2.5 grams. The sodium and chlorine react to form salt. What is the mass of the salt?

 Research and Inquiry Use the internet, the library, or your science book to answer these questions.

1. What are the chemical formulas of sugar and salt? What elements are they made of?
2. What are covalent and ionic chemical bonds?
3. Why does an iron chain gain mass as it rusts?

Writing You see a commercial for a new machine. The commercial says that the machine can create new matter. Write a paragraph explaining why this cannot be true.

Radiation and Radioactivity

FOCUS QUESTION
Why do scientists use special clothing when they work with radioactive materials?

CD 4
TR 26

1 radioactive sample

2 radiation

3 radioactive symbol

4 alpha particles

5 beta particles

6 gamma rays

7 paper

8 aluminum

9 concrete

10 atom

11 nucleus

Word Study

Multiple-Meaning Words

Particle has different meanings.

Particle can mean "a very small piece or part."

> **Particles** of sand covered the road.

Particle can mean "a piece of matter that is smaller than an atom."

> An atom is made from **particles.**

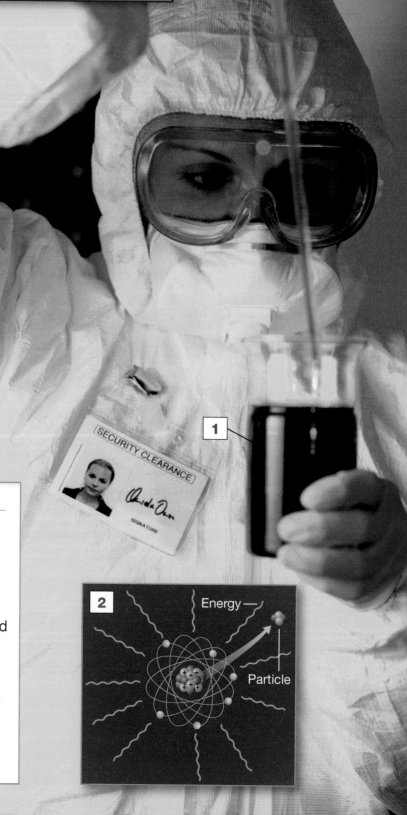

Energy

Particle

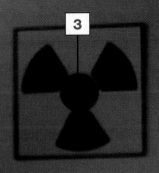

3

Vocabulary in Context CD 4 TR 27

Some kinds of matter give off energy and particles. These materials are **radioactive.** They have an unstable **nucleus.** They give off energy and particles to become more stable. **Alpha particles** are the least powerful. They are slow and large. A sheet of **paper** can stop alpha particles. **Beta particles** are smaller and faster than alpha particles. A sheet of **aluminum** foil can stop beta particles. **Gamma rays** are the most powerful. It takes a thick block of **concrete** to stop gamma rays. Exposure to **radiation** of any kind can be dangerous, so scientists use special clothing and equipment.

➤ For information on the nucleus of an atom, see pages 170–173.

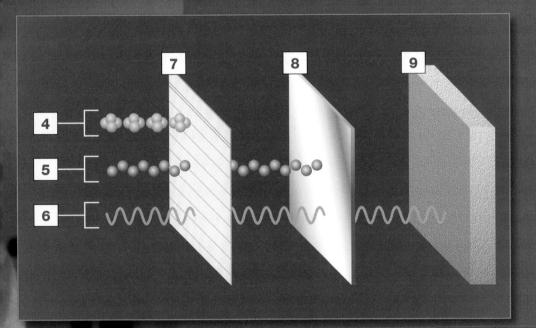

7 **8** **9**

4

5

6

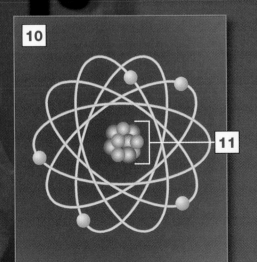

10

11

✅ Check Your Understanding

1. Look at the pictures. What can beta particles pass through?

2. Which are faster, alpha particles or beta particles?

3. Why do scientists use special clothing when they work with radioactive materials?

Critical Thinking Making Inferences

4. Why should radioactive samples have a symbol that is easy to recognize?

Workbook page 181

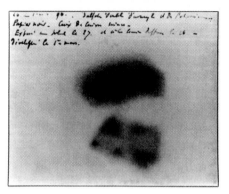

■ Becquerel's Photographic Plate

● For information on protons, neutrons, and electrons, see pages 170–172.

Discovery of Radioactivity

CD 4
TR 28

In 1869, French scientist Antoine-Henri Becquerel put some **uranium** (a kind of metal) in a drawer. A photographic plate was also in the drawer. When Becquerel looked a few days later, an image of the uranium sample was on the plate! Only an energy source can make an image on a photographic plate. The uranium gave off energy. Becquerel accidentally discovered radioactivity.

Radioactive Decay

CD 4
TR 29

When something **decays,** it breaks down into smaller parts. An atom decays when it gives off particles or energy. An atom may release an alpha particle. This is made from two **protons** and two **neutrons.** The atom may release a beta particle. This is usually an **electron.** An atom can also emit energy instead of particles. Gamma rays are a form of energy that comes from the decay of an atom.

The time it takes for half the atoms in a sample to decay is its **half-life.** Some kinds of radioactive materials have half-lives that last only a fraction of a second. Others have half-lives that last billions of years.

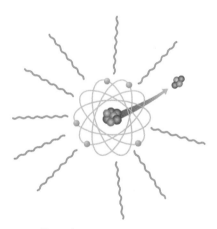

■ Radioactive Decay

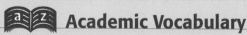

Academic Vocabulary

An atom decays when it	gives off	particles or energy.
	releases	
	emits	

Uses of Radiation CD 4 TR 30

Radiation can be dangerous. It can make people and animals sick or even kill them. But radiation can also help people when used carefully. Doctors use radiation to find out what is making people sick. They use **X-rays** to check for broken bones. Radiation also helps treat **cancer.** And it is used to clean instruments used in **surgery.**

Most people use radioactive materials every day. They might not even know it. A smoke detector contains a small amount of radioactive material.

Word Study

Suffixes

The suffix **tion** changes a verb into a noun.

Radiate means "to send out energy."

radiate + tion = radiation

Radiation means "energy that is sent out."

Science Skill   Comparing Data

Scientists often compare data. Placing data in a table makes the data easier to compare. The table lists the uses and half-lives of some radioactive elements.

1. Which element in the table has the longest half-life?

2. How can carbon-14 be used?

3. Which element can help a doctor?

Element	Half-Life	Use
carbon-14	5,730 years	We use it to find out how old a fossil or an artifact is.
cobalt-60	5.3 years	We use it to sterilize surgical instruments.
uranium-238	4.47 billion years	We use it as fuel for nuclear power.

■ Uses and Half-Lives of Some Radioactive Elements

✔ Check Your Understanding

1. Who discovered radioactivity?

2. What are gamma rays?

3. What is one way people use radioactive materials in their homes?

Critical Thinking Applying Information

4. A scientist has a 2-gram sample of radioactive material. It has a half life of 1 hour. How much of the sample will decay in 1 hour?

 Research and Inquiry Use the internet, the library, or your science book to answer these questions.

1. Who were Marie and Pierre Curie?

2. Where are natural sources of radioactive materials found?

3. How is radioactivity measured?

 Writing How are radioactive substances used to help people who are sick? Write a short paragraph. Explain how doctors and hospitals use radiation.

Forces

FOCUS QUESTION
What is a force?

CD 4
TR 31

1 **balanced**

2 **unbalanced**

3 **friction**

4 **push**

5 **pull**

6 **move**

7 **stop**

8 **gravity**

Word Study

Multiple-Meaning Words

The word **force** has different meanings.

Force can mean "a group organized to maintain law and order."

New York City has a large police **force**.

Force can mean "a push or pull that acts on an object."

Gravity is the **force** that causes Earth to orbit the sun.

▶ For information on Earth's orbit, see pages 114–115.

Vocabulary in Context
🎧 CD 4 TR 32

What makes a skateboard **move** across the ground? What makes it **stop**? What makes the skateboard go faster down a hill? Forces make these things happen. A force is a **push** or a **pull** on an object. The push or pull changes the object's motion. A push from the skateboarder's leg causes the skateboard to move. When objects rub against each other, **friction** is the result. The force of friction between the wheels and the ground causes the skateboard to slow down and stop. Objects also pull on each other. The name of this force is **gravity.** Earth's gravity pulls us toward the ground. The force of gravity makes the skateboard go faster down a hill.

✔ Check Your Understanding

1. Look at the pictures. Find two examples of friction.
2. Why do skateboarders go fast down hills?
3. What is a force?

Critical Thinking Applying Information

4. What forces affect a soccer ball when you kick it down a hill? How does each force affect the ball?

📖 Workbook page 185

Gravity CD 4 TR 33

Gravity is the force of **attraction** between objects. Earth's gravity pulls us toward the ground. The sun's gravity pulls on the planets and keeps them in their orbits.

Objects with more **mass** have more gravity. Earth has more mass than the moon. It has about six times more gravity than the moon. The measure of the pull of gravity on an object is its **weight.** Weight is measured in units called newtons (N).

Planet	Weight of an Average Person in Newtons (N)
Mercury	302.4 N
Venus	725.6 N
Earth	800 N
Mars	301.6 N
Jupiter	2,026.4 N
Saturn	851.2 N
Uranus	711.2 N
Neptune	900 N

■ Gravity and Weight on Different Planets

◉ For more information on mass and weight, see page 169.

◉ For information on motion, see pages 190–193.

Science Skill Using Numbers to Compare

You can use the numbers in a table to compare things. The table to the left shows the weight of an average person on the planets in our solar system. Think about what you can learn about weight, gravity, and mass by looking at the table.

1. On which planet is a person's weight closest to what it is on Earth?
2. Which planet has the greatest gravity?
3. Which planet has the least mass?

Friction  CD 4 TR 34

Have you ever tried to push a heavy box over a rough surface? Have you ever rubbed your hands together to make heat? Then you have felt the effects of friction. Friction happens when surfaces rub against each other.

Friction always works against motion. When you push a box across the floor, friction makes pushing the box harder.

Pushing force

Force of friction

■ Friction always opposes motion. Friction makes pushing a box harder.

Academic Vocabulary

Friction	works against	motion.
	opposes	

Balanced and Unbalanced Forces CD 4 TR 35

Look at the picture of people playing tug-of-war. If the students on each side pull the rope with exactly the same amount of force, the flag will not move. The forces are balanced. When balanced forces act on an object, the object is in **equilibrium.**

If another student joins the game, the forces acting on the rope will be unbalanced, and the flag will move. There is no longer equilibrium. Unbalanced forces cause a change in motion.

Flag   Rope

■ When forces are balanced, an object won't move.

Word Study

Antonyms

Antonyms are words that mean the opposite of each other.

Push and **pull** are antonyms.

> You **push** a swing.

> You **pull** a wagon.

Move and **stop** are antonyms.

> When you **move,** you are running or walking.

> When you **stop,** you are standing still.

✔ Check Your Understanding

1. What force keeps the planets in their orbits?

2. What does friction do?

3. What happens when the forces acting on an object are unbalanced?

Critical Thinking Inferring from Evidence

4. Two dogs are playing with a rope toy. Each dog pulls on the toy, but the toy does not move. Are the forces balanced or unbalanced? How do you know?

 Research and Inquiry Use the internet, the library, or your science book to answer these questions.

1. How does the distance between objects affect the force of gravity?

2. What is magnetic force?

3. How does a compass work?

 Writing You are on a spaceship. You travel in space to Mars. Write a paragraph about the pull of gravity on Mars. Is it stronger or weaker than the gravity on Earth? How do you move? How do you feel?

Forces and Motion

FOCUS QUESTION
What makes objects move?

CD 4
TR 36

1 **velocity**

2 **mass**

3 **force**

4 **speed**

5 **acceleration**

6 **action force**

7 **reaction force**

[1]

[2]

Word Study
Related Meanings

Velocity, speed, and **acceleration** have related meanings.

Speed means "how fast something is moving."

The roller coaster car moves at a high **speed.**

Velocity means "speed in a direction."

The roller coaster car's **velocity** changed as it turned a corner.

Acceleration means "change in speed or direction."

The roller coaster's rate of **acceleration** increased as it raced down the hill and decreased when it rolled to a stop.

600 g

500 kg

▶ For information on measuring an object's mass, see pages 166–169.

▶ For information on forces, see pages 186–189.

Vocabulary in Context 🎧 CD 4 TR 37

When you roll a ball, you cause motion. **Force** makes the ball, or any object, move. The **speed** of the ball depends on how much force you used. The ball's **velocity** is its speed in a direction. **Acceleration** is a change in speed or direction. When an object accelerates, it changes direction or speed. For example, the roller coaster is always accelerating because it's always changing speed and direction. The acceleration of an object is related to its **mass.** The larger the mass of an object, the more force is needed to change its speed or direction. Forces always happen in pairs. For example, when the baseball hits the glove, an **action force** affects the baseball glove. It moves back. At the same time, a **reaction force** affects the ball. The ball stops moving.

3

5

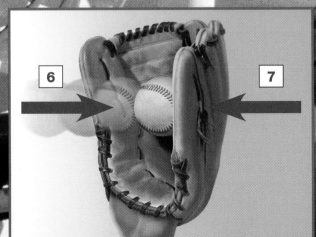

6   7

✔ Check Your Understanding

1. Look at the pictures. Which pictures show motion?

2. What is velocity?

3. What makes objects move?

Critical Thinking Analyzing Information

4. What words can you use to describe an object's motion?

■ Newton's first law explains why the car stops moving but a safety belt and airbag are needed to stop the dummy.

⊙ For information on friction, see pages 186–189.

Newton's First Law CD 4 TR 38

Isaac Newton lived from 1643 to 1727. His three laws of motion describe how forces change motion. His first law explains that objects resist any change in their motion. This is called **inertia.** An object at rest will stay at rest unless a force affects it. For example, you roll a ball. The law also says that an object in motion will stay in motion unless a force stops it. The force that stops the ball is **friction.**

Inertia causes a crash-test dummy to keep moving forward when the car suddenly stops. A force stops the car, but a safety belt and an airbag are needed to stop the dummy.

Newton's Second Law CD 4 TR 39

Acceleration is the rate at which velocity changes. Velocity is speed in a direction. It is expressed as **meters per second (m/s).** Velocity changes when an object's speed or direction, or both, change. On a roller coaster, your speed, your direction, or both are always changing. So you are always accelerating. Acceleration tells you how quickly your velocity changes, expressed as **m/s per second (m/s/s).**

Newton's second law of motion explains that more force causes more acceleration. It also says that more force is needed to move an object with more mass.

> *F* (force) = *m* (mass) × *a* (acceleration)

■ Newton's Second Law

Science Skill Using Math to Solve Problems

Newton's second law in equation form is $F = m \times a$. This means that the force (F) acting on an object is equal to its mass (m) multiplied by its acceleration (a). If the acceleration is 10 m/s/s and the mass is 2 kg, the force is 20 newtons.

1. What is the force if the acceleration is 8 m/s/s and the mass is 5 kg?

2. What is the force if the acceleration is 10 m/s/s and the mass is 7 kg?

Newton's Third Law CD 4 TR 40

Newton's third law explains that forces always happen in pairs. When a basketball player jumps, her feet push against the floor. This is the action force. But the floor also pushes against the player's feet. This is the reaction force. Newton's law states that the action and reaction forces are always **equal** and always occur in **opposite** directions.

 Academic Vocabulary

Forces can	**change**	an object's motion.
	affect	

Word Study

Prefixes

A prefix is added to the beginning of a word. It changes the meaning of the word.

The prefix **re** can mean "back" or "against."

Reaction means "an action against."

The **action** caused a **reaction.**

■ Newton's third law says that the action and reaction forces are always equal and opposite.

✔ Check Your Understanding

1. What does Newton's first law say will happen to an object at rest?
2. You increase the force on an object. What also increases?
3. What two things are true about action and reaction forces?

Critical Thinking Applying Information

4. You push a door open. What is the action force? What is the reaction force?

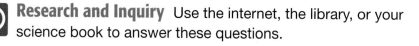 **Research and Inquiry** Use the internet, the library, or your science book to answer these questions.

1. What is momentum? How is it calculated?
2. What is Newton's law of gravitation?
3. Research the story of Newton and the falling apple. What is it?

 Writing A shopping cart full of groceries rolls away down a steep hill. Halfway down, it hits a very large rock. What happens? How do Newton's laws explain what happens? Write a paragraph.

Work, Power, and Machines

How do machines make work easier?

CD 4
TR 41

1 **load**

2 **simple machines**

3 **lever**

4 **inclined plane**

5 **wedge**

6 **screw**

7 **pulley**

8 **wheel and axle**

9 **fulcrum**

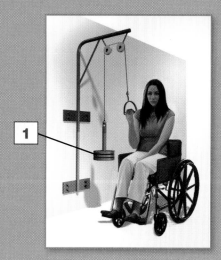

2 | Simple Machines

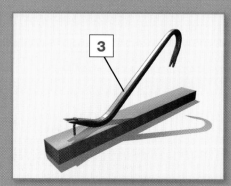

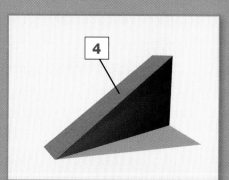

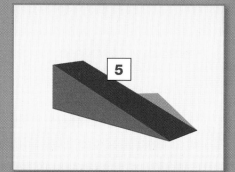

Word Study

Homonyms

The words **plane** and **plain** are homonyms. They are pronounced the same way. But they are spelled differently and have different meanings.

Plane means "a flat surface."

    An inclined **plane** is a simple machine.

Plain means "simple" or "not fancy."

    We did not decorate the room, so it looked **plain.**

▶ For information on forces, see pages 186–189.

Vocabulary in Context 🎧 CD 4 TR 42

Did you ever play on a seesaw when you were a child? Did you know you were using a **lever?** A lever is a board or rod that turns on a fixed point called a **fulcrum.** The lever is one example of a **simple machine.** There are six kinds of simple machines: **pulleys,** levers, **wedges, screws, wheels and axles,** and **inclined planes.** Machines change the distance or direction of the force you use to do work. Machines do not change the amount of work. They make the work easier. A seesaw changes the direction of force. Instead of trying to lift a person off the ground using an upward force, you use a downward force and the lever. You are still doing the same amount of work, but it is much easier.

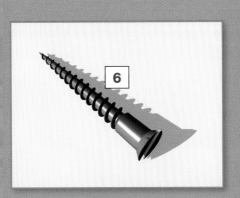

6

7

8

Axle

Wheel

9

■ A Seesaw

✓ Check Your Understanding

1. Look at the pictures. How many types of simple machines do you see?

2. What kind of simple machine is a seesaw?

3. How do machines make work easier?

Critical Thinking Applying Information

4. Name a simple machine you have used. How did it make work easier?

📖 Workbook page 193

▶ For information on energy, see pages 206–209.

Effort force

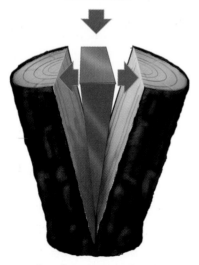

■ A wedge can change the direction of a force and split wood.

Force and Distance CD 4 TR 43

Suppose you want to climb a hill. One side of the hill is steep. The other is a long, gentle slope. Which is easier? Climbing either side of the hill is the same amount of work. But the gentle slope spreads the work over a greater distance. It makes the work easier. The slope of a hill is an example of an inclined plane.

You can calculate **work** by multiplying force and distance ($W = F \times d$). A simple machine such as the inclined plane makes work easier by making the distance greater. When the distance is greater, you use less force to do the same amount of work.

A

B

■ Using an Inclined Plane

Science Skill   Interpreting a Simple Machine Diagram

The diagram above shows two people trying to move a box onto another box. One is using a ramp and pushing the box up to the top. The other is lifting the box straight up.

1. Which person is moving the box the greater distance?

2. Which person is using the most force?

3. Is person A doing less work than person B? How do you know?

The Wedge CD 4 TR 44

A wedge is thin at one end and thick at the other. You can use it to separate two objects. You can use it to split a single object. You can use a wedge to split wood.

A wedge changes the direction of force. To use a wedge, you put its thin end on the object you want to split. Then you apply an **effort force** to the thick edge. Effort force is the force you use to try to move something. You use force to push the wedge downward into the wood. The wedge changes the direction of the force. It pushes sideways on the inside of the wood and splits the wood apart.

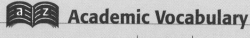

Academic Vocabulary

Machines reduce the force you	use	to do work.
	apply	
	exert	

Compound Machines CD 4 TR 45

A **compound machine** is made up of two or more simple machines. Many things we use every day are compound machines. A shovel is made of a wedge and a lever. The part of the shovel that scoops snow is the wedge. The handle of the shovel is a lever that has its fulcrum at one end. What you lift with the shovel is a load.

A compound machine makes work even easier than a simple machine. You exert less force to do the same work.

■ A shovel is a compound machine.

✔ Check Your Understanding

1. Why does an inclined plane make work easier?
2. What can you use a wedge to do?
3. What is a compound machine?

Critical Thinking Drawing Conclusions
4. Scissors are a kind of compound machine. What kind of simple machine are the blades of scissors? How do the blades help make work easier?

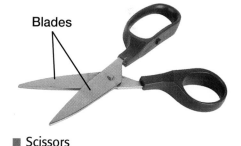

■ Scissors

 Research and Inquiry Use the internet, the library, or your science book to answer these questions.

1. What is a block and tackle? What is it used for?
2. What happens when you move the fulcrum of a lever?
3. What are three of the simple machines that make up a bicycle? What jobs do these machines do?

 Writing You are carrying some heavy boxes inside school. At the front of the school you can walk up 5 steps or use a ramp. Which is less work? Explain why. Write a paragraph.

Waves

CD 4
TR 46

FOCUS QUESTION
How does energy travel?

1 waves

2 transverse waves

3 crest

4 trough

5 wavelength

6 amplitude

7 water waves

8 longitudinal waves

9 sound waves

10 compression

11 rarefaction

| 2 | Transverse Waves |

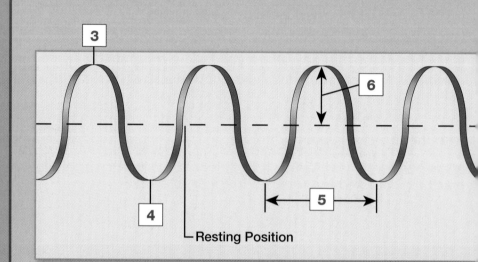

3

6

4

5

Resting Position

7

Word Study

Multiple-Meaning Words

The word **wave** has different meanings.

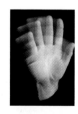

Wave can mean "to communicate with a back-and-forth hand gesture."

I **wave** good-bye to my sister when I leave for school.

Wave can also mean "a movement of energy."

Energy travels through water in **waves.**

198

8 | **Longitudinal Waves**

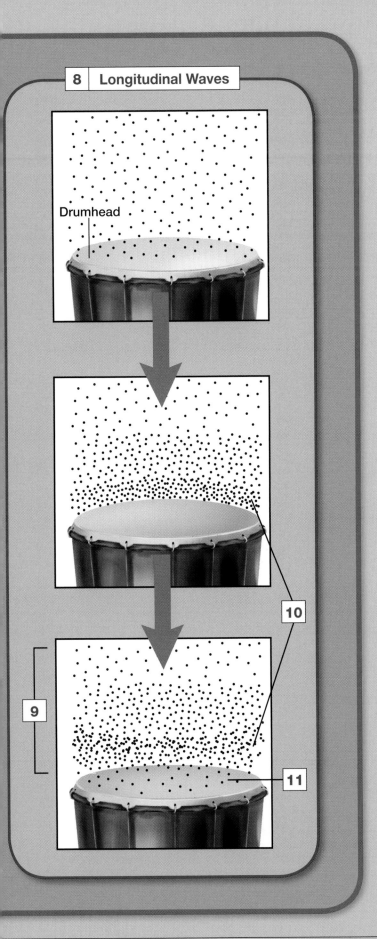

Drumhead

10

9

11

Vocabulary in Context CD 4 TR 47

Waves are movements that carry energy without carrying matter. The tiny waves on the surface of a pond carry energy from one place to another. But the water does not move along with the wave.

Water waves are **transverse waves.** In transverse waves, the water particles move up and down, but the wave moves forward. Transverse waves have **crests** and **troughs.** The crest is the highest part of the wave. The trough is the lowest part of the wave. The distance between two crests (or troughs) is the **wavelength.** The height of a transverse wave is its **amplitude.**

Sound waves are **longitudinal waves.** A drumhead moving up causes air particles above it to be squeezed together. This forms a **compression.** When the drumhead moves downward, air particles spread out. This forms a **rarefaction.** In sound waves, the particles move back and forth as the wave moves forward. You can measure the wavelength of both kinds of waves.

✅ Check Your Understanding

1. Look at the pictures. What is a crest? What is a trough? What kind of wave has them?

2. What kind of waves are water waves? What kind of waves are sound waves?

3. How does energy travel?

Critical Thinking Making Inferences

4. What matter do sound waves usually move through to get to your ear?

📖 Workbook page 197

Word Study

Multiple-Meaning Words

The word **medium** has different meanings.

The word **medium** can mean "the size of something."

> This shirt comes in sizes small, **medium,** and large.

It can also mean "a type of material."

> Waves travel through a **medium** such as air or water.

Medium has an irregular plural: **media.**

> Waves can travel through many different kinds of **media.**

▶ For information on sound energy, see pages 206–209.

Longitudinal and Transverse Waves 🎧 CD 4 TR 48

Sound waves and water waves carry energy through **matter.** The matter that waves move through is called a **medium.** The medium that water waves travel through is water. Sound waves can travel through different media, such as air, water, or steel.

In longitudinal waves, some particles of the medium are pushed together, while others are spread apart. Particles in the medium move back and forth as the wave travels forward.

In transverse waves, the particles in the medium move in an up-and-down pattern as the wave travels forward.

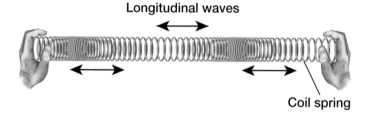

Longitudinal waves

Coil spring

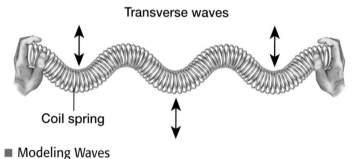

Transverse waves

Coil spring

■ Modeling Waves

Science Skill — Interpreting a Model

A model can help us understand a science concept. For example, we can use a coil spring to model longitudinal waves and transverse waves. Look at the drawings of the two wave models above.

1. What kind of wave is modeled by back-and-forth motion?
2. What kind of wave is modeled by up-and-down motion?

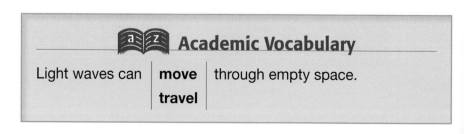

Academic Vocabulary

| Light waves can | **move** | through empty space. |
| | **travel** | |

Electromagnetic Spectrum CD 4 TR 49

Light, **X-rays,** and **radio waves** are all **electromagnetic waves.** These kinds of waves can travel through empty space. Different parts of the **electromagnetic spectrum** have different wavelengths. Waves with long wavelengths are at one end of the electromagnetic spectrum. Waves with short wavelengths are at the other end. In the center are visible light waves. This is the part of the spectrum we see with our eyes.

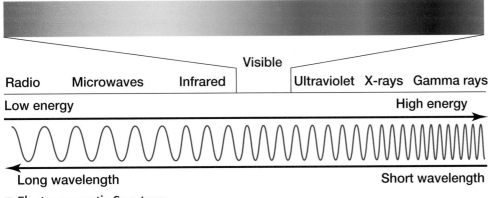

Visible

| Radio | Microwaves | Infrared | | Ultraviolet | X-rays | Gamma rays |

Low energy High energy

Long wavelength   Short wavelength

■ Electromagnetic Spectrum

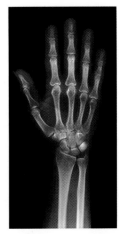

■ An X-ray Picture of the Bones in a Hand

Uses of Electromagnetic Waves CD 4 TR 50

Many kinds of electromagnetic waves are useful. We use radio waves to send radio and TV signals. We use microwaves to cook food. We use X-rays to take pictures of the insides of people.

✅ Check Your Understanding

1. What kinds of media can sound waves travel through?
2. What kinds of waves are part of the electromagnetic spectrum?
3. What is one use of microwaves?

Critical Thinking Comparing and Contrasting
4. How are X-rays and radio waves alike? How are they different?

 Research and Inquiry Use the internet, the library, or your science book to answer these questions.

1. Which kind of wave causes most skin cancer? How can people protect themselves from this kind of wave?
2. How fast do sound waves travel? How fast do electromagnetic waves travel?
3. What kinds of waves does the sun produce?

 Writing Think about three devices you have at home that use different kinds of waves. Write a paragraph describing how you use these devices.

Light

FOCUS QUESTION
What happens when light strikes an object?

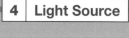

CD 4
TR 51

1 transparent	6 sun	11 reflect
2 translucent	7 natural light	12 refract
3 opaque	8 candle	13 absorb
4 light source	9 lamp	14 prism
5 stars	10 artificial light	15 colors

5

6

7 | Natural Light

1

2

3

Word Study

Multiple-Meaning Words

The word **reflect** has different meanings.

Reflect can mean "to think deeply."
The boy **reflected** on his studies.

Reflect can also mean "to show an image."
A mirror **reflects** your face.

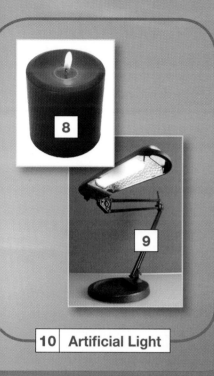

8

9

10 | Artificial Light

Vocabulary in Context 🎧 CD 4 TR 52

Light is energy that we can see. A **light source** is something that gives off its own light. **Natural light** comes from nature. Some natural light sources are the **sun** and **stars**. **Artificial light** is any light that people produce. Some artificial light sources are **lamps** and **candles**.

We see the world around us because of light. Light is **absorbed, reflected,** or **refracted** when it strikes an object. Absorbed light is taken in by the object. Reflected light bounces off an object. Refracted light bends when it passes through an object. We see an object when light reflected from the object reaches our eyes. Moonlight is reflected sunlight.

➤ For information on light waves, see pages 198–201.

➤ For information on forms of energy, see pages 206–207.

11

■ Light bounces off a mirror.

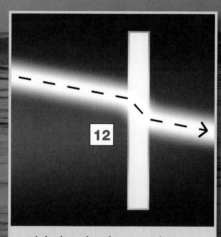

12

■ Light bends when passing through a transparent object.

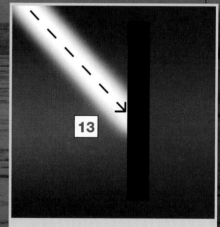

13

■ Light is taken in by an opaque object.

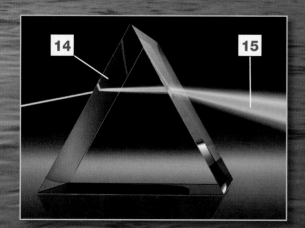

14   15

✅ Check Your Understanding

1. Look at the pictures of light sources. Which light sources are natural? Which ones are artificial?

2. What is moonlight?

3. What happens when light strikes an object?

Critical Thinking Making Observations

4. What sources of light do you use during the day? What about at night?

📖 Workbook page 201

■ Refraction makes the pencil look bent or broken.

❯ For information on the colors of light, see page 201.

Reflection and Refraction CD 4 TR 53

When you shine a light on a mirror, light bounces off. This is called reflection. Smooth, shiny surfaces reflect the most light.

Sometimes light bends as it passes through a material. This is called refraction. You can see refraction if you place a pencil in a glass of water. The pencil looks bent or broken.

Seeing Colors CD 4 TR 54

White light contains all the colors of light. When white light shines on objects, you see colors. An object's color depends on the colors of light it reflects and absorbs. A green leaf absorbs all colors except green. It reflects green light to your eyes. A white object reflects all colors of light. A black object absorbs all colors of light.

A prism divides light into its colors. As light enters the prism, the light refracts. Each color of light bends differently. The light passes through the prism and separates into different colors.

■ A White Truck Under Different Colors of Light

Word Study

Antonyms

Antonyms are words that have opposite meanings.

Reflect and **absorb** are opposites.

A red shirt **reflects** red light and **absorbs** all other colors.

Natural and **artificial** are opposites.

The sun is a **natural** light source. A lamp is an **artificial** light source.

Science Skill Interpreting Photos

The two photos above show the same white model truck. But the truck doesn't look white in the photos. The reflection of light explains why.

1. What color of light is shining on the truck in each photo? What color of light is the truck reflecting?

2. What color would the truck look in red light?

3. You shine a flashlight on another model truck. The truck absorbs all the colors in the light. What color is the truck?

Academic Vocabulary

A prism	**divides**	light into different colors.
	separates	

Transparent, Translucent, or Opaque? 🎧 CD 4 TR 55

Some materials let light pass through them. If all the light passes through, the material is transparent. The windshield of a car is transparent. If some light passes through, the material is translucent. Frosted glass is translucent. If no light passes through, the material is opaque. The car body is opaque.

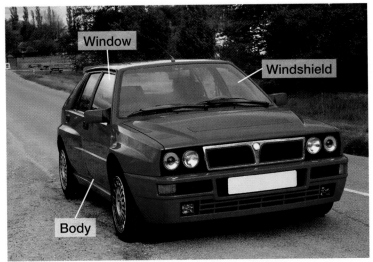

Window
Windshield
Body

■ Transparent Windshield and Windows, and Opaque Body

■ Translucent Frosted Glass

✅ Check Your Understanding

1. What type of surfaces reflect the most light? Give examples.
2. What causes an apple to look red?
3. What type of material does not let any light pass through?

Critical Thinking Classifying Information

4. List ten objects you see in the room around you. Classify each as transparent, translucent, or opaque.

 Research and Inquiry Use the internet, the library, or your science book to answer these questions.

1. How does the human eye see color?
2. How is a shadow formed?
3. There is some light that we cannot see. What are some kinds of light we cannot see?

 Writing Imagine that the sun stops giving off red light. What will the world look like? How will it change? Write a paragraph that explains your answer.

Forms of Energy

CD 4
TR 56

FOCUS QUESTION
How do we use energy?

1 renewable energy

2 nonrenewable energy

3 sound energy

4 thermal energy

5 light energy

6 chemical energy

7 electrical energy

8 mechanical energy

9 potential energy

10 kinetic energy

1

Wind energy

2

Gasoline

3

Fire

Guitar

4

Word Study

Word Families

The word **heat** can be a noun or a verb.

I can feel the **heat** coming from the stove. (noun)

Heat the soup in this pan. (verb)

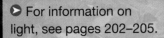
For information on light, see pages 202–205.

For information on renewable and nonrenewable energy sources, see pages 158–161.

Vocabulary in Context CD 4 TR 57

You can see, hear, and feel energy. A fire gives off **thermal energy** and **light energy.** Thermal energy makes you warm. Light energy lets you see. You hear **sound energy** when you listen to music. **Electrical energy** powers the lights in your home. And the battery in your wristwatch has **chemical energy.**

Mechanical energy is the ability to do work. There are two kinds of mechanical energy. You have both kinds. You have **potential energy** when you are on your bike at the top of a hill. As you ride down the hill, you have **kinetic energy.**

6

Battery

7

8

9

10

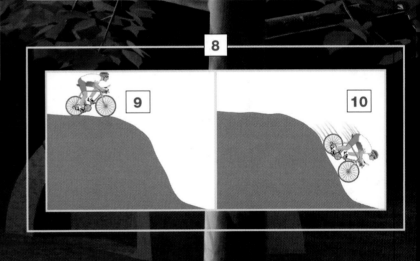

5

✅ Check Your Understanding

1. Look at the pictures. What is an example of renewable energy?

2. What kind of energy is in the battery of a wristwatch?

3. How do we use energy? Give some examples.

Critical Thinking Making Inferences

4. What forms of energy help you learn in school?

📖 Workbook page 205

Forms of Energy

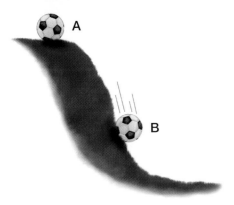

■ A soccer ball has potential energy at the top of the hill (A) and kinetic energy as it rolls down the hill (B).

Potential and Kinetic Energy 🎧 CD 4 TR 58

Mechanical energy is the ability to do work. Mechanical energy can be classified as potential energy or kinetic energy. Things with mechanical potential energy have the possibility of moving. An object's position can give it potential energy. A soccer ball at the top of a steep hill has potential energy. Objects can also store potential energy. A stretched rubber band has stored potential energy. Kinetic energy is the energy of motion. A soccer ball has kinetic energy as it rolls down the hill. A stretched rubber band has kinetic energy as it snaps back to its original shape.

Science Skill Visualizing

When you visualize, you use your imagination to "see" a picture of something. Visualizing can help you when you read. Visualize an example of an object or person that has potential energy. Then visualize the same object or person with kinetic energy. Describe the scenes you pictured.

1. When did the object or person have potential energy?
2. When did the object or person have kinetic energy?

▶ For information on renewable and nonrenewable energy sources, see pages 158–161.

■ Coal, a fossil fuel, is a nonrenewable energy source.

Renewable and Nonrenewable Energy 🎧 CD 4 TR 59

You can group energy sources into renewable and nonrenewable. Renewable sources can be **replaced** as quickly as they are used. Wind energy and **hydropower,** energy from moving water, are renewable.

Nonrenewable sources of energy cannot be replaced quickly. We can run out of them. **Fossil fuels,** such as coal, oil, and gasoline, are nonrenewable energy sources. Fossil fuels are the remains of organisms that lived long ago. They are found deep in Earth.

■ Hydropower: A Renewable Energy Source

Grand Coulee Dam in Washington State

<hr />

Word Study

Prefixes

A prefix is added to the beginning of a word. It changes the meaning of the word. The prefix **non** means "not." The prefix **re** means "do again."

Nonrenewable means "not able to be made new again."

Fossil fuels are **nonrenewable.**

<hr />

 Academic Vocabulary

You can | **classify** / **group** | energy and energy sources different ways.

Sound Energy CD 4 TR 60

A musician pulls her bow across the strings of a violin. The strings start to **vibrate,** or move back and forth very fast. These vibrations travel from the strings to other parts of the instrument. Then the air **molecules** around the violin begin to vibrate. The vibrations travel through the air to your ear. Tiny bones inside your ear vibrate. Sound energy from the violin has made it all the way to your ear!

■ When the musician plays the violin, sound energy travels through the air.

▷ For information on molecules, see page 172.

✔ Check Your Understanding

1. When does a soccer ball have kinetic energy?
2. What are three renewable energy sources?
3. How does sound energy travel from an instrument to your ear?

Critical Thinking Applying Information

4. You hold a ball high above the ground. Then you drop it. When did the ball have the **most** potential energy? When did it have the **least** potential energy?

 Research and Inquiry Use the internet, the library, or your science book to answer these questions.

1. What is biomass? How is it used?
2. How does an object's mass affect its potential energy?
3. How does a turbine convert wind energy into electricity?

 Writing You are at home. You go to the kitchen and turn on the light. Then you turn on the radio. Then you make a cup of hot chocolate. What forms of energy do you use? Write a paragraph.

Energy Transformations

FOCUS QUESTION
What are some ways that energy changes form?

1 thermal energy

2 sound energy

3 electrical energy

4 chemical energy

5 heat

6 potential energy

7 kinetic energy

8 light energy

9 temperature

■ Fireworks have many kinds of energy. We can see the light energy. Thermal energy makes them hot. Kinetic energy shoots them high into the sky.

1

■ The thermal energy from a toaster feels hot. We can use this energy to toast bread.

3

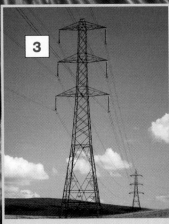

■ The wires on this tower carry electrical energy.

4

■ The materials in batteries have chemical energy. This energy can change to electrical energy.

Word Study

Suffixes

The suffix **ation** changes a verb into a noun.

The verb **transform** means "change."

transform + **ation** = **transformation**

A radio **transforms** electrical energy into sound energy. This is one kind of **transformation.**

5

■ When we boil water, heat moves from the stove to the water.

■ A radio produces sound energy. When the sound waves reach our ears, we hear music.

Vocabulary in Context CD 4 TR 62

We use energy to run and play. We use energy to cook food. We use energy to play a CD. Energy comes in many forms. Energy can also change forms. Do you want to make toast? A toaster uses **electrical energy.** It changes electrical energy to **thermal energy** and **light energy.** Do you want to listen to music? A radio changes electrical energy into **sound energy.** A flashlight transforms the **chemical energy** in the battery into light energy. The energy in people and things can change forms, too. A bicycle and its rider have **potential energy** at the top of the hill. They have **kinetic energy** as they go down the hill. Fireworks show many kinds of changes in energy. Chemical energy is transformed into sound energy, light energy, thermal energy, and kinetic energy. Sometimes, energy can move without changing form. **Heat** is the movement of thermal energy from one object to another.

▶ For information on forms of energy, see pages 206–209.

▶ For more information on waves, see pages 198–201.

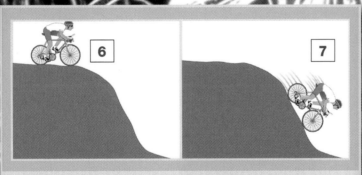

6 **7**

■ Potential energy is energy from position. At the top of the hill, the bicycle has potential energy. Kinetic energy is energy of movement. When the bicycle is going down the hill it has kinetic energy.

9

■ A thermometer shows temperature.

8

✓ Check Your Understanding

1. Look at the pictures. Name three kinds of energy.
2. What energy change occurs in a radio?
3. What are some ways that energy changes form?

Critical Thinking Applying Information

4. What form of energy do you use most in your daily activities? How does this energy change when you use it?

Workbook page 209

211

Energy Transformations

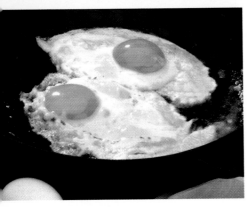

■ Heating Eggs

■ Heat travels from hot chocolate to the spoon by conduction.

Pan

Convection

Hot plate

OFF — HOT

■ Convection is the flow of heat by movement in a liquid or a gas.

■ Energy travels from the sun to Earth in waves.

Heat and Temperature CD 4 TR 63

Heat is the transfer of thermal energy from one object to another. Heat always moves from warmer matter to cooler matter. Solids, liquids, and gases are made of particles that are always moving. Temperature is a measure of how fast those particles are moving. Have you ever seen someone fry an egg? When the cold egg touches the hot pan, thermal energy from the pan moves to the egg. The particles in the egg begin to move faster. Then the temperature of the egg increases.

Heating Matter CD 4 TR 64

Thermal energy can move in three ways. **Conduction** is the transfer of heat when fast-moving particles hit slower-moving particles. Think about what happens when you put a metal spoon in a cup of hot chocolate. The particles of the hot liquid bump into the spoon. Thermal energy moves directly from the hot drink to the spoon. The temperature of the spoon goes up.

Convection is the flow of heat from one place to another by movement in a liquid or a gas. You heat water in a pot. The water at the bottom of the pot heats up. The warm water rises, and cooler water takes its place. A circular movement of water gradually heats all the water in the pan.

Radiation is heat transfer in waves. Waves are movements that carry energy but not matter. When you are outside on a sunny day, energy travels by radiation from the sun to your body. Some of this energy changes into thermal energy. You get warm.

Science Skill — Thinking about Systems

A system is made of parts that work together. Look at the drawing of the pan of water on a hot plate.

1. What are the parts of the system in the drawing?
2. How does thermal energy move through the water?
3. How does thermal energy move from the hot plate to the pan? Explain.

Academic Vocabulary

A toaster	changes converts transforms	electrical energy into thermal energy.

Conservation of Energy CD 4 TR 65

Energy can change from one form into another. For example, we can convert chemical energy to sound energy in a battery-powered radio. Energy can move from place to place. But energy cannot be made or destroyed. This is the **law of conservation of energy.**

A pendulum is a good example of how this law works. When the ball is at points A and C, it has potential energy, or energy because of its position. At point B, all of its energy has been converted to kinetic energy, or energy because it is moving. Halfway between points A and B, its energy changes to half kinetic and half potential. Halfway between points B and C, its energy is half kinetic and half potential. The total energy always stays exactly the same. Energy transforms from kinetic to potential, but is not lost. Energy is conserved.

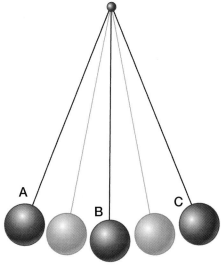

■ Energy is not gained or lost when the potential energy in the pendulum changes to kinetic energy.

❯ For information on potential and kinetic energy, see pages 208–211.

Word Study
Word Origins

Transfer comes from Latin word roots.

- **Trans** means "across."
- **Ferre** means "to carry."

Transfer means "movement from one place to another."

✓ Check Your Understanding

1. What is heat? What is temperature?
2. What are the three ways that thermal energy can move?
3. What is the law of conservation of energy?

Critical Thinking Inferring from Evidence

4. You put a hot object in a bowl of ice. The object gets cold. Was the thermal energy destroyed? How do you know?

Research and Inquiry Use the internet, the library, or your science book to answer these questions.

1. What type of heat transfer does not need to travel through matter? How does this kind of transfer affect Earth?
2. Why does boiling water bubble?
3. How does energy transfer affect the particles of matter?

 Writing Think about the energy transformations you see on a typical day. Write a short paragraph explaining what happens during three of these transformations.

Energy and Life

FOCUS QUESTION

What process changes stored energy into energy you can use?

CD 4
TR 66

1 **leaves**

2 **sun**

3 **light energy**

4 **chemical energy**

5 **photosynthesis**

6 **cellular respiration**

7 **chloroplast**

8 **chlorophyll**

▶ For information on photosynthesis, see pages 42–45.

Word Study

Syllabification

Syllabification means "breaking a word into its syllables." You can use syllabification to make long words such as **photosynthesis** and **respiration** easier to read and say.

photosynthesis = pho • to • **syn** • the • sis

  Photosynthesis is the way plants use light energy to make food.

respiration = res • pi • **ra** • tion

  Respiration is the way animals change stored energy into forms they can use.

Vocabulary in Context CD 4 TR 67

All living things, including you, need energy. You get energy from the food you eat. How did energy get into the food? The energy comes from the **sun.**

Plants trap **light energy** from the sun in a process called **photosynthesis. Chlorophyll** inside plant **chloroplasts** in **leaves** uses sunlight, water, and carbon dioxide. The plant cells make a kind of sugar. Sugar contains **chemical energy.** The plant stores this energy. When you eat part of a plant, you are eating some of the plant's stored energy.

Your body changes this chemical energy into energy to move and grow. Your body needs oxygen to use chemical energy. The process of changing stored energy into other forms of energy is called **cellular respiration.**

5

light energy + water + carbon dioxide → sugar (chemical energy) + oxygen

6

sugar (chemical energy) + oxygen → energy + carbon dioxide + water

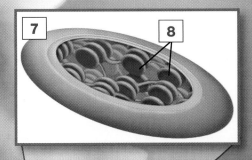

▶ For information on light and chemical energy, see pages 206–209.

▶ For information on how energy changes form, see pages 210–213.

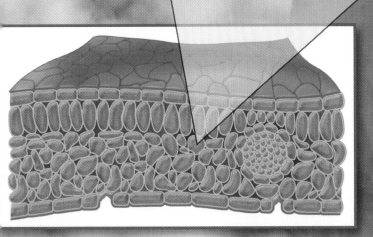

✅ Check Your Understanding

1. Where is chlorophyll found?
2. What living things make chemical energy from sunlight?
3. What process changes stored energy into energy you can use?

Critical Thinking Making Inferences

4. What is the source of the energy you use to move and grow?

Workbook page 213

215

Living Things Use the Sun's Energy 🎧 CD 4 TR 68

The sun provides energy for all life on Earth. Without the sun, Earth would be too cold for living things. The sun supplies the heat that seeds need to grow. Plants need the sun's light energy to grow and to make food. People, animals, and many other living things can't make their own food. These living things depend on plants for food.

■ Plants use the sun's energy to grow and to make food.

◉ For information on the transfer of energy between living things, see pages 86–89.

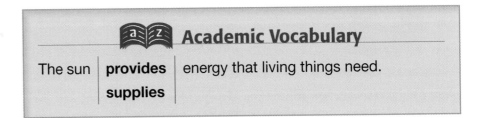

a z	**Academic Vocabulary**	
The sun	**provides**	energy that living things need.
	supplies	

Photosynthesis 🎧 CD 4 TR 69

Living things need food. In photosynthesis, plants use energy from the sun to make the food they need. This food is **glucose,** which is a type of sugar. Chlorophyll is the green matter found in plant chloroplasts. Chlorophyll traps light energy and uses it to make glucose. Glucose contains chemical energy.

Light energy — Oxygen — Atmosphere — Glucose (chemical energy) storage — Carbon dioxide — Water — Ground

■ Photosynthesis

Science Skill   Making Observations

When you make an observation, you look at something and learn something from it. Look at the diagram of photosynthesis. Plants need energy, water, and carbon dioxide. Arrows in the diagram show where these things come from. The lines and arrows also show where glucose is stored and where oxygen goes when it is released.

1. Where does the light energy come from? Where do carbon dioxide and water come from?

2. What happens to the glucose that the plant makes? Where does the oxygen go?

⊙ For information on the parts of a cell, see pages 22–25.

Word Study

Word Origins

The word **chlorophyll** is made up of two Greek words.

- **Chloros** means "green."
- **Phyllon** means "leaf."

    Chlorophyll gives leaves their green color.

Cellular Respiration 🎧 CD 4 TR 70

Cellular respiration is the opposite of photosynthesis. Plants take energy from the sun during photosynthesis. They store it as glucose. Cellular respiration takes place in the **mitochondria** of plant and animal cells. In cellular respiration, the mitochondria of cells change this chemical energy. The plant or animal uses the energy to grow. It uses the energy to build new cells and body parts.

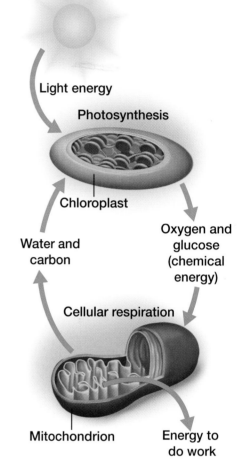

Light energy

Photosynthesis

Chloroplast

Oxygen and glucose (chemical energy)

Water and carbon

Cellular respiration

Mitochondrion

Energy to do work

■ Photosynthesis and Cellular Respiration

✅ Check Your Understanding

1. Why is the sun important to Earth?
2. What energy change happens during photosynthesis?
3. What energy change happens in cellular respiration?

Critical Thinking Making Inferences

4. Why is cellular respiration the opposite of photosynthesis?

Research and Inquiry Use the internet, the library, or your science book to answer these questions.

1. Why is oxygen important in cellular respiration?
2. What are autotrophs and heterotrophs?
3. Where did the chemical energy in fossil fuels come from?

Writing Eva planted a rosebush in the sun. The rosebush grew and produced many flowers. Then she planted a tall tree near the rosebush. The rosebush was in the shade most of the day. Explain what you think happened to the rosebush. Write a paragraph.

Electricity and Magnetism

FOCUS QUESTION
What is a magnet?

CD 4
TR 71

1 static electricity
2 charge
3 electron
4 conductor
5 insulator
6 electromagnet

7 magnetic poles
8 magnet
9 magnetic field
10 electric generator
11 electric current
12 circuit

1

2

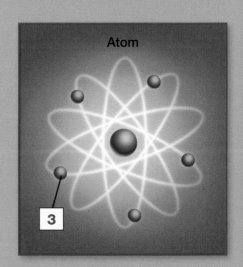

Atom

3

▸ For information on protons and electrons, see pages 172–175.

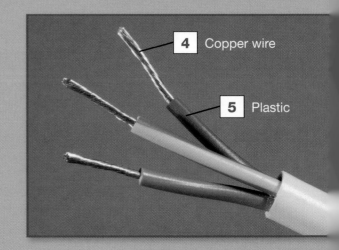

4 Copper wire

5 Plastic

Word Study

Multiple-Meaning Words

The words **positive** and **negative** have special meanings in math and science.

In math, a **positive** number is a number greater than zero. A **negative** number is a number less than zero.

In science, protons have a **positive** electrical charge. Electrons have a **negative** electrical charge.

218

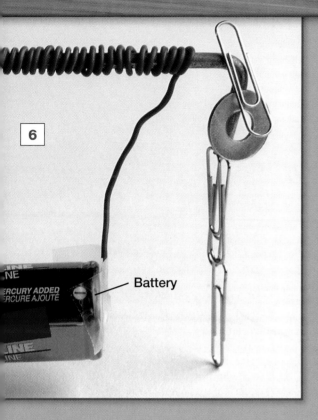

6

Battery

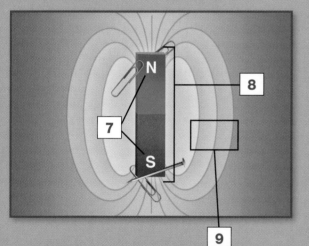

7

8

N

S

9

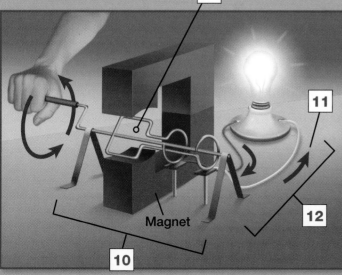

Magnet

10

11

12

Vocabulary in Context CD 4 TR 72

A **magnet** is an object that pulls some metals, such as iron, to itself. A magnet has a **magnetic field** around it. The magnetic field is the area the magnet affects. The magnetic field is stronger at the **magnetic poles.** A magnet has two magnetic poles—a north pole and a south pole. Both poles attract other metals. The north pole will also attract the south pole of another magnet. Magnets will push away from each other if the north poles or south poles are together.

An electric **charge** is caused by **electrons** moving between atoms. **Static electricity** is a charge that doesn't flow. It can only jump from place to place. If you rub a balloon on a cat's fur, static electricity causes the cat's fur to rise. **Electric current** is a charge that flows along a **circuit.** A circuit is a path electricity can follow. A **conductor,** such as copper wire, makes the path. A conductor is any material that can carry electricity. Many metals are conductors.

We can use magnetism to make electric current. In an **electric generator,** metal wires spin inside a magnetic field. This makes electricity.

An **electromagnet** uses electricity to create a magnetic field. An electromagnet is a metal bar with wire around it. An electric current in the wire creates a magnetic field. The bar now attracts metals.

✔ Check Your Understanding

1. What caused the cat's fur to stand up?
2. How does the electric generator make electricity?
3. What is a magnet?

Critical Thinking Understanding Cause and Effect

4. Look at the electric generator. What will happen if the person stops turning the handle?

📖 Workbook page 217

Static and Current Electricity CD 4 TR 73

There are two basic kinds of electricity. Static electricity is a buildup of electric charge. To make static electricity, you rub two objects together. One of the objects loses electrons. It now has a positive electric charge. The other object gains electrons. It now has a negative charge. The charge stays in one place until the electrons jump to another object.

Current electricity moves along a path. To make current electricity, you need an **energy source** such as a **battery** or an electric generator. An energy source produces a flow of electrons. This is called an electric current.

Circuits CD 4 TR 74

In a **flashlight,** a battery is connected to a **wire.** The wire goes to a **lightbulb.** Another wire goes from the lightbulb back to the battery, forming a path. The flow of electrons along this path from the battery to the bulb and back is called a circuit.

A break, or opening, in the circuit stops the current from traveling along the path. The bulb will not light up. A **switch** turns the light on and off by closing and opening the circuit.

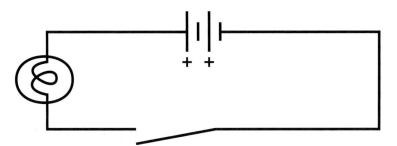

■ A Flashlight Circuit Diagram

■ Lightning: Static Electricity from Clouds

▶ For information on sources of electrical energy, see pages 206–209.

Science Skill   Reading a Circuit Diagram

A **circuit diagram** uses a special symbol to represent each part. Look at the circuit diagram. The symbol that looks like a spring stands for a lightbulb. The symbol that looks like two lines with a plus sign (+) stands for the battery. Look at the flashlight circuit diagram.

1. What is the straight line that joins the battery symbol and the lightbulb symbol?
2. The circuit diagram includes a symbol that looks like a door that opens and closes. What do you think this stands for?

Conductors and Insulators CD 4 TR 75

Electrical wire is made of metal, such as copper. The metal is often covered by a plastic coating. The electric current moves along the copper wire because the wire is a conductor. This means electricity flows easily through it.

Electricity does *not* flow easily through the plastic. Plastic is an insulator. The wire is enclosed in the plastic, so the electricity does not leave the path.

■ Electrical Wire

Word Study

Multiple-Meaning Words

Conductor has different meanings.

Conductor can mean "a person who leads an orchestra."

The **conductor** of the orchestra wears a tuxedo.

Conductor can also mean "a material that lets electricity flow through it."

Metal is a good **conductor**.

Academic Vocabulary

| The metal wire is | **covered by** | plastic. |
| | **enclosed in** | |

✔ Check Your Understanding

1. When an object gains electrons, what charge does it have?
2. What parts make up the circuit in a flashlight?
3. What is an insulator?

Critical Thinking Integrating Information

4. Copper wire is a good conductor, and plastic is a good insulator. Name two more conductors and two more insulators.

 Research and Inquiry Use the internet, the library, or your science book to answer these questions.

1. What is a series circuit? Draw a diagram of one.
2. What is a parallel circuit? Draw a diagram of one. What is one advantage a parallel circuit has over a series circuit?
3. How are electromagnets used?

 Writing Imagine you are an electron inside a battery. You join up with other electrons to form an electric current. Describe your journey along the copper wire of a circuit. Write a paragraph.

Periodic Table of the Elements

Period / **Group**

1	**H** hydrogen 1

Element box key:

O oxygen **8**

- Symbol for element
- Element name
- Atomic number

Period	1	2	3	4	5	6	7	8	9
1	**H** hydrogen 1								
2	**Li** lithium 3	**Be** beryllium 4							
3	**Na** sodium 11	**Mg** magnesium 12							
4	**K** potassium 19	**Ca** calcium 20	**Sc** scandium 21	**Ti** titanium 22	**V** vanadium 23	**Cr** chromium 24	**Mn** manganese 25	**Fe** iron 26	**Co** cobalt 27
5	**Rb** rubidium 37	**Sr** strontium 38	**Y** yttrium 39	**Zr** zirconium 40	**Nb** niobium 41	**Mo** molybdenum 42	**Tc** technetium 43	**Ru** ruthenium 44	**Rh** rhodium 45
6	**Cs** cesium 55	**Ba** barium 56	Lanthanide series	**Hf** hafnium 72	**Ta** tantalum 73	**W** tungsten 74	**Re** rhenium 75	**Os** osmium 76	**Ir** iridium 77
7	**Fr** francium 87	**Ra** radium 88	Actinide series	**Rf** rutherfordium 104	**Db** dubnium 105	**Sg** seaborgium 106	**Bh** bohrium 107	**Hs** hassium 108	**Mt** meitnerium 109

Lanthanide series

La lanthanum 57	**Ce** cerium 58	**Pr** praseodymium 59	**Nd** neodymium 60	**Pm** promethium 61	**Sm** samarium 62	**Eu** europium 63

Actinide series

Ac actinium 89	**Th** thorium 90	**Pa** protactinium 91	**U** uranium 92	**Np** neptunium 93	**Pu** plutonium 94	**Am** americium 95

							18
							He helium 2

13	14	15	16	17	
B boron 5	C carbon 6	N nitrogen 7	O oxygen 8	F fluorine 9	Ne neon 10
Al aluminum 13	Si silicon 14	P phosphorus 15	S sulphur 16	Cl chlorine 17	Ar argon 18

10	11	12	13	14	15	16	17	18
Ni nickel 28	Cu copper 29	Zn zinc 30	Ga gallium 31	Ge germanium 32	As arsenic 33	Se selenium 34	Br bromine 35	Kr krypton 36
Pd palladium 46	Ag silver 47	Cd cadmium 48	In indium 49	Sn tin 50	Sb antimony 51	Te tellurium 52	I iodine 53	Xe xenon 54
Pt platinum 78	Au gold 79	Hg mercury 80	Tl thallium 81	Pb lead 82	Bi bismuth 83	Po polonium 84	At astatine 85	Rn radon 86
Ds darmstadtium 110	Rg roentgenium 111	Uub ununbium 112	Uut ununtrium 113	Uuq ununquadium 114	Uup ununpentium 115	Uuh ununhexium 116	Uus ununseptium 117	Uuo ununoctium 118

Gd gadolinium 64	Tb terbium 65	Dy dysprosium 67	Ho holmium 67	Er erbium 68	Tm thulium 69	Yb ytterbium 70	Lu lutetium 71
Cm curium 96	Bk berkelium 97	Cf californium 98	Es einsteinium 99	Fm fermium 100	Md mendelevium 101	No nobelium 102	Lr lawrencium 103

Glossary
with Spanish Translations

Pronunciation Key			
a	apple	o	fox
ah	father	oh	know, go
air	where, pear	oo	through, to
ar	hard	yoo	few, music
ay	away, they	or	orange, door
aw	law, off	oi	oil, annoy
e	let, thread	ow	how, about
ee	tree, sea	u	put, book
eer	fear, here	uh	cut, awake
eye	nine, by	er	were, water
i	lips		

A

abrasion /uh-BRAY-zhuhn/ *(noun)* Abrasion is the gradual wearing away of the surface of rock as a result of other rock or sand particles rubbing against it. *page 142* [abrasión]

absorb /uhb-ZORB/ *(verb)* To absorb a substance means to soak it up or take it in. *page 202* [absorber]

acceleration /ak-sehl-uh-RAY-shuhn/ *(noun)* Acceleration is the rate at which the speed of an object increases. *page 190* [aceleración]

action force /ak-SHUHN fors/ *(noun)* In physics, for every action force there is an equal in size and opposite in direction reaction force. *page 190* [fuerza de acción]

adaptation /ad-uhp-TAY-shuhn/ *(noun)* Adaptation is the act of changing something to make it suitable for a new purpose or situation. *page 74* [adaptación]

adapted /uh-DAP-tid/ *(adjective)* Changed to fit a new situation. *page 84* [adaptado]

adenine /AD-uh-neen/ *(noun)* Adenine is an organic molecule that forms an important part of the structure of DNA. *page 70* [adenina]

air /air/ *(noun)* Air is the mixture of gases that forms the earth's atmosphere and that we breathe. *pages 46, 146, 174* [aire]

air mass /air mas/ *(noun)* An air mass is a large area of air that has the same temperature and amount of moisture throughout. *page 150* [masa de aire]

algae /AL-jee/ *(noun)* Algae are plants with no stems or leaves that grow in water or on damp surfaces. *page 26* [alga]

alpha particle /al-FUH PAR-ti-kl/ *(noun)* Alpha particles are subatomic particles that are emitted by radioactive substances such as uranium and radium. *page 182* [partícula alfa]

aluminum /ah-LOOM-in-uhm/ *(noun)* Aluminum is a lightweight metal used, for example, for making cooking equipment and aircraft parts. *pages 174, 182* [aluminio]

amoeba /uh-MEE-buh/ (noun) An amoeba is the smallest kind of living creature. Amoebae consist of only one cell, and are found in water or soil. *pages 26, 62* [amiba]

amphibian /am-FIB-ee-yuhn/ (noun) Amphibians are animals such as frogs and toads that can live both on land and in water. *page 54* [anfibio]

amplitude /AM-pluh-tood/ (noun) In physics, the amplitude of a sound wave or electrical signal is its strength. *page 198* [amplitud]

analyze /AN-uh-leyez/ (verb) **1.** If you analyze something, you consider it carefully or use statistical methods in order to fully understand it. *page 2* [analizar]

(verb) **2.** If you analyze something, you examine it using scientific methods in order to find out what it consists of. *page 2* [análisis]

anaphase /an-UH-fayz/ (noun) Anaphase is a stage in the process of cell division that takes place within animals and plants. *page 64* [anafase]

anemometer /an-uh-MAHM-uht-uhr/ (noun) An anemometer is an instrument that is used to measure wind speeds. *page 6* [anemómetro]

animal kingdom /AN-i-muhl KING-dom/ (noun) All the animals, birds, and insects in the world can be referred to together as the animal kingdom. *page 78* [reino animal]

annual ring /AN-yoo-uhl ring/ (noun) An annual ring is the layer of wood that forms during a single year in a plant such as a tree. Annual rings can be used to measure the age of plants. *page 45* [anillo anual]

anther /AN-ther/ (noun) The anther is the male part of a flower, which produces pollen. *page 40* [antera]

archeobacteria /ar-kee-oh-bak-TEER-ee-uh/ (noun) Archaea or archeobacteria are a type of bacteria that can live in extreme environments such as volcanoes. *page 78* [arqueobacteria]

artificial light /ahr-ti-FISH-uhl leyet/ (noun) Artificial light is light from a source such as an electric light or a gas lamp rather than from the sun. *page 202* [luz artificial]

asexual reproduction /ay-SEK-shoo-uhl ree-proh-DUHK-SHUYN/ (noun) Asexual reproduction is a form of reproduction that involves no sexual activity. *page 62* [asexual]

asteroid /AS-tuh-roid/ (noun) An asteroid is one of the very small planets that move around the sun between Mars and Jupiter. *page 110* [asteroide]

astronaut /AS-troh-nawt/ (noun) An astronaut is a person who is trained for traveling in a spacecraft. *page 122* [astronauta]

astronomical unit /as-troh-NOM-i-kuhl YOO-nit/ (noun) An astronomical unit is a unit of distance used in astronomy that is equal to the average distance between the Earth and the sun. The abbreviation AU is also used. *page 104* [unidad astronómica]

atmosphere /AT-muhs-feer/ (noun) A planet's atmosphere is the layer of air or other gases around it. *pages 136, 146* [atmósfera]

atmospheric pressure /AT-muhs-FEER-ik PRESH-er/ (noun) Atmospheric pressure is the amount of pressure that is produced by the weight of the Earth's atmosphere. *page 152* [presión atmosférica]

atom /AT-uhm/ (noun) An atom is the smallest amount of a substance that can take part in a chemical reaction. *pages 170, 178, 182* [átomo]

atomic number /uh-TOM-ik nuhm-ber/ (noun) The atomic number of a chemical element is the number of protons in the nucleus of one atom of the element. *page 173* [número atómico]

attraction /uh-TRAK-shuhn/ (noun) Attraction is the force that exists between two objects when they are pulled toward one another, for example by magnetism or gravity. *page 188* [atracción]

axis /AK-sihs/ (noun) An axis is an imaginary line through the middle of something. *page 114* [eje]

backbone /BAK-bohn/ *(noun)* Your backbone is the column of small linked bones down the middle of your back. *pages 46, 50, 54* [columna vertebral, espina dorsal]

bacteria /bak-TEER-ee-uh/ *(noun)* Bacteria are very small organisms. Some bacteria can cause disease. *pages 25, 26, 62, 78, 92* [bacterias]

balance /BAL-ins/ *(noun)* A balance is a scientific instrument that is used for weighing things. *pages 6, 166* [balanza]

balanced forces /BAL-insed FORS-es/ *(noun)* In physics, balanced forces are forces that are equal and opposite to each other, so that an object to which the forces are applied does not move. *page 186* [fuerzas equilibradas]

bar graph *(noun)* /Bahr graf/ A bar graph is a graph which uses parallel rectangular shapes to represent changes in the size, value or rate of something. *page 14* [gráfica de barras]

basalt /buh-SAWLT/ *(noun)* Basalt is a type of black rock that is produced by volcanoes. *page 126* [basalto]

base /bays/ *(noun)* Referring to the bottom of a tree. *page 76* [base]

basket sponge /BAS-ket spuhnj/ *(noun)* A basket sponge is a type of primitive sea creature with a hollow body that is open at the top. *page 50* [esponja de canasta]

battery /BAT-er-ee/ *(noun)* Batteries are small devices that provide the power for electrical items such as radios and children's toys. *page 220* [batería]

beak /beek/ *(noun)* A bird's beak is the hard curved or pointed part of its mouth. *page 74* [pico]

beaker /BEEK-er/ *(noun)* A beaker is a large cup or glass. *page 6* [vaso de precipitado]

bear /bair/ *(noun)* A bear is a large, strong wild animal with thick fur and sharp claws. *page 54* [oso]

beetle /BEET-uhl/ *(noun)* A beetle is an insect with a hard covering to its body. *page 50* [escarabajo]

behavior /bee-HAYV-yor/ *(noun)* In science, the behavior of something is the way that it behaves. *page 97* [comportamiento]

beta particle /BAY-tuh PAR-ti-kl/ *(noun)* Beta particles are atomic particles that are released by the nuclei of certain radioactive substances. Compare alpha particle and gamma ray. *page 182* [partícula beta]

binomial nomenclature /beye-NOH-mee-uhl NOH-muhn-klay-cher/ *(noun)* Binomial nomenclature is a system of scientifically classifying plants and animals by giving them a name consisting of two parts, first the genus and then the species. *page 81* [nomenclatura binomial]

biomass /BEYE-oh-mas/ *(noun)* Biomass is biological material such as dead plants that is used to provide fuel or energy. *page 160* [biomasa]

biome /BEYE-ohm/ *(noun)* A biome is a group of plants and animals that live in a particular region because they are suited to its physical environment. *page 82* [bioma]

bird /bird/ *(noun)* A bird is a creature with feathers and wings. *pages 46, 48, 54* [ave]

black hole /blak hohl/ *(noun)* Black holes are areas in space where gravity is so strong that nothing, not even light, can escape from them. Black holes are thought to be formed by collapsed stars. *page 106* [agujero negro]

black rhino /blak REYE-noh/ *(noun)* A black rhino is a type of rhinoceros with gray skin and two horns on its nose, that lives in Africa. *page 98* [rinoceronte negro]

blood vessel /bluhd VES-uhl/ *(noun)* Blood vessels are the narrow tubes through which your blood flows. *page 58* [vaso sanguíneo]

boiling point /BOI-ling point/ *(noun)* The boiling point of a liquid is the temperature at which it starts to change into steam or vapor. For example, the boiling point of water is 212° Fahrenheit. *page 166* [punto de ebullición]

bond /bond/ *(verb)* When one thing bonds with another, it sticks to it or becomes joined to it in some way. *page 178* [enlazar]

bone /bohn/ *(noun)* Your bones are the hard parts inside your body that together form your skeleton. *page 58* [hueso]

booster rocket /BOOS-ter ROK-it/ *(noun)* A combustible device, shaped like a long tube, used to put a space vehicle in orbit. *page 122* [cohete suplementario, impulsor auxiliar]

brain /brayn/ *(noun)* Your brain is the organ inside your head that controls your body's activities and enables you to think and to feel things such as heat and pain. *pages 49, 58* [cerebro]

bulb /bulb/ *(noun)* A bulb is a root shaped like an onion that grows into a flower or plant. *page 62* [bulbo]

buoyant force /BOI-yuhnt fors/ *(noun)* The buoyant force of an object immersed in a fluid is the physical force that causes the object to float or to rise upward. *page 168* [fuerza de flotación]

burn /bern/ *(verb)* If a substance burns, it produces flames or smoke when heated. *pages 162, 178* [quemar]

C

cancer /KAN-ser/ *(noun)* Cancer is a serious disease in which abnormal body cells increase, producing growths. *page 185* [cáncer]

candle /KAN-duhl/ *(noun)* A candle is a stick of hard wax with a piece of string called a wick through the middle, that you set fire to in order to provide light. *page 202* [vela]

canyon /KAN-yuhn/ *(noun)* A canyon is a long, narrow valley with very steep sides. *page 134* [cañón]

carbon /KAR-buhn/ *(noun)* Carbon is a chemical element that diamonds and coal are made of. *pages 170, 176* [carbono]

carbon dioxide /KAR-buhn deye-OKS-eyed/ *(noun)* Carbon dioxide is a gas that animals and people breathe out. *pages 44, 148, 176* [bióxido de carbono, dióxido de carbono]

carnivore /KAHRN-i-vor/ *(noun)* A carnivore is an animal that eats meat. *page 86* [carnívoro]

caterpillar /KAT-er-pil-er/ *(noun)* A caterpillar is a small, worm-like animal that eventually develops into a butterfly or moth. *page 52* [oruga]

cell /sel/ *(noun)* A cell is the smallest part of an animal or plant. Every animal or plant is made up of millions of cells. *pages 22, 30, 48* [célula]

cell division /sel dee-VI-zhuhn/ *(noun)* Cell division is the biological process by which a cell inside an animal or a plant divides into two new cells during growth or reproduction. *pages 33, 62, 66* [división celular]

cell membrane /sel MEM-brayn/ *(noun)* Cell membranes are the thin outer layers of the cells inside an animal. *page 22* [membrana celular]

cellular respiration /SEL-yoo-ler res-per-AY-shuhn/ *(noun)* Cellular respiration is the biological process by which substances within a plant or an animal are converted into energy. *page 214* [respiración celular]

cell wall /sel wawl/ *(noun)* Cell walls are the thin outer layers of the cells inside plants and bacteria. *page 22* [pared celular]

Celsius /SEL-see-uhs/ *(adjective)* Celsius is a scale for measuring temperature, in which water freezes at 0° and boils at 100°. *page 10* [centígrado]

centimeter /SEN-tuh-mee-ter/ *(noun)* A centimeter is a unit of length in the metric system equal to ten millimeters or one-hundredth of a meter. *page 10* [centímetro]

centipede /SEN-tuh-peed/ *(noun)* A centipede is a long, thin creature with a lot of legs. *page 50* [ciempiés]

charge /chahrj/ (*noun*) An electrical charge is an amount of electricity that is held in or carried by something. *page 218* [**carga**]

chemical /KEM-i-kuhl/ (*noun*) Chemicals are substances that are used in a chemical process or made by a chemical process. *pages 37, 101* [**sustancia química, producto químico**]

chemical change /KEM-i-kuhl chaynj/ (*noun*) A chemical change is a change in a substance that results in a new or different substance, such as the conversion of wood to smoke and ash when it is burned. *pages 162, 177* [**cambio químico**]

chemical energy /KEM-i-kuhl EN-er-jee/ (*noun*) Chemical energy is the energy that is released during a chemical reaction or a chemical change. *pages 206, 210, 214* [**energía química**]

chemical property /KEM-i-kuhl PROP-er-tee/ (*noun*) The chemical properties of a substance are the physical qualities that determine how it will react with other substances. *page 165* [**propiedad química**]

chemical weathering /KEM-i-kuhl WETH-er-ing/ (*noun*) Chemical weathering is the change that takes place in the structure of rocks and minerals as a result of their exposure to water and the atmosphere. *page 144* [**erosión química**]

chlorine /KLOR-een/ (*noun*) Chlorine is a gas that is used to disinfect water and to make cleaning products. *page 176* [**cloro**]

chlorophyll /KLOR-oh-fil/ (*noun*) Chlorophyll is a green substance in plants which enables them to use the energy from sunlight in order to grow. *pages 42, 214* [**clorofila**]

chloroplast /KLOR-oh-plast/ (*noun*) A chloroplast is the part of a plant cell that contains chlorophyll and is involved in photosynthesis. *pages 22, 27, 42, 214* [**cloroplasto**]

chromosome /KROHM-oh-sohm/ (*noun*) A chromosome is a part of a cell in an animal or plant. It contains genes which determine what characteristics the animal or plant will have. *pages 33, 62, 66, 70* [**cromosoma**]

chrysalis /KRIS-ah-lis/ (*noun*) A chrysalis is a butterfly or moth in the stage between being a larva and an adult. A chrysalis is the hard, protective covering that a chrysalis has. *page 52* [**crisálida**]

cilia /SIL-ee-ah/ (*noun*) Cilia are short thin structures, resembling hairs, on the surfaces of some types of cells and organisms. *page 26* [**cilio**]

circuit /SER-kit/ (*noun*) An electrical circuit is a complete route which an electric current can flow around. *page 218* [**circuito**]

clam /klam/ (*noun*) Clams are a kind of shellfish. *page 50* [**almeja**]

class /klas/ (*noun*) A class of things is a group of them with similar characteristics. *page 80* [**clase**]

clay /klay/ (*noun*) Clay is a kind of earth that is soft when it is wet and hard when it is dry. Clay is shaped and baked to make things such as pots and bricks. *page 36* [**arcilla**]

climate /KLEYE-mit/ (*noun*) The climate of a place is the general weather conditions that are typical of it. *pages 84, 153* [**clima**]

cloud /klowd/ (*noun*) A cloud is a mass of water vapor that floats in the sky. Clouds are usually white or gray in color. *pages 90, 146, 150* [**nube**]

coal /kohl/ (*noun*) Coal is a hard, black substance that is extracted from the ground and burned as fuel. *page 158* [**carbón**]

coarse adjustment /kors a-JUHST-ment/ (*noun*) The part of a microscope that controls the coarse adjustment is the part that allows you to obtain the correct general focus for the object you are looking at. *page 8* [**ajuste grueso**]

cold-blooded /kohld BLUHD-ed/ (*adjective*) Cold-blooded animals have a body temperature that changes according to the surrounding temperature. Reptiles, for example, are cold-blooded. *page 56* [**de sangre fría**]

cold front /kohld fruhnt/ (noun) A cold atmospheric air mass moving against a warm air mass. *page 150* [frente frío]

color /KUHL-er/ (noun) The color of something is the appearance that it has as a result of the way in which it reflects light. Red, blue, and green are colors. *pages 162, 202* [color]

column /KAHL-uhm/ (noun) On a printed page such as a page of a dictionary, newspaper, or printed chart, a column is one of two or more vertical sections which are read downward. *page 16* [columna]

comet /KOM-it/ (noun) A comet is a bright object with a long tail that travels around the sun. *page 110* [cometa]

command module /kuh-MAND MOD-joo-uhl/ (noun) The command module is the part of a spacecraft in which the astronauts live and operate the controls. *page 124* [módulo de comando]

commensalism /kuh-MEN-suh-liz-em/ (noun) A commensalism between two species of plants or animals is a relationship which benefits one of the species and does not harm the other species. *page 88* [comensalismo]

common ancestor /KAH-muhn AN-ses-tor/ (noun) The common ancestor of a group of human beings or animals is the individual who is an ancestor of all of them. *page 74* [ancestro común]

community /kuh-MYOO-ni-tee/ (noun) A community is a group of plants and animals that live in the same region and interact with one another. *page 82* [comunidad]

compare /kuhm-PAIR/ (verb) When you compare things, you consider them and discover the differences or similarities between them. *page 16* [comparar]

compound /kom-POWND/ (noun) In chemistry, a compound is a substance that consists of two or more elements. *pages 174, 178* [compuesto]

compound machine /kom-POWND muh-SHEEN/ (noun) A compound machine is a machine that consists of two or more smaller machines working together. Compare simple machine. *page 197* [máquina compuesta]

compression /kuhm-PRESH-uhn/ (noun) Compression is the process of pressing or squeezing something so that it takes up less space. *page 198* [compresión]

computer /kuhm-PYOO-ter/ (noun) A computer is an electronic machine that can store and deal with large amounts of information. *page 6* [computadora]

conclusion /kuhn-KLOO-zhuhn/ (noun) When you come to a conclusion, you decide that something is true after you have thought about it carefully. *page 2* [conclusión]

concrete /KON-kreet/ (noun) Concrete is a substance used for building which is made from cement, sand, small stones, and water. *page 182* [concreto]

condensation /kon-din-SAY-shuhn/ (noun) Condensation consists of small drops of water which form when warm water vapor or steam touches a cold surface such as a window. *page 90* [condensación]

conduction /kuhn-DUK-shuhn/ (noun) Conduction is the process by which heat or electricity passes through or along something. *page 212* [conducción]

conductor /kuhn-DUK-tor/ (noun) A conductor is a substance that heat or electricity can pass through or along. *page 218* [conductor]

cone /kohn/ (noun) A cone is the fruit of a tree such as a pine or fir. *pages 34, 38* [piña]

conifer /KON-uh-fer/ (noun) Conifers are a type of trees and shrubs such as pine trees and fir trees. They have fruit called cones, and very thin leaves called needles which they do not normally lose in winter. *page 38* [conífera]

conservation of energy /kon-ser-VAY-zhuhn uhv EN-er-jee/ (noun) The law of conservation of energy is a principle in physics which states that energy cannot be created or destroyed. *page 213* [conservación de energía]

conservation of mass /kon-ser-VAY-zhuhn uhv mas/ (*noun*) The law of conservation of mass is a principle in physics which states that matter cannot be created or destroyed. *page 181* [conservación de masa]

constellation /kon-stuh-LAY-zhuhn/ (*noun*) A constellation is a group of stars which form a pattern and have a name. *page 106* [constelación]

consumer /kuhn-SOOM-er/ (*noun*) A consumer is a plant or animal that obtains energy by eating other plants or animals. *page 86* [consumidor]

continent /KON-tin-ent/ (*noun*) A continent is a very large area of land, such as Africa or Asia, that consists of several countries. *pages 130, 134* [continente]

continental drift /KON-tin-ent-uhl drift/ (*noun*) Continental drift is the slow movement of the Earth's continents toward and away from each other. *page 132* [deriva continental]

convection /kuhn-VEK-zhuhn/ (*noun*) Convection is the process by which heat travels through air, water, and other gases and liquids. *page 212* [convección]

converge /kuhn-VERJ/ (*verb*) If roads or lines converge, they meet or join. *page 140* [converger]

copper wire /KOP-er weyer/ (*noun*) Copper wire is a type of cable made of copper that is good at conducting heat and electricity. *page 221* [alambre de cobre]

correlational design /kor-uh-LAY-shuhn-uhl dee-ZEYEN/ (*noun*) Research that has a correlational design involves studying the relationship between two or more things. *page 2* [diseño de correlación]

crab /krab/ (*noun*) A crab is a sea creature with a flat round body covered by a shell, and five pairs of legs with large claws on the front pair. Crabs usually move sideways. *page 46* [cangrejo]

crater /KRAYT-er/ (*noun*) A crater is a very large hole in the ground, which has been caused by something hitting it or by an explosion. *page 138* [cráter]

crest /krest/ (*noun*) The crest of a hill or a wave is the top of it. *page 198* [cima]

crocodile /KROK-oh-deyel/ (*noun*) A crocodile is a large reptile with a long body and strong jaws. Crocodiles live in rivers. *page 54* [cocodrilo]

crossing over /KROS-ing OH-ver/ (*noun*) In biology, crossing over is a process in which genetic material is exchanged between two chromosomes, resulting in new combinations of genes. *page 68* [entrecruzamiento]

crust /kruhst/ (*noun*) The outer layer of the Earth. *pages 29, 130* [corteza]

crystal /KRIS-tuhl/ (*noun*) **1.** A crystal is a small piece of a substance that has formed naturally into a regular symmetrical shape. *page 126* [cristal]

(*noun*) **2.** Crystal is a transparent rock used in jewelry and ornaments. *page 126* [cristal]

cubic /KYOO-bik/ (*adjective*) Cubic is used in front of units of length to form units of volume such as 'cubic meter' and 'cubic foot'. *page 10* [cúbico]

current electricity /KUHR-ent ee-lek-TRIS-i-tee/ (*noun*) Current electricity is electricity that is flowing through a circuit. Compare static electricity. *page 220* [corriente eléctrica]

cyanobacteria /seye-an-oh-bak-TEER-ee-uh/ (*noun*) Cyanobacteria are bacteria that obtain their energy through photosynthesis. *page 78* [cianobacteria]

cycle /seyekl/ (*noun*) **1.** A cycle is a series of events or processes that is repeated again and again, always in the same order. *page 90* [ciclo]

(*noun*) **2.** A cycle is a single complete series of movements in an electrical, electronic, or mechanical process. *page 90* [circuito]

cytoplasm /SEYE-toh-plaz-uhm/ (*noun*) Cytoplasm is the material that surrounds the nucleus of a plant or animal cell. *page 22* [citoplasma]

cytosine /SEYE-toh-seen/ *(noun)* Cytosine is one of the four basic components of the DNA molecule. It bonds with guanine. *page 70* [citosina]

D

data /DAY-tuh/ *(noun)* Data is information that can be stored and used by a computer program. *page 2* [datos]

data table /DAY-tuh TAY-buhl/ *(noun)* A data table is a chart containing a set of data. *page 14* [tabla de datos]

daughter cell /DAW-ter sel/ *(noun)* A daughter cell is one of the two cells that are formed when a single cell divides. *pages 62, 66* [célula hija]

day /day/ *(noun)* A day is one of the seven twenty-four hour periods of time in a week. *page 114* [día]

decay *(verb)* /di-KAY/ The decomposition of matter. *page 184* [descomponerse, pudrirse]

deciduous /dee-SIDJ-yoo-uhs/ *(adjective)* A deciduous tree or bush is one that loses its leaves in the fall every year. *page 82* [caducifolio, de hoja caduca]

decomposer /dee-kuhm-POHZ-er/ *(noun)* Decomposers are organisms such as bacteria, fungi, and earthworms that feed on dead plants and animals and convert them into soil. *page 86* [descomponedor]

deer /deer/ *(noun)* A deer is a large wild animal that eats grass and leaves. A male deer usually has large, branching horns. *page 46* [venado]

degree /duh-GREE/ *(noun)* A degree is a unit of measurement that is used to measure temperatures. It is often written as °, for example, 23°. *page 10* [grado]

delta /DEL-tuh/ *(noun)* A delta is an area of low, flat land shaped like a triangle, where a river splits and spreads out into several branches before entering the sea. *pages 134, 142* [delta]

density /DEN-suh-tee/ *(noun)* In science, the density of a substance or object is the relation of its mass or weight to its volume. *page 168* [densidad]

deposition /dep-oh-ZISH-uhn/ *(noun)* Deposition is a geological process in which material that has been carried by the wind or water from one area is deposited on the surface of another area. *pages 142* [sedimentación]

descriptive design /dee-SKRIP-tiv dee-ZEYEN/ *(noun)* Research that has a descriptive design involves studying the similarities and differences between two or more things. *page 2* [diseño descriptivo]

desert /DEZ-ert/ *(noun)* A desert is a large area of land, usually in a hot region, where there is almost no water, rain, trees, or plants. *page 82* [desierto]

diamond /DEYEM-uhnd/ *(noun)* A diamond is a hard, bright, precious stone which is clear and colorless. Diamonds are used in jewelry and for cutting very hard substances. *page 126* [diamante]

digest /DEYE-jest/ *(verb)* When food digests, or when you digest it, it passes through your body to your stomach. Your stomach removes the substances that your body needs and gets rid of the rest. *page 37* [digerir]

dinoflagellate /deye-noh-FLAJ-uh-layt/ *(noun)* Dinoflagellates are tiny organisms that live in sea water and fresh water and are found in plankton. *page 26* [dinoflagelado]

dinosaur /DEYE-noh-sor/ *(noun)* Dinosaurs were large reptiles which lived in prehistoric times. *page 98* [dinosaurio]

dissolve /di-ZOLV/ *(verb)* If a substance dissolves in liquid or if you dissolve it, it becomes mixed with the liquid and disappears. *page 176* [disolver]

diverge /deye-VERJ/ *(verb)* If roads or lines diverge, they separate and go in different directions. *page 140* [divergir]

DNA /dee-en-AY/ *(noun)* DNA is an acid in the chromosomes in the center of the cells of living things. DNA determines the particular structure and functions of every cell and is responsible for characteristics being passed on from parents to their children. DNA is an abbreviation for "deoxyribonucleic acid." *pages 70, 80* [DNA]

dodo /DOH-doh/ *(noun)* A dodo was a very large bird that was unable to fly. Dodos are now extinct. *page 98* [dodo]

dog /dawg/ *(noun)* A dog is a very common four-legged animal that is often kept by people as a pet or to guard or hunt. There are many different breeds of dog. *page 78* [perro]

dominant /DOM-i-nuhnt/ *(adjective)* In genetics, a gene is dominant when a single copy of the gene is all that is necessary for a particular characteristic to develop. *page 72* [dominante]

double helix /DUB-uhl HEEL-iks/ *(noun)* The double helix is a term used to describe the shape of the DNA molecule, which resembles a long ladder twisted into a coil. *page 70* [doble hélice]

downdraft /down-draft/ *(noun)* A downdraft is a downward current of air, usually accompanied by rain. *page 154* [corriente descendente]

duck /duhk/ *(noun)* A duck is a common water bird with short legs, a short neck, and a large flat beak. *page 46* [pato]

dust /duhst/ *(noun)* Dust is very small dry particles of earth or sand. *page 152* [polvo]

dwarf planet /dworf PLAN-it/ *(noun)* A dwarf planet is a round object that orbits the sun and is larger than an asteroid but smaller than a planet. *page 110* [planeta enano]

E

earth /erth/ *(noun)* Earth or the Earth is the planet on which we live. People usually say Earth when they are referring to the planet as part of the universe, and the Earth when they are talking about the planet as the place where we live. *pages 110, 114* [tierra]

earthquake /ERTH-kwayk/ *(noun)* An earthquake is a shaking of the ground caused by movement of the earth's crust. *page 138* [terremoto]

earthworm /ERTH-werm/ *(noun)* An earthworm is a kind of worm that lives in the ground. *pages 16, 50* [lombriz de tierra]

eclipse /ee-KLIPS/ *(noun)* An eclipse of the sun is an occasion when the moon is between the earth and the sun, so that for a short time you cannot see part or all of the sun. An eclipse of the moon is an occasion when the earth is between the sun and the moon, so that for a short time you cannot see part or all of the moon. *page 118* [eclipse]

ecological succession /ee-KOH-loj-i-kuhl suk-SESH-zhuhn/ *(noun)* Ecological succession is the process in which one population of plants and animals gradually replaces another population in a particular area as a result of changing environmental conditions. *page 84* [sucesión ecológica]

ecosystem /ee-KOH-sis-tuhm/ *(noun)* An ecosystem is all the plants and animals that live in a particular area together with the complex relationship that exists between them and their environment. *page 82* [ecosistema]

effort force /EF-ert fors/ *(noun)* In physics, effort force is force that is used to move an object. *page 196* [fuerza de esfuerzo]

electrical energy /ee-LEK-tri-kuhl EN-er-jee/ *(noun)* Electrical energy is energy in the form of electricity. *pages 206, 210* [energía eléctrica]

electric current /ee-LEK-trik KUH-rent/ *(noun)* An electric current is a flow of electricity through a wire or circuit. *page 218* [corriente eléctrica]

electric generator /ee-LEK-trik JEN-er-ay-tor/ *(noun)* An electric generator is a machine which produces electricity. *page 218* [generador eléctrico]

electromagnet /ee-lek-troh-MAG-nit/ *(noun)* An electromagnet is a magnet that consists of a piece of iron or steel surrounded by a coil. The metal becomes magnetic when an electric current is passed through the coil. *page 218* [electroimán]

electromagnetic spectrum /ee-lek-troh-MAG-net-ik SPEK-truhm/ (noun) The electromagnetic spectrum is the complete range of electromagnetic radiation, from the longest radio waves to the shortest gamma rays. *page 201* [espectro electromagnético]

electromagnetic wave /ee-lek-troh-MAG-net-ik wayv/ (noun) Electromagnetic waves are waves of energy inside an electromagnetic field. *page 201* [onda electromagnética]

electron /ee-LEK-tron/ (noun) An electron is a tiny particle of matter that is smaller than an atom and has a negative electrical charge. *pages 170, 178, 184, 218* [electrón]

element /EL-uh-ment/ (noun) An element is a substance such as gold, oxygen, or carbon that consists of only one type of atom. *pages 170, 174, 178* [elemento]

endangered species /in-DAYN-jerd SPEE-seez/ (noun) An endangered species is an animal species that is in danger of becoming extinct. *page 98* [especie en peligro de extinción]

endoplasmic reticulum /en-DOH-plaz-mik ri-TIK-yoo-luhm/ (noun) The endoplasmic reticulum is a network of tubes and membranes within cells that is involved in the making and movement of proteins. *page 22* [retículo endoplasmático]

endothermic /en-doh-THER-mik/ (adjective) An endothermic chemical reaction or process is one that takes in heat from its surroundings, such as when ice melts. *page 180* [endotérmico]

energy /EN-er-jee/ (noun) Energy is the power from sources such as electricity and coal that makes machines work or provides heat. *pages 28, 60* [energía]

energy pyramid /EN-er-jee PEER-uh-mid/ (noun) An energy pyramid is a diagram that shows the amount of energy that is available at each level of a food chain. *page 88* [pirámide del flujo de energía]

energy source /EN-er-jee sors/ (noun) An energy source is any substance or system from which energy can be obtained, such as coal, gas, water, or sunlight. *page 220* [fuente de energía]

epicenter /EP-ee-sen-ter/ (noun) The epicenter of an earthquake is the place on the earth's surface directly above the point where it starts, and is the place where it is felt most strongly. *page 138* [epicentro]

equal /EE-kwuhl/ (adjective) If two things are equal, or if one thing is equal to another, they are the same in size, number, standard, or value. *page 193* [igual]

equation /ee-KWAY-shuhn/ (noun) An equation is a mathematical statement saying that two amounts or values are the same, for example 6 x 4 = 12 x 2. *page 178* [ecuación]

equilibrium /ee-kwuh-LIB-ree-uhm/ (noun) Equilibrium is a balance between several different influences or aspects of a situation. *page 189* [equilibrio]

erosion /ee-ROH-zhuhn/ (noun) Erosion is the gradual destruction and removal of rock or soil in a particular area by rivers, the sea, or the weather. *pages 128, 142* [erosión]

eruption /ee-RUHP-shuhn/ (verb) When a volcano erupts, it throws out a lot of hot, melted rock called lava, as well as ash and steam. *page 138* [erupción]

estivation /es-ti-VAY-shuhn/ (noun) Estivation is a period during which some animals become inactive because the weather is very hot or dry. *page 94* [estivación]

eubacteria /yoo-bak-TEER-ee-uh/ (noun) Eubacteria are all bacteria except for archaebacteria. *page 78* [eubacteria]

euglena /yoo-GLEE-nuh/ (noun) Euglena is a type of single-celled organism that lives mainly in fresh water. *page 28* [euglena]

evaporation /ee-VAP-or-ay-shuhn/ (noun) Evaporation is the process in which a liquid changes from a liquid state to a gas because its temperature has been raised. *page 90* [evaporación]

evolution /ev-uh-LOO-shuhn/ (noun) Evolution is a process of gradual development in a particular situation or thing over a period of time. *page 76* [evolución]

exosphere /EKS-oh-sfeer/ (noun) The exosphere is the highest layer of the Earth's atmosphere. *page 149* [exósfera]

exothermic /EKS-oh-ther-mik/ (adjective) An exothermic chemical reaction or process is one that releases heat. *page 180* [exotérmica, exotérmico]

experiment /ek-SPE-ruh-ment/ (noun) **1.** An experiment is a scientific test done in order to discover what happens to something in particular conditions. *page 2* [experimento]

(verb) **2.** If you experiment with something or experiment on it, you do a scientific test on it in order to discover what happens to it in particular conditions. *page 2* [experimentar]

experimental design /ek-SPE-ruh-ment-uhl dee-ZEYEN/ (noun) Research that has an experimental design involves carrying out scientific experiments. *page 2* [diseño experimental]

external fuel tank /eks-TERN-uhl fyool taynk/ (noun) An external fuel tank is a container for fuel that is fitted to the outside of a spacecraft. *page 122* [tanque externo de combustible]

extinct /eks-TINKT/ (adjective) A species of animal or plant that is extinct no longer has any living members, either in the world or in a particular place. *pages 76, 98* [extinta]

eye /eye/ (noun) The eye of a storm, tornado, or hurricane is the center of it. *page 154* [ojo]

eyepiece /EYE-pees/ (noun) The eyepiece of a microscope or telescope is the piece of glass at one end, where you put your eye in order to look through the instrument. *page 8* [ocular]

F

family /FAM-uh-lee/ (noun) A family of animals or plants is a group of related species. *page 80* [familia]

fault /fawlt/ (noun) A fault is a large crack in the surface of the earth. *page 138* [falla]

feldspar /FELD-spar/ (noun) Feldspar is a mineral that forms rocks and makes up most of the Earth's crust. *page 126* [feldespato]

fern /fern/ (noun) A fern is a plant that has long stems with feathery leaves and no flowers. *pages 38, 78* [helecho]

fertilize /FER-tuh-leyez/ (verb) When an egg from the ovary of a woman or female animal is fertilized, a sperm from the male joins with the egg, causing a baby or young animal to begin forming. A female plant is fertilized when its reproductive parts come into contact with pollen from the male plant. *page 40* [fecundar]

fine adjustment /feyen a-JUHST-ment/ (noun) The part of a microscope that controls the fine adjustment is the part that allows you to obtain the best possible focus for the object you are looking at. *page 8* [ajuste fino]

fire alarm /feyer uh-LARM/ (noun) A fire alarm is a device that makes a noise, for example, with a bell, to warn people when there is a fire. *page 18* [alarma contra incendios]

fire extinguisher /feyer ek-STING-gwish-er/ (noun) A fire extinguisher is a metal cylinder which contains water or chemicals at high pressure which can put out fires. *page 18* [extinguidor]

first aid kit /ferst ayd kit/ (noun) A first aid kit is a bag or case containing basic medical supplies that are designed to be used on someone who is injured or who suddenly becomes ill. *page 18* [botiquín de primeros auxilios]

fish /fish/ (noun) A fish is a creature that lives in water and has a tail and fins. *pages 48, 54* [pez]

flagella /fluh-JEL-uh/ (noun) Flagella are the long, thin extensions of cells in some microorganisms that help them move. *page 26* [flagelos]

flamingo /fluh-MING-goh/ (noun) A flamingo is a bird with pink feathers, long thin legs, a long neck, and a curved beak. Flamingos live near water in warm areas. *page 54* [flamenco]

flashlight /FLASH-leyet/ *(noun)* A flashlight is a small electric light which gets its power from batteries and which you can carry in your hand. *page 220* [linterna]

float /floht/ *(verb)* If something or someone is floating in a liquid, they are in the liquid, on or just below the surface, and are being supported by it. You can also float something on a liquid. *page 166* [flotar]

flood /fluhd/ *(noun)* If there is a flood, a large amount of water covers an area which is usually dry, for example, when a river flows over its banks or a pipe bursts. *page 154* [inundación]

flowchart /FLOH-chart/ *(noun)* A flowchart or a flow diagram is a diagram which represents the sequence of actions in a particular process or activity. *page 14* [diagrama de flujo]

flower /FLOW-er/ *(noun)* A flower is the part of a plant which is often brightly colored and grows at the end of a stem. *page 34* [flor]

flowering /FLOW-er-ing/ *(adjective)* Flowering shrubs, trees, or plants are those which produce noticeable flowers. *page 38* [que da flores]

focus /FOH-kuhs/ *(noun)* The focus of an earthquake is the point within the Earth where the earthquake starts. *page 138* [foco]

fog /fog/ *(noun)* When there is fog, there are tiny drops of water in the air which form a thick cloud and make it difficult to see things. *pages 146, 150* [niebla]

food /food/ *(noun)* Food is what people and animals eat. *pages 46, 86* [comida]

food chain /food chayn/ *(noun)* The food chain is a series of living things which are linked to each other because each thing feeds on the one next to it in the series. *page 86* [cadena trófica, cadena alimentaria]

food web /food web/ *(noun)* A food web is a network of interconnected food chains. *page 86* [red trófica, red alimentaria]

force /fors/ *(noun)* In physics, a force is the pulling or pushing effect that something has on something else. *pages 168, 190* [fuerza]

formula /FOR-myoo-la/ *(noun)* **1.** A formula is a group of letters, numbers, or other symbols which represents a scientific or mathematical rule. *page 178* [fórmula]

(noun) **2.** In science, the formula for a substance tells you what amounts of other substances are needed in order to make that substance. *page 178* [fórmula]

fossil /FAH-suhl/ *(noun)* A fossil is the hard remains of a prehistoric animal or plant that are found inside a rock. *pages 74, 126, 130* [fósil]

fossil fuel /FAH-suhl fyool/ *(noun)* Fossil fuel is fuel such as coal or oil that is formed from the decayed remains of plants or animals. *pages 158, 208* [combustible]

freezing point /FREE-zing point/ *(noun)* **1.** Freezing point is 32° Fahrenheit or 0° Celsius, the temperature at which water freezes. Freezing point is often used when talking about the weather. *page 166* [punto de congelación]

(noun) **2.** The freezing point of a particular substance is the temperature at which it freezes. *page 166* [punto de congelación]

fresh water /fresh WUH-ter/ *(adjective)* Fresh water is water that is not salty. *page 136* [agua dulce]

friction /FRIK-shuhn/ *(noun)* Friction is the force that makes it difficult for things to move freely when they are touching each other. *pages 186, 192* [fricción]

frog /frahg/ *(noun)* A frog is a small creature with smooth skin, big eyes, and long back legs which it uses for jumping. *pages 46, 54* [rana]

fruit /froot/ *(noun)* Fruit or a fruit is something which grows on a tree or bush and which contains seeds or a pit covered by a substance that you can eat. *page 34* [fruto]

fulcrum /FUL-kruhm/ *(noun)* In physics, the fulcrum is the central point on which a lever balances when it is lifting or moving something. *page 194* [punto de apoyo]

fungi /FUHN-geye/ *(noun)* Fungi is the plural of fungus. *page 78* [hongos]

fungus /FUHN-guhs/ *(noun)* A fungus is a plant that has no flowers, leaves, or green coloring, such as a mushroom or a toadstool. *pages 26, 78* [hongo]

funnel /FUHN-nuhl/ *(noun)* **1.** A funnel is an organ on the bodies of some animals such as octopuses, which is used for breathing, laying eggs, and getting rid of waste. *page 49* [embudo]

(noun) **2.** A funnel or funnel cloud is a rotating column of air below a cumulonimbus cloud, which can become part of a tornado. *page 156* [embudo]

G

galaxy /GA-luhks-ee/ *(noun)* **1.** A galaxy is an extremely large group of stars and planets that extends over many billions of light years. *page 102* [galaxia]

(noun) **2.** The Galaxy is the extremely large group of stars and planets to which the Earth and the solar system belong. *page 102* [galaxia]

gamma rays /GAM-muh rayz/ *(noun)* Gamma rays are a type of electromagnetic radiation that has a shorter wavelength and higher energy than X-rays. *page 182* [rayos gamma]

gas /gas/ *(noun)* A gas is any substance that is neither liquid nor solid, for example oxygen or hydrogen. *pages 32, 146, 162, 166, 172* [gas]

gene /jeen/ *(noun)* A gene is the part of a cell in a living thing which controls its physical characteristics, growth, and development. *page 70* [gen]

genus /JEE-nuhs/ *(noun)* A genus is a class of similar things, especially a group of animals or plants that includes several closely related species. *page 80* [género]

geostationary /jee-oh-STAY-shuhn-air-ee/ *(adjective)* A satellite that is in geostationary orbit is positioned directly above the equator and moves at the same speed as the Earth's rotation, so that it appears to be stationary. *page 9* [geoestacionario]

geothermal energy /jee-oh-THER-muhl EN-er-jee/ *(noun)* Geothermal energy is energy that comes from hot water and steam beneath the Earth's surface. *page 158* [energía geotérmica]

germinate /JER-min-ayt/ *(verb)* If a seed germinates or if it is germinated, it starts to grow. *page 41* [germinar]

giant panda /JEYE-uhnt PAN-duh/ *(noun)* A giant panda or a panda is a large animal like a bear that has black and white fur and lives in the bamboo forests of China. *page 98* [panda gigante]

glacier /GLAY-sher/ *(noun)* A glacier is an extremely large mass of ice which moves very slowly, often down a mountain valley. *pages 136, 142* [glaciar]

glass slide /glas sleyed/ *(noun)* A glass slide is a piece of glass on which you put something that you want to examine through a microscope. *page 8* [portaobjetos]

glove /gluhv/ *(noun)* Gloves are pieces of clothing which cover your hands and wrists and have individual sections for each finger. You wear gloves to keep your hands warm or dry or to protect them. *page 18* [guante]

glucose /GLOO-kohs/ *(noun)* Glucose is a type of sugar that gives you energy. *pages 44, 216* [glucosa]

GOES /gohz/ *(noun)* The GOES program is a series of satellites that send back information to Earth about environmental and weather conditions. GOES is an abbreviation for 'Geostationary Operational Environmental Satellite'. *page 9* [GOES, Satélites Meteorológicos Geoestacionarios de la Serie GOES]

goggles /GAHG-uhlz/ *(noun)* Goggles are large glasses that fit closely to your face around your eyes to protect them from such things as water, wind, or dust. *page 18* [lentes protectores]

gold /gohld/ *(noun)* Gold is a valuable, yellow-colored metal that is used for making jewelry and ornaments, and as an international currency. *page 170* [oro]

Golgi complex /GOHL-jee KAHM-pleks/ *(noun)* The Golgi complex is a structure inside the cells of animals and plants, which controls the production and secretion of substances such as proteins. *page 22* [**complejo de Golgi**]

graduated cylinder /grad-JYOO-ayt-ed SIL-in-der/ *(noun)* Graduated cylinders are marked with lines and numbers and used to measure volume of liquids or solids. *pages 6, 166* [**probeta**]

gram /gram/ *(noun)* A gram is a unit of weight. One thousand grams are equal to one kilogram. *page 10* [**gramo**]

granite /GRAN-it/ *(noun)* Granite is a very hard rock used in building. *pages 126, 174* [**granito**]

grassland /GRAS-land/ *(noun)* Grassland is land covered with wild grass. *page 82* [**pradera**]

gravitropism /grav-i-TROHP-iz-uhm/ *(noun)* Gravitropism is the tendency of a plant to grow either downward or upward in response to the force of gravity. *page 96* [**gravitropismo, geotropismo**]

gravity /GRAV-i-tee/ *(noun)* Gravity is the force that causes things to drop to the ground. *pages 152, 168, 186* [**gravedad**]

Great Red Spot /grayt red spot/ *(noun)* The Great Red Spot is a large area in the atmosphere of the planet Jupiter where a powerful storm has been taking place for hundreds of years. *page 112* [**Gran Mancha Roja**]

green plant /green plant/ *(noun)* Green plants are plants that get their energy by means of photosynthesis. *page 42* [**planta verde**]

groundwater /grownd-WUH-ter/ *(noun)* Groundwater is water that is found under the ground. Groundwater has usually passed down through the soil and become trapped by rocks. *pages 90, 136* [**aguas subterráneas**]

guanine /GWAH-neen/ *(noun)* Guanine is one of the four basic components of the DNA molecule. It bonds with cytosine. *page 70* [**guanina**]

guard cell /gard sel/ *(noun)* Guard cells are pairs of cells on the leaves of plants, which control things such as how much air a plant takes in and how much water it releases. *page 42* [**célula oclusiva**]

H

H /heye PRESH-er/ *(adjective)* On a weather map, H is an abbreviation for "high pressure." *page 152* [**A**]

habitat /HAB-i-tat/ *(noun)* The habitat of an animal or plant is the natural environment in which it normally lives or grows. *pages 85, 100* [**hábitat**]

hail /hayl/ *(noun)* Hail consists of small balls of ice that fall like rain from the sky. *pages 150, 154* [**granizo**]

half-life /haf lif/ *(noun)* The half-life of a radioactive substance is the amount of time that it takes to lose half its radioactivity. *page 184* [**media vida**]

Halley's comet /HAL-eez KOM-it/ *(noun)* Halley's comet is a comet that is visible from the Earth every 76 years. *page 112* [**cometa Halley**]

halophile /HAL-oh-feyel/ *(noun)* Halophiles are bacteria that need salt in order to grow. *page 78* [**halófilo**]

heart /hart/ *(noun)* Your heart is the organ in your chest that pumps the blood around your body. People also use heart to refer to the area of their chest that is closest to their heart. *page 58* [**corazón**]

heartworm /HART-werm/ *(noun)* Heartworms are parasitic worms that are spread through mosquito bites and affect cats, dogs, foxes and some other animals. You can also use heartworm to mean the disease caused by heartworms. *page 50* [**gusano de corazón**]

heat /heet/ *(noun)* **1.** Heat is warmth or the quality of being hot. *pages 88, 210* [**calor**]

(verb) **2.** When you heat something, you raise its temperature. *pages 88, 210* [**calentar**]

hedgehog cactus /HEJ-hog KAK-tuhs/ *(noun)* Hedgehog cactus is a name given to several types of cactus with short prickly spines, especially a type that has edible fruit. *page 98* [cacto fresa]

herbivore /ERB-i-vor/ *(noun)* A herbivore is an animal that only eats plants. *page 86* [herbívoro]

heterogeneous mixture /het-er-oh-JEEN-ee-uhs MIKS-cher/ *(noun)* In chemistry, a heterogeneous mixture is a mixture of two or more substances that remain separate, for example oil and water. *page 174* [mezcla heterogénea]

hibernation /HEYE-ber-nay-shuhn/ *(noun)* Hibernation is the act or state of spending the winter in a state like a deep sleep. *page 94* [hibernación]

high power lens /heye POW-er lenz/ *(noun)* A high power lens is a very powerful lens on an instrument such as a microscope. *page 8* [lente de alta potencia]

high tide /heye teyed/ *(noun)* At the coast, high tide is the time when the sea is at its highest level because the tide is in. *page 118* [marea alta]

hill /hil/ *(noun)* A hill is an area of land that is higher than the land that surrounds it. *page 136* [colina]

homogeneous mixture /hoh-moh-JEE-nee-uhs MIKS-cher/ *(noun)* In chemistry, a homogeneous mixture is a mixture of two or more substances that have mixed completely, for example salt and water. *page 174* [mezcla homogénea]

host /hohst/ *(noun)* The host of a parasite is the plant or animal which it lives on or inside and from which it gets its food. *page 88* [huésped]

human /HYOO-muhn/ *(adjective)* **1.** Human means relating to or concerning people. *page 54* [humano]

(noun) **2.** You can refer to people as humans, especially when you are comparing them with animals or machines. *page 54* [humano]

humpback whale /HUHMP-bak wayl/ *(noun)* A humpback whale is a large whale with long front fins. *page 98* [yubarta]

humus /HUHM-uhs/ *(noun)* Humus is the part of soil which consists of dead plants that have begun to decay. *page 36* [humus]

hunt /huhnt/ *(verb)* When animals hunt something, they chase and kill wild animals for food. *page 89* [cazar]

hurricane /HUH-ri-kayn/ *(noun)* A hurricane is an extremely violent storm that begins over ocean water. *page 154* [huracán]

hydropower /HEYE-droh-pow-er/ *(noun)* Hydropower is the use of energy from running water, especially in hydroelectricity. *page 208* [energía hidráulica]

hypothesis /heye-POHTH-uh-sis/ *(noun)* A hypothesis is an idea which is suggested as a possible explanation for a particular situation or condition, but which has not yet been proved to be correct. *page 2* [hipótesis]

I

ice wedging /eyes WEJ-ing/ *(noun)* Ice wedging is a geological process in which rocks are broken because water freezes in gaps or cracks in the rocks. *page 142* [gelifracción]

igneous /IG-nee-uhs/ *(adjective)* In geology, igneous rocks are rocks that were once so hot that they were liquid. *page 126* [ígneas]

inclined plane /in-KLEYEND playn/ *(noun)* An inclined plane is a flat, level surface that is sloping at a particular angle. *page 194* [plano inclinado]

inertia /in-ER-shuh/ *(noun)* Inertia is the tendency of a physical object to remain still or to continue moving, unless a force is applied to it. *page 192* [inercia]

inherit /in-HE-rit/ *(verb)* If you inherit a characteristic or quality, you are born with it, because your parents or ancestors also had it. *page 72* [heredar]

inner core /IN-er kor/ *(noun)* The inner core of the Earth is the deepest part of the Earth's interior. It is solid and made of nickel and iron. *page 130* [núcleo, endosfera]

insect /IN-sekt/ *(noun)* An insect is a small animal that has six legs. Most insects have wings. *pages 48, 50* [insecto]

instinct /IN-stinkt/ *(noun)* Instinct is the natural tendency that a person or animal has to behave or react in a particular way. *page 97* [instinto]

insulator /IN-suhl-ay-tor/ *(noun)* An insulator is a material that protects something from cold, heat, electricity or noise. *pages 218, 221* [aislante]

intestine /in-TES-tin/ *(noun)* Your intestines are the tubes in your body through which food passes when it has left your stomach. *pages 58, 88* [intestino]

invertebrate /in-VER-tuh-brayt/ *(noun)* An invertebrate is a creature that does not have a spine such as an insect, a worm, or an octopus. *page 50* [invertebrado]

isobar /EYE-soh-bar/ *(noun)* An isobar is a line on a weather map that connects points of equal atmospheric pressure. *page 152* [isobara]

J

jellyfish /JEL-ee-fish/ *(noun)* A jellyfish is a sea creature that has a clear soft body and can sting you. *pages 48, 50* [medusa]

Jupiter /JOO-pit-er/ *(noun)* Jupiter is the fifth planet from the sun and the largest in our solar system. *page 110* [Júpiter]

K

kangaroo rat /kayn-guh-ROO rat/ *(noun)* A kangaroo rat is a small rodent that lives in North and Central America. It has long back legs, which it uses in order to hop. *page 85* [rata canguro]

kidney /KID-nee/ *(noun)* Your kidneys are the organs in your body that take waste matter from your blood and send it out of your body as urine. *page 58* [riñón]

kilogram /KI-loh-gram/ *(noun)* A kilogram is a metric unit of weight. One kilogram is a thousand grams, and is equal to 2.2 pounds. *page 10* [kilogramo]

kilometer /ki-LOM-eter/ *(noun)* A kilometer is a metric unit of distance or length. One kilometer is a thousand meters and is equal to 0.62 miles. *page 10* [kilómetro]

kinetic energy /ki-NET-ik EN-er-jee/ *(noun)* In physics, kinetic energy is the energy that is produced when something moves. *pages 206, 210* [energía cinética]

kingdom /KING-duhm/ *(noun)* All the animals, birds, and insects in the world can be referred to together as the animal kingdom. All the plants can be referred to as the plant kingdom. *page 78* [reino]

L

L /lohw PRESH-er/ *(adjective)* On a weather map, L is an abbreviation for "low pressure." *page 152* [B]

lab apron /lab AY-pruhn/ *(noun)* A lab apron is a piece of clothing that you put on over the front of your normal clothes and tie around your waist when you are working in a laboratory, in order to prevent your clothes from getting dirty. *page 18* [delantal de laboratorio]

lake /layk/ *(noun)* A lake is a large area of fresh water, surrounded by land. *page 134* [lago]

lamp /lamp/ *(noun)* A lamp is a light that works by using electricity or by burning oil or gas. *page 202* [lámpara]

landform /LAND-form/ *(noun)* A landform is any natural feature of the earth's surface, such as a hill, a lake, or a beach. *page 136* [formación terrestre]

launchpad /LAWNCH-pad/ *(noun)* A launchpad or launching pad is a platform from which rockets, missiles, or satellites are launched. *page 122* [plataforma de lanzamiento]

lava /LAH-vah/ (*noun*) Lava is the very hot liquid rock that comes out of a volcano. *page 138* [**lava**]

law /law/ (*noun*) A law is a scientific rule that someone has invented to explain a particular natural process. *pages 181, 213* [**ley**]

layer /LAY-er/ (*noun*) A layer of a material or substance is a quantity or piece of it that covers a surface or that is between two other things. *pages 126, 149* [**capa**]

leaf /leef/ (*noun*) The leaves of a tree or plant are the parts that are flat, thin, and usually green. Many trees and plants lose their leaves in the winter and grow new leaves in the spring. *pages 34, 38, 42, 62, 214* [**hoja**]

learned behavior /lernd bee-HAYV-yor/ (*noun*) Learned behavior is behavior that someone has learned through experience or observation rather than because it is a natural instinct. *page 97* [**comportamiento aprendido**]

length /lenth/ (*noun*) The length of something is the amount that it measures from one end to the other along the longest side. *page 12* [**longitud**]

lever /LEV-er/ (*noun*) A lever is a long bar, one end of which is placed under a heavy object so that when you press down on the other end you can move the object. *page 194* [**palanca**]

lightbulb /leyet bulb/ (*noun*) A lightbulb or bulb is the round glass part of an electric light or lamp which light shines from. *page 220* [**foco**]

light energy /leyet EN-er-jee/ (*noun*) Light energy is energy in the form of electromagnetic waves. *pages 206, 210, 214* [**energía luminosa**]

lightning /LEYET-ning/ (*noun*) Lightning is the very bright flashes of light in the sky that happen during thunderstorms. *page 154* [**rayo, relámpago**]

light source /leyet sors/ (*noun*) A light source is any object or device that gives off light, such as the sun or an electric light bulb. *page 202* [**fuente de luz**]

light year /leyet yeer/ (*noun*) A light year is the distance that light travels in a year. *page 104* [**año luz**]

limestone /LEYEM-stohn/ (*noun*) Limestone is a whitish-colored rock which is used for building and for making cement. *page 126* [**piedra caliza**]

line graph /leyen graf/ (*noun*) A line graph is a graph in which the data are represented by points connected by one or more lines. *page 14* [**gráfica lineal**]

liquid /LIK-wid/ (*adjective*) **1.** A liquid is a substance which is not solid but which flows and can be poured, for example, water. *pages 162, 166, 172* [**líquido**]

(*noun*) **2.** A liquid substance is in the form of a liquid rather than being solid or a gas. *pages 162, 166, 172* [**líquido**]

liter /LEE-ter/ (*noun*) A liter is a metric unit of volume that is a thousand cubic centimeters. It is equal to 2.11 pints. *page 10* [**litro**]

liver /LIV-er/ (*noun*) Your liver is a large organ in your body which processes your blood and helps to clean unwanted substances out of it. *page 58* [**hígado**]

liverwort /LIV-er-wert/ (*noun*) A liverwort is a plant with no leaves or stem that grows in wet places and resembles seaweed or moss. *page 38* [**hepática**]

load /lohd/ (*noun*) **1.** The load of a system or piece of equipment, especially a system supplying electricity or a computer, is the extent to which it is being used at a particular time. *page 194* [**carga**]

(*noun*) **2.** The load on something is the amount of weight that is pressing down on it or the amount of strain that it is under. *page 194* [**carga**]

loam /lohm/ (*noun*) Loam is soil that is good for growing crops and plants in because it contains a lot of decayed vegetable matter and does not contain too much sand or clay. *page 36* [**marga**]

lobster /LOB-ster/ (noun) A lobster is a sea creature that has a hard shell, two large claws, and eight legs. *page 50* [langosta]

longitudinal wave /lon-juh-TOOD-in-uhl wayv/ (noun) Longitudinal waves are waves such as sound waves in which the material that the waves are passing through moves in the same direction as the waves. Compare transverse wave. *page 198* [onda longitudinal]

lower mantle /LOW-wer MAN-tuhl/ (noun) The lower mantle is the part of the Earth's interior that lies between the upper mantle and the outer core. *page 130* [manto bajo]

low tide /low teyed/ (noun) At the coast, low tide is the time when the sea is at its lowest level because the tide is out. *page 118* [marea baja]

lunar eclipse /LOO-ner ee-KLIPS/ (noun) A lunar eclipse is an occasion when the Earth is between the sun and the moon, so that for a short time you cannot see part or all of the moon. Compare solar eclipse. *page 118* [eclipse lunar]

lunar module /LOO-ner MOD-joo-uhl/ (noun) A lunar module is a part of a spacecraft that is designed to separate from the rest of the spacecraft and land on the moon. *page 124* [módulo lunar]

lung /luhng/ (noun) Your lungs are the two organs inside your chest which fill with air when you breathe in. *page 58* [pulmón]

lysosome /LEYE-suh-sohm/ (noun) A lysosome is a part of a cell that contains enzymes which can break down many different substances. *page 22* [lisosoma]

M

magma /MAG-muh/ (noun) Magma is molten rock that is formed in very hot conditions inside the earth. *pages 132, 138* [magma]

magnet /MAG-nit/ (noun) A magnet is a piece of iron or other material which attracts iron toward it. *page 218* [imán]

magnetic field /mag-NET-ik feeld/ (noun) A magnetic field is an area around a magnet, or something functioning as a magnet, in which the magnet's power to attract things is felt. *page 218* [campo magnético]

magnetic pole /mag-NET-ik pohl/ (noun) The magnetic poles of a magnet are the two areas at opposite ends of the magnet where the magnetic field is strongest. The magnetic poles of the Earth are the two areas near the North and South Poles where the Earth's magnetic field is strongest. *page 218* [polo magnético]

magnitude /MAG-ni-tood/ (noun) A star's magnitude is its brightness. *page 108* [magnitud]

main-sequence star /mayn SEE-kwens star/ (noun) A main-sequence star is the most common type of star, which gets its energy by converting hydrogen into helium. *page 106* [estrella de secuencia principal]

mammal /MAM-uhl/ (noun) Mammals are animals such as humans, dogs, lions, and whales. In general, female mammals give birth to babies rather than laying eggs, and feed their young with milk. *pages 48, 54* [mamífero]

mammoth /MAM-uhth/ (noun) A mammoth was an animal like an elephant, with very long tusks and long hair, that lived a long time ago but no longer exists. *page 98* [mamut]

map /map/ (noun) A map is a drawing of a particular area such as a city, a country, or a continent, showing its main features as they would appear if you looked at them from above. *page 14* [mapa]

map key /map kee/ (noun) A map key is a list which explains the meaning of the symbols and abbreviations used on a map. *page 14* [clave]

marble /MAR-buhl/ (noun) Marble is a type of very hard rock which feels cold when you touch it and which shines when it is cut and polished. Statues and parts of buildings are sometimes made of marble. *page 126* [mármol]

Mars /marz/ (noun) Mars is the fourth planet from the sun, between the Earth and Jupiter. *page 110* [Marte]

mass /mas/ (*noun*) In physics, the mass of an object is the amount of physical matter that it has. *pages 12, 166, 188, 190* [masa]

matter /MAT-er/ (*noun*) Matter is the physical part of the universe consisting of solids, liquids, and gases. *page 200* [materia]

mechanical energy /muh-KAN-i-kuhl EN-er-jee/ (*noun*) Mechanical energy is the energy that an object such as a machine has because of its movement or position. *page 206* [energía mecánica]

mechanical weathering /muh-KAN-i-kuhl WETH-er-ing/ (*noun*) Mechanical weathering is a geological process in which rock is broken down into smaller pieces, for example because of frost. *page 144* [erosión mecánica]

medicine /MED-i-suhn/ (*noun*) Medicine is a substance that you drink or swallow to cure an illness. *page 100* [medicina, medicamento]

medium /MEE-dee-uhm/ (*noun*) **1.** A medium is a substance or material which is used for a particular purpose or in order to produce a particular effect. *page 200* [medio]

(*adjective*) **2.** If something is of medium size, it is neither large nor small, but approximately halfway between the two. *page 8* [medio]

meiosis /meye-OH-sis/ (*noun*) Meiosis is a type of cell division that results in egg and sperm cells with only half the usual number of chromosomes. *page 66* [meiosis]

melting point /MELT-ing point/ (*noun*) The melting point of a substance is the temperature at which it melts when you heat it. *page 166* [punto de fusión]

meniscus /mi-NIS-kuhs/ (*noun*) A curve in the surface of a liquid in a container. *page 8* [menisco]

Mercury /MER-kyer-ee/ (*noun*) Mercury is the planet that is closest to the sun. *page 110* [Mercurio]

mesa /ME-suh/ (*noun*) A mesa is a large hill with a flat top and steep sides; used mainly of hills in the southwestern United States. *page 134* [meseta]

metal /MET-uhl/ (*noun*) Metal is a hard substance such as iron, steel, gold, or lead. *page 170* [metal]

metamorphic /met-uh-MOR-fik/ (*adjective*) Metamorphic rock is rock that is formed from other rock as a result of heat or pressure beneath the surface of the Earth. Compare igneous, sedimentary. *page 126* [metamórfico]

metamorphosis /met-uh-MOR-foh-sis/ (*noun*) When a metamorphosis occurs, a person or thing develops and changes into something completely different. *page 52* [metamorfosis]

metaphase /MET-uh-fayz/ (*noun*) Metaphase is a stage in the process of cell division in which the chromosomes line up before they separate. *page 64* [metafase]

meteoroid /MEET-ee-or-oid/ (*noun*) A meteoroid is a piece of rock or dust that travels around the sun. *page 110* [meteoroide]

meter /MEET-er/ (*noun*) A meter is a metric unit of length equal to 100 centimeters. *page 10* [metro]

meters per second /MEET-erz per SEK-uhnd/ (*noun*) Meters per second is a unit of speed in physics. An object that is moving at a particular number of meters per second travels that number of meters in one second. The abbreviation m/s is also used. *page 192* [metros por segundo]

methanogen /muh-THAN-uh-jen/ (*noun*) Methanogens are bacteria that produce methane. *page 78* [metanógeno]

metric system /ME-trik SIS-tuhm/ (*noun*) The metric system is the system of measurement that uses meters, grams, and liters. *page 12* [sistema métrico]

microscope /MEYE-kruh-skohp/ (*noun*) A microscope is a scientific instrument which makes very small objects look bigger so that more detail can be seen. *pages 6, 24* [microscopio]

migration /meye-GRAY-shuhn/ (*noun*) Migration is the movement of birds, fish, or animals at a particular season from one part of the world or from one part of a country to another, usually in order to breed or to find new feeding grounds. *page 94* [migración]

milliliter /MIL-uh-lee-ter/ (*noun*) A milliliter is a unit of volume for liquids and gases that is equal to a thousandth of a liter. *page 10* [mililitro]

millimeter /MIL-uh-mee-ter/ (*noun*) A millimeter is a metric unit of length that is equal to a tenth of a centimeter or a thousandth of a meter. *page 10* [milímetro]

mineral /MIN-er-uhl/ (*noun*) A mineral is a substance such as tin, salt, or sulfur that is formed naturally in rocks and in the earth. Minerals are also found in small quantities in food and drink. *pages 36, 126, 158* [mineral]

mitochondrion /meyet-oh-KON-dree-uhn/ (*noun*) Mitochondria are the parts of a cell that convert nutrients into energy. *pages 22, 217* [mitocondrio]

mitosis /meye-TOH-sis/ (*noun*) Mitosis is the process by which a cell divides into two identical halves. *page 62* [mitosis]

mixture /MIKS-cher/ (*noun*) A mixture is a substance that consists of other substances which have been stirred or shaken together. *page 174* [mezcla]

mold /mohld/ (*noun*) Mold is a soft gray, green, or blue substance that sometimes forms in spots on old food or on damp walls or clothes. *page 78* [moho]

molecule /MAH-luh-kyool/ (*noun*) A molecule is the smallest amount of a chemical substance which can exist by itself. *pages 170, 172, 178, 209* [molécula]

molting /MUHLT-ing/ (*verb*) Molting is a process in which an animal or bird gradually loses its coat or feathers so that a new coat or feathers can grow. *page 52* [mudar]

moon /moon/ (*noun*) **1.** The moon is the object that you can often see in the sky at night. It goes around the earth once every four weeks, and as it does so its appearance changes from a circle to part of a circle. *pages 110, 112, 114* [luna]

(*noun*) **2.** A moon is an object similar to a small planet that travels around a planet. *pages 110, 112, 114* [luna]

moraine /MOR-ayn/ (*noun*) A moraine is a pile of rocks and soil left behind by a glacier. *page 142* [morrena]

moss /maws/ (*noun*) Moss is a very small, soft, green plant which grows on damp soil, or on wood or stone. *page 38* [musgo]

mountain /MOWN-tuhn/ (*noun*) A mountain is a very high area of land with steep sides. *page 134* [montaña]

mountain gorilla /MOWN-tuhn guh-RIL-uh/ (*noun*) A mountain gorilla is a type of gorilla that has long, dark hair and lives in central Africa. *page 98* [gorila de montaña]

move /moov/ (*verb*) When you move something or when it moves, its position changes and it does not remain still. *page 186* [mover]

m/s /MEET-erz per SEK-uhnd/ (*noun*) m/s is an abbreviation for meters per second. *page 192* [mts/seg, metros por segundo]

m/s/s /MEET-erz per SEK-uhnd per SEK-uhnd/ (*noun*) m/s/s or m/s per second is a unit of acceleration in physics. m/s/s is an abbreviation for 'meters per second per second'. *page 192* [mts/seg/seg metros por segundo por segundo]

muscle /MUHS-uhl/ (*noun*) A muscle is a piece of tissue inside your body that connects two bones and which you use when you make a movement. *page 58* [músculo]

mushroom /MUHSH-room/ (*noun*) Mushrooms are fungi that you can eat. They have short stems and round tops. *page 78* [champiñón]

mutualism /MYOO-choo-uhl-iz-uhm/ (noun) Mutualism is a relationship between two species of animals or plants from which both species benefit. *page 88* [mutualismo]

N

natural gas /NACH-er-uhl gas/ (noun) Natural gas is gas which is found underground or under the sea. It is collected and stored, and piped into people's homes to be used for cooking and heating. *page 158* [gas natural]

natural light /NACH-er-uhl leyet/ (noun) Natural light is light from the sun rather than from an artificial source such as an electric light. *page 202* [luz natural]

natural selection /NACH-er-uhl suh-LEK-shuhn/ (noun) Natural selection is a process by which species of animals and plants that are best adapted to their environment survive and reproduce, while those that are less well adapted die out. *page 77* [selección natural]

neap tide /neep teyed/ (noun) A neap tide is a tide with a smaller rise and fall than normal, which occurs when the moon is halfway between a new moon and a full moon. *page 121* [marea muerta]

nebula /NEB-yoo-lah/ (noun) A nebula is a cloud of dust and gas in space. New stars are produced from nebulae. *page 106* [nebulosa]

nectar /NEK-ter/ (noun) Nectar is a sweet liquid produced by flowers, which bees and other insects collect. *page 4* [néctar]

Neptune /NEP-toon/ (noun) Neptune is the eighth planet from the sun. *page 110* [Neptuno]

nest /nest/ (noun) A bird's nest is the home that it makes to lay its eggs in. *page 46* [nido]

neutron /NOO-tron/ (noun) A neutron is an atomic particle that has no electrical charge. *pages 170, 184* [neutrón]

neutron star /NOO-tron star/ (noun) A neutron star is a star that has collapsed under the weight of its own gravity. *page 106* [estrella de neutrones]

night /neyet/ (noun) The night is the part of each period of twenty-four hours when the sun has set and it is dark outside, especially the time when people are sleeping. *page 114* [noche]

nitrogen /NEYE-troh-jin/ (noun) Nitrogen is a colorless element that has no smell and is usually found as a gas. It forms about 78 percent of the earth's atmosphere, and is found in all living things. *pages 37, 92, 148* [nitrógeno]

nonmetal /non-MET-uhl/ (noun) Nonmetals are chemical elements that are not metals. *page 170* [no metal]

nonrenewable /non-ree-NOO-uh-buhl/ (adjective) Nonrenewable resources are natural materials such as coal, oil and gas that exist in limited amounts and take a very long time to replace. You can refer to nonrenewable resources as nonrenewables. *pages 160, 206* [no renovable]

nonvascular plant /non-VAS-kyoo-ler plant/ (noun) Nonvascular plants are plants such as mosses and algae that are unable to move water or nutrients through themselves. *page 38* [planta no vascular]

nuclear energy /NOO-klee-er EN-er-jee/ (noun) Nuclear energy is energy that is released when the nuclei of atoms are split or combined. *page 158* [energía nuclear]

nucleus /NOO-klee-uhs/ (noun) The nucleus of an atom or cell is the central part of it. *pages 22, 170, 172, 182* [núcleo]

nutrient /NOO-tree-int/ (noun) Nutrients are substances that help plants and animals to grow. *page 36* [nutriente]

O

objective lens /uhb-JEK-tiv lenz/ (noun) The objective lens of a microscope is the lens that is closest to the object being observed and farthest from the eyepiece. *page 8* [lente objetivo]

observation /ob-zer-VAY-shuhn/ (noun) **1.** Observation is the action or process of carefully watching someone or something. *page 2* [observación]

(noun) **2.** An observation is something that you have learned by seeing or watching something and thinking about it. *page 2* [observación]

ocean /OH-shuhn/ (noun) **1.** The ocean is the salty water that covers much of the earth's surface. *page 134* [océano]

(noun) **2.** An ocean is one of the five very large areas of sea on the Earth's surface. *page 134* [océano]

oceanic ridge /oh-shee-AN-ik rij/ (noun) A mountain range under the sea. *page 132* [dorsal oceánica]

octopus /OK-toh-pus/ (noun) An octopus is a soft sea creature with eight long arms called tentacles. *page 46* [pulpo]

odor /OH-dor/ (noun) An odor is a smell. *page 162* [olor]

offspring /AWF-spring/ (noun) You can refer to a person's children or to an animal's young as their offspring. *page 72* [descendencia]

opaque /oh-PAYK/ (adjective) If an object or substance is opaque, you cannot see through it. *page 202* [opaco]

opossum /uh-POS-uhm/ (noun) An opossum is a small animal that lives in America and Australia. It carries its young in a pouch on its body, and has thick fur and a long hairless tail. *page 46* [zarigüeya]

opposite /OP-oh-zit/ (adjective) **1.** The opposite side or part of something is the side or part that is farthest away from you. *page 193* [opuesto]

(noun) **2.** Opposite is used to describe things of the same kind which are completely different in a particular way. *page 193* [opuesto]

orbit /OR-bit/ (noun) **1.** An orbit is the curved path in space that is followed by an object going around and around a planet, moon, or the sun. *pages 110, 114* [órbita]

(noun) **2.** If something such as a satellite orbits a planet, moon, or sun, it moves around it in a continuous, curving path. *pages 110, 114* [órbita]

order /OR-der/ (noun) In biology, an order of animals or plants is a group of related species. Compare class, family. *page 80* [orden]

organ /OR-guhn/ (noun) An organ is a part of your body that has a particular purpose or function, for example, your heart or lungs. *page 30* [órgano]

organelle /or-guh-NEL/ (noun) Organelles are structures within cells that have a specialized function, such as mitochondria or the nucleus. *page 24* [organela]

organism /OR-guhn-iz-uhm/ (noun) An organism is an animal or plant, especially one that is so small that you cannot see it without using a microscope. *page 74* [organismo]

organize /OR-guhn-eyez/ (verb) If you organize a set of things, you arrange them in an ordered way or give them a structure. *page 16* [organizar]

organ system /OR-guhn SIS-tuhm/ (noun) An organ system is a group of related organs within an organism, for example the nervous system. *pages 30, 60* [sistema orgánico]

outer core /OW-ter kor/ (noun) The outer core of the Earth is the layer of the Earth's interior between the mantle and the inner core. *page 130* [núcleo exterior]

ovule /OV-yool/ (noun) An ovule is the part of a plant that develops into a seed. *page 40* [óvulo]

oxygen /OKS-i-jin/ (noun) Oxygen is a colorless gas in the air which is needed by all plants and animals. *pages 44, 148, 170, 174* [oxígeno]

P

Pangaea /pan-JEE-uh/ (noun) Pangaea is the name given by scientists to the huge landmass that existed on the Earth millions of years ago, before it split into separate continents. *page 132* [pangea]

paper /PAY-per/ (noun) **1.** Paper is a material that you write on or wrap things with. The pages of this book are made of paper. *page 182* [papel]

paramecium /pa-ruh-MEE-see-uhm/ (noun) Paramecia are a type of protozoa that are found in fresh water. *page 26* [paramecio]

parasitism /PA-ruh-seyet-iz-uhm/ (noun) In biology, parasitism is the state of being a parasite. *page 88* [parasitismo]

parent cell /PA-rent sel/ (noun) A parent cell is a cell in an organism which divides to produce other cells. Compare daughter cell. *pages 62, 66* [célula madre]

partial eclipse /PAR-shuhl ee-KLIPS/ (noun) A partial eclipse of the sun is an occasion when the moon is between the earth and the sun, so that for a short time you cannot see part of the sun. A partial eclipse of the moon is an occasion when the earth is between the sun and the moon, so that for a short time you cannot see part of the moon. Compare total eclipse. *page 118* [eclipse parcial]

particle /PART-i-kuhl/ (noun) In physics, a particle is a piece of matter smaller than an atom such as an electron or a proton. *pages 146, 164* [partícula]

penguin /PEN-gwin/ (noun) A penguin is a type of large black and white sea bird found mainly in the Antarctic. Penguins cannot fly but use their short wings for swimming. *page 54* [pingüino]

percentage /per-SENT-ij/ (noun) A percentage is a fraction of an amount expressed as a particular number of hundredths of that amount. *page 17* [porcentaje]

periodic table /peer-ee-OD-ik TAY-buhl/ (noun) In chemistry, the periodic table is a table showing the chemical elements arranged according to their atomic numbers. *page 173* [tabla periódica]

Petri dish /PEE-tree dish/ (noun) A Petri dish is a shallow circular dish that is used in laboratories for producing groups of microorganisms. *page 6* [placa de Petri]

petroleum /puh-TROHL-ee-uhm/ (noun) Petroleum is oil that is found under the surface of the earth or under the sea bed. Gasoline and kerosene are obtained from petroleum. *page 158* [petróleo]

phase /fayz/ (noun) The phases of the moon are the different stages of the moon's appearance, for example a new moon or a full moon. *page 117* [fase]

phloem /FLOH-uhm/ (noun) Phloem is the layer of material in plants that carries food from the leaves to the rest of the plant. Compare xylem. *pages 38, 42* [floema]

photosynthesis /foh-toh-SIN-thuh-sis/ (noun) Photosynthesis is the way that green plants make their food using sunlight. *pages 42, 214* [fotosíntesis]

phototropism /foh-toh-TROHP-iz-uhm/ (noun) Phototropism is the tendency of a plant to grow in the direction of a light source. *page 94* [fototropismo]

phylum /FEYE-luhm/ (noun) A phylum is a group of related species of animals or plants. Compare kingdom, class. *page 80* [fílum]

physical change /FIZ-i-kuhl chaynj/ (noun) When there is a physical change to a substance, its form or appearance changes but it does not become a different substance. *page 177* [cambio físico]

physical property /FIZ-i-kuhl PROP-er-tee/ (noun) The physical properties of a substance are qualities such as its size and shape, which can be measured without changing what the substance is. *page 165* [propiedad física]

pie chart /peye chart/ (noun) A pie chart is a circle divided into sections to show the relative proportions of a set of things. *page 14* [gráfico circular, gráfico de sectores]

pine /peyen/ (noun) A pine tree or a pine is a tall tree that has very thin, sharp leaves called needles and a fresh smell. Pine trees have leaves all year round. *page 78* [pino]

pistil /PIS-til/ (*noun*) The pistil is the female part of a flower, which produces seeds. *page 40* [pistilo]

plain /playn/ (*noun*) A plain is a large flat area of land with very few trees on it. *page 134* [llanura]

planet /PLAN-it/ (*noun*) A planet is a large, round object in space that moves around a star. The Earth is a planet. *page 102* [planeta]

plant kingdom /plant KING-duhm/ (*noun*) The plants of the world. *page 78* [reino vegetal]

plate /playt/ (*noun*) In geology, a plate is a large piece of the Earth's surface, perhaps as large as a continent, which moves very slowly. *pages 130, 138* [placa]

plate boundary /playt BOWN-duh-ree/ (*noun*) A plate boundary is a place on the Earth's surface where two or more tectonic plates meet. *pages 130, 133, 140* [límite de placa]

plate tectonics /playt tek-TON-iks/ (*noun*) Plate tectonics is the way that large pieces of the earth's surface move slowly around. *page 133* [placa tectónica]

polar /POH-ler/ (*adjective*) Polar means near the North or South Poles. *page 153* [polar]

pollen /POL-in/ (*noun*) Pollen is a fine powder produced by flowers. It fertilizes other flowers of the same species so that they produce seeds. *page 40* [polen]

pollinate /POL-in-ayt/ (*verb*) Pollination is the process of fertilizing a plant or tree with pollen. *page 40* [polinizar]

pollution /poh-LOO-shuhn/ (*noun*) **1.** Pollution is the process of polluting water, air, or land, especially with poisonous chemicals. *pages 101, 146* [polución, contaminación]

(*noun*) **2.** Pollution is poisonous or dirty substances that are polluting the water, air, or land somewhere. *pages 101, 146* [polución, contaminación]

population /pop-yoo-LAY-shuhn/ (*noun*) **1.** The population of a country or area is all the people who live in it. *page 82* [población]

(*noun*) **2.** If you refer to a particular type of population in a country or area, you are referring to all the people or animals of that type there. *page 82* [población]

pore /por/ (*noun*) Your pores are the tiny holes in your skin. *page 53* [poro]

potential energy /poh-TEN-chuhl EN-er-jee/ (*noun*) Potential energy is the energy that an object has because of its position or condition, for example because it is raised above the ground. Compare kinetic energy. *pages 206, 210* [energía potencial]

precipitation /pree-sip-uh-TAY-shuhn/ (*noun*) **1.** Precipitation is rain, snow, or hail. *pages 90, 150* [precipitación]

(*noun*) **2.** Precipitation is a process in a chemical reaction that causes solid particles to become separated from a liquid. *pages 90, 150* [precipitación]

predator /PRED-uh-ter/ (*noun*) A predator is an animal that kills and eats other animals. *page 89* [predador, depredador]

prediction /pree-DIK-shuhn/ (*noun*) If you make a prediction about something, you say what you think will happen. *page 2* [predicción]

press together /pres too-GETH-er/ (*verb*) When substances such as sand or gravel press together or when they are pressed together, they are pushed hard against each other so that they form a single layer. *page 126* [comprimir, apretar]

prey /pray/ (*noun*) A creature's prey are the creatures that it hunts and eats in order to live. *page 89* [presa]

prism /PRIZ-uhm/ (*noun*) A prism is a block of clear glass or plastic that separates the light passing through it into different colors. *page 202* [prisma]

process /PRO-ses/ (noun) A process is a series of things that happen naturally and result in a biological or chemical change. *page 68* [proceso]

producer /proh-DOOS-er/ (noun) In biology, producers are plants or bacteria that can produce their own food, especially by means of photosynthesis. *page 86* [productor]

property /PROP-er-tee/ (noun) The properties of a substance or object are the ways in which it behaves in particular conditions. *page 172* [propiedad]

prophase /PROH-fayz/ (noun) Prophase is the first stage of cell division, in which the DNA inside a cell forms into chromosomes. *page 64* [profase]

protist /PROHT-ist/ (noun) Protists are organisms such as algae and molds that are not animals, plants or fungi. *page 78* [protisto]

proton /PROH-ton/ (noun) A proton is an atomic particle that has a positive electrical charge. *pages 170, 184* [protón]

protozoan /proht-oh-ZOH-uhn/ (noun) Protozoa are very small organisms that often live inside larger animals. *pages 26, 78* [protozoo]

pseudopod /SOO-doh-pod/ (noun) Pseudopods are the tiny extensions of cells within some microorganisms that are used for movement and feeding. *page 26* [seudópodo]

pull /pul/ (verb) A pull is a strong physical force that causes things to move in a particular direction. *page 186* [jalar]

pulley /PUL-ee/ (noun) A pulley is a device consisting of a wheel over which a rope or chain is pulled in order to lift heavy objects. *page 194* [polea]

Punnett square /PUN-et skwair/ (noun) A Punnett square is a diagram used by biologists to predict the genetic makeup of an organism. *page 73* [tablero de Punnett]

pure /pyor/ (adjective) A pure substance is not mixed with anything else. *page 174* [pura]

push /push/ (verb) When you push something, you use force to make it move away from you or away from its previous position. *page 186* [empujar]

Q

quagga /KWAG-uh/ (noun) A quagga was a type of zebra that is now extinct. *page 98* [cuaga]

quartz /kwortz/ (noun) Quartz is a hard, shiny crystal used in making electronic equipment and very accurate watches and clocks. *page 126* [cuarzo]

question /KWES-chuhn/ (noun) A question is a problem, matter, or point which needs to be considered. *page 2* [cuestión]

R

raccoon /ra-KOON/ (noun) A nocturnal carnivore that lives in North and Central America. *page 46* [mapache]

radiation /ray-dee-AY-shuhn/ (noun) **1.** Radiation consists of very small particles of a radioactive substance. Large amounts of radiation can cause illness and death. *pages 182, 212* [radiación]

(noun) **2.** Radiation is energy, especially heat, that comes from a particular source. *pages 182, 212* [radiación]

radioactive /ray-dee-oh-AK-tiv/ (adjective) Something that is radioactive contains a substance that produces energy in the form of powerful and harmful rays. *page 182* [radioactivo, radioactiva]

radioactive symbol /ray-dee-oh-AK-tiv SIM-buhl/ (noun) A radioactive symbol is a printed sign which shows that a place or an object contains dangerous amounts of radiation. *page 182* [símbolo radioactivo]

radio telescope /RAY-dee-oh TEL-uh-skohp/ (noun) A radio telescope is an instrument that receives radio waves from space and finds the position of stars and other objects in space. *page 102* [radiotelescopio]

radio wave /RAY-dee-oh wayv/ *(noun)* Radio waves are the form in which radio signals travel. *pages 105, 201* **[onda de radio]**

rain /rayn/ *(noun)* Rain is water that falls from the clouds in small drops. *pages 90, 146, 150* **[lluvia]**

rainfall /RAYN-fawl/ *(noun)* Rainfall is the amount of rain that falls in a place during a particular period. *page 84* **[pluviosidad]**

rain forest /rayn FOR-ist/ *(noun)* A rain forest is a thick forest of tall trees which is found mainly in tropical areas where there is a lot of rain. *pages 82, 100* **[bosque tropical]**

rarefaction /rair-uh-FAK-shuhn/ *(noun)* Rarefaction is a reduction in the density of something, especially the density of the atmosphere. *page 198* **[rarefacción]**

react /ree-AKT/ *(verb)* When one chemical substance reacts with another, or when two chemical substances react, they combine chemically to form another substance. *page 144* **[reaccionar]**

reaction force /ree-AK-shuhn fors/ *(noun)* In physics, for every action force there is an equal in size and opposite in direction reaction force. *page 190* **[fuerza de reacción]**

recessive /ree-SES-iv/ *(adjective)* A recessive gene produces a particular characteristic only if a person has two of these genes, one from each parent. Compare dominant. *page 72* **[recesivo]**

recycle /ree-SEYE-kuhl/ *(verb)* If you recycle things that have already been used, such as bottles or sheets of paper, you process them so that they can be used again. *page 158* **[reciclar]**

red blood cell /red bluhd sel/ *(noun)* Your red blood cells are the cells in your blood which carry oxygen around your body. Compare white blood cell. *page 32* **[glóbulo rojo]**

red giant /red JEYE-uhnt/ *(noun)* A red giant is a very large, relatively cool star that is in the final stages of its life. *page 106* **[estrella gigante]**

reduce /ree-DOOS/ *(verb)* If you reduce something, you make it smaller in size or amount, or less in degree. *page 160* **[reducir]**

reflect /ree-FLEKT/ *(verb)* **1.** When light, heat, or other rays reflect off a surface or when a surface reflects them, they are sent back from the surface and do not pass through it. *page 202* **[reflejar]**

(verb) **2.** When something is reflected in a mirror or in water, you can see its image in the mirror or in the water. *page 202* **[reflejar]**

reflex /REE-fleks/ *(noun)* A reflex or a reflex action is a normal, uncontrollable reaction of your body to something that you feel, see, or experience. *page 97* **[reflejo]**

refract /ree-FRAKT/ *(verb)* When a ray of light or a sound wave refracts or is refracted, the path it follows bends at a particular point, for example when it enters water or glass. *page 202* **[refractar]**

relationship /ree-LAY-shuhn-ship/ *(noun)* The relationship between an organism and its environment is the way that the organism and its environment interact and the effect they have on each other. *page 4* **[relación]**

renewable /ree-NOO-uh-buhl/ *(adjective)* Renewable resources are natural ones such as wind, water, and sunlight which are always available. You can refer to renewable resources as renewables. *pages 160, 206* **[renovable]**

replace /ree-PLAYS/ *(verb)* If one thing or person replaces another, the first is used or acts instead of the second. *page 208* **[reemplazar]**

reproduce /ree-proh-DOOS/ *(verb)* When people, animals, or plants reproduce, they produce young. *page 48* **[reproducir]**

reptile /REP-teyel/ *(noun)* Reptiles are a group of cold-blooded animals which lay eggs and have skins covered with small, hard plates called scales. Snakes, lizards, and crocodiles are reptiles. *pages 48, 54* **[reptil]**

respiratory system /RES-per-uh-tor-ee SIS-tuhm/ *(noun)* Your body's respiratory system is the group of organs that are involved in breathing, including the nose, mouth, and lungs. *page 30* [**sistema respiratorio**]

response /ree-SPONS/ *(noun)* The response of an organism to a stimulus is the way that the organism reacts to it. *page 94* [**respuesta**]

reuse /ree-YOOZ/ *(verb)* When you reuse something, you use it again instead of throwing it away. *page 160* [**reutilizar**]

revolve /ree-VOLV/ *(verb)* **1.** If one object revolves around another object, the first object turns in a circle around the second object. *page 114* [**girar alrededor de**]

(verb) **2.** When something revolves or when you revolve it, it moves or turns in a circle around a central point or line. *page 114* [**girar**]

ribosome /REYE-buh-sohm/ *(noun)* Ribosomes are structures within the cells of an organism that produce proteins. *page 22* [**ribosoma**]

river /RIV-er/ *(noun)* A river is a large amount of fresh water flowing continuously in a long line across the land. *page 134* [**río**]

rock /rok/ *(noun)* Rock is the hard substance which the earth is made of. *pages 36, 126* [**roca**]

root /root/ *(noun)* The roots of a plant are the parts of it that grow under the ground. *pages 34, 38, 42, 62* [**raíz**]

root system /root SIS-tuhm/ *(noun)* A plant's root system is the part of the plant that contains the roots. Compare shoot system. *page 30* [**sistema radical**]

rotate /ROH-tayt/ *(verb)* When something rotates or when you rotate it, it turns with a circular movement. *page 114* [**girar**]

rotation /roh-TAY-shuhn/ *(noun)* Rotation is circular movement. A rotation is the movement of something through one complete circle. *pages 114, 154* [**rotación**]

row /rohw/ *(noun)* A row of things or people is a number of them arranged in a line. *page 16* [**fila**]

runner /RUN-er/ *(noun)* On a plant, runners are long shoots that grow from the main stem and put down roots to form a new plant. *page 65* [**rama rastrera**]

runoff /RUN-of/ *(noun)* Runoff is rainwater that forms a stream rather than being absorbed by the ground. *page 90* [**agua de escorrentía**]

rust /rust/ *(noun)* **1.** Rust is a brown substance that forms on iron or steel, for example when it comes into contact with water. *pages 162, 178* [**óxido**]

(verb) **2.** When a metal object rusts, it becomes covered in rust and often loses its strength. *pages 162, 178* [**oxidar**]

S

salamander /SAL-uh-man-der/ *(noun)* A salamander is an animal that looks rather like a lizard, and that can live both on land and in water. *page 54* [**salamandra**]

salt /sawlt/ *(noun)* Salts are substances that are formed when an acid reacts with an alkali. *page 152* [**sal**]

salt water /sawlt WUH-ter/ *(noun)* **1.** Salt water is water, especially from the ocean, which has salt in it. *page 136* [**agua salada**]

(adjective) **2.** Salt water fish live in water which is salty. Salt water lakes contain salt. *page 136* [**de agua salada**]

sand /sand/ *(noun)* Sand is a substance that looks like powder, and consists of very small pieces of stone. Some deserts and many beaches are made up of sand. *page 142* [**arena**]

sand dune /sand doon/ *(noun)* A sand dune is a hill of sand near the sea or in a sand desert. *page 142* [**duna**]

sandstone /SAND-stohn/ *(noun)* Sandstone is a type of rock which contains a lot of sand. *page 126* [**arenisca**]

sandy /SAN-dee/ *(adjective)* A sandy area is covered with sand. *page 36* [**arenosa**]

satellite /SAT-uh-leyet/ (noun) **1.** A satellite is an object which has been sent into space in order to collect information or to be part of a communications system. pages 9, 122 [satélite]

(noun) **2.** A satellite is a natural object in space that moves around a planet or star. page 9 [satélite]

Saturn /SAT-ern/ (noun) Saturn is the sixth planet from the sun. It is surrounded by rings made of ice and dust. page 110 [Saturno]

scallop /SKAL-uhp/ (noun) Scallops are large shellfish with two flat fan-shaped shells. Scallops can be eaten. page 50 [vieira]

screw /skroow/ (noun) A screw is a metal object similar to a nail, with a raised spiral line around it. You turn a screw using a screwdriver so that it goes through two things, for example, two pieces of wood, and fastens them together. page 194 [tornillo]

sea-floor spreading /see-flor SPRED-ing/ (noun) Sea-floor spreading is the expansion of the ocean floor that occurs when two tectonic plates move apart and new rock is formed. page 132 [expansión del fondo oceánico]

seahorse /SEE-hors/ (noun) A seahorse is a type of small fish which appears to swim in a vertical position and whose head looks a little like the head of a horse. page 54 [caballito de mar]

season /SEE-zuhn/ (noun) The seasons are the periods into which a year can be divided and which each have their own typical weather conditions. page 114 [estación]

sea star /see star/ (noun) A sea star is a flat, star-shaped creature, usually with five arms, that lives in the sea. page 50 [estrella de mar]

seaweed /SEE-weed/ (noun) Seaweed is a plant that grows in the sea. page 78 [alga marina]

sediment /SED-i-ment/ (noun) Sediment is solid material that settles at the bottom of a liquid. page 128 [sedimento]

sedimentary /sed-i-MEN-ter-ee/ (adjective) Sedimentary rocks are formed from

sediment left by water, ice, or wind. page 126 [sedimentarias]

seed /seed/ (noun) A seed is the small, hard part of a plant from which a new plant grows. pages 34, 38 [semilla]

seed fern /seed fern/ (noun) A seed fern was a plant, with leaves resembling those of a fern, that is now extinct. page 98 [helecho con semillas]

seedling /SEED-ling/ (noun) A seedling is a young plant that has been grown from a seed. page 41 [plántula]

seismic wave /SEYEZ-mik wayv/ (noun) A seismic wave is a sudden increase in heat or energy that travels through the earth, as the result of an earthquake or an explosion. page 138 [onda sísmica]

sense /sens/ (noun) Your senses are the physical abilities of sight, smell, hearing, touch, and taste. pages 48, 162 [sentido]

sex cell /seks sel/ (noun) Sex cells are the two types of male and female cells that join together to make a new creature. page 66 [célula sexual]

sexual reproduction /SEK-shoo-uhl ree-proh-DUHK-shuhn/ (noun) Sexual reproduction is the creation of new people, animals or plants as a result of sexual activity. page 66 [reproducción sexual]

shadow /SHAD-oh/ (noun) **1.** A shadow is a dark shape on a surface that is made when something stands between a light and the surface. page 118 [sombra]

(noun) **2.** Shadow is darkness in a place caused by something preventing light from reaching it. page 118 [sombra]

shark /shark/ (noun) A shark is a very large fish. Some sharks have very sharp teeth and may attack people. page 46 [tiburón]

shell /shel/ (noun) A hard outer covering of an animal. page 50 [caparazón, concha]

shellfish /SHEL-fish/ (noun) Shellfish are small creatures that live in the sea and have a shell. page 49 [moluscos, crustáceos]

shelter /SHEL-ter/ (*noun*) If a place provides shelter, it provides you with a place to stay or live, especially when you need protection from bad weather or danger. *page 46* [refugio]

shoot system /shoot SIS-tuhm/ (*noun*) A plant's shoot system is the part of the plant that is above the ground, including the stem and leaves. Compare root system. *page 30* [sistema de ramificación]

Siberian tiger /seye-BEER-ee-uhn TEYE-ger/ (*noun*) A Siberian tiger is a species of large tiger that lives in parts of Russia. *page 98* [tigre siberiano]

silver /SIL-ver/ (*noun*) Silver is a valuable pale gray metal that is used for making jewelry and ornaments. *page 170* [plata]

simple machine /SIM-puhl muh-SHEEN/ (*noun*) A simple machine is a device such as a lever, wheel or screw that forms a part of other, more complex machines. Compare compound machine. *page 194* [máquina simple]

sink /sink/ (*verb*) If something sinks, it disappears below the surface of a mass of water. *page 166* [hundir]

six kingdoms /siks KING-duhmz/ (*noun*) The six kingdoms are the six general types of organisms that make up all living things: Animalia, Plantae, Fungi, Protista, Archaebacteria and Eubacteria. *page 78* [seis reinos]

skin /skin/ (*noun*) Your skin is the natural covering of your body. *page 58* [piel]

slate /slayt/ (*noun*) Slate is a dark gray rock that can be easily split into thin layers. Slate is often used for covering roofs. *page 126* [pizarra]

snake /snayk/ (*noun*) A snake is a long, thin reptile without legs. *page 54* [serpiente]

snow /snohw/ (*noun*) **1.** Snow consists of a lot of soft white pieces of frozen water that fall from the sky in cold weather. *pages 90, 150* [nieve]

(*verb*) **2.** When it snows, snow falls from the sky. *pages 90, 150* [nevar]

soap and water /sohp and WUH-ter/ (*noun*) You wash your hands with soap and water. *page 18* [agua y jabón]

sodium /SOH-dee-uhm/ (*noun*) Sodium is a silvery white chemical element which combines with other chemicals. Salt is a sodium compound. *page 176* [sodio]

soil /soil/ (*noun*) Soil is the substance on the surface of the earth in which plants grow. *pages 34, 42 142* [tierra]

solar eclipse /SOH-ler ee-KLIPS/ (*noun*) A solar eclipse is an occasion when the moon is between the Earth and the sun, so that for a short time you cannot see part or all of the sun. Compare lunar eclipse. *page 118* [eclipse solar]

solar energy /SOH-ler EN-er-jee/ (*noun*) Solar power or solar energy is obtained from the sun's light and heat. *page 158* [energía solar]

solar system /SOH-ler SIS-tuhm/ (*noun*) The solar system is the sun and all the planets that go around it. *page 102* [sistema solar]

solid /SAHL-id/ (*adjective*) **1.** A solid substance or object stays the same shape whether it is in a container or not. *pages 162, 166, 168* [sólida, sólido]

(*noun*) **2.** A solid is a substance that stays the same shape whether it is in a container or not. *pages 162, 166, 168* [sólida, sólido]

solution /suh-LOO-shuhn/ (*noun*) A solution is a liquid in which a solid substance has been dissolved. *page 176* [solución]

sound energy /sownd EN-er-jee/ (*noun*) Sound energy is energy in the form of sound waves. *page 206, 210* [energía sónica]

sound wave /sownd wayv/ (*noun*) Sound waves are the waves of energy that we hear as sound. *page 198* [onda sonora]

space /spays/ (*noun*) Space is the area beyond the earth's atmosphere, where the stars and planets are. *page 102* [espacio]

spacecraft /spays-kraft/ (noun) A spacecraft is a rocket or other vehicle that can travel in space. *page 122* [nave espacial]

space probe /spays prohb/ (noun) A space probe is a spacecraft with no people in it which is sent into space in order to study the planets and send information about them back to earth. *page 122* [sonda espacial]

space shuttle /spays SHUHT-uhl/ (noun) A space shuttle or a shuttle is a spacecraft that is designed to travel into space and back to earth several times. *page 122* [transbordador espacial]

space station /spays STAY-shuhn/ (noun) A space station is a place built for astronauts to live and work in, which is sent into space and then keeps going around the earth. *page 122* [estación espacial]

space suit /spays soot/ (noun) A space suit is a special protective suit that is worn by astronauts in space. *page 122* [traje espacial]

species /SPEE-seez/ (noun) A species is a class of plants or animals whose members have the same main characteristics and are able to breed with each other. *pages 74, 80, 82, 100* [especie]

speed /speed/ (noun) The speed of something is the rate at which it moves, happens or is done. *page 190* [velocidad]

sperm /sperm/ (noun) A sperm is a cell which is produced in the sex organs of a male animal and can enter a female animal's egg and fertilize it. *page 68* [esperma, semen]

spider /SPEYE-der/ (noun) A spider is a small creature with eight legs. *page 50* [araña]

spin /spin/ (verb) If something spins or if you spin it, it turns quickly around a central point. *page 114* [girar]

spiral galaxy /SPEYE-ruhl GA-luhks-ee/ (noun) A spiral galaxy is a galaxy consisting of a flat disk at the center and spiral arms that contain many young stars. *page 104* [galaxia espiral]

sponge /spuhnj/ (noun) **1.** Sponge is a very light soft substance with lots of little holes in it, which can be either artificial or natural. It is used to clean things or as a soft layer. *page 48* [esponja]

(noun) **2.** A sponge is a sea animal with a soft round body made of natural sponge. *page 48* [esponja]

spore /spor/ (noun) Spores are cells produced by bacteria and fungi which can develop into new bacteria or fungi. *pages 34, 40* [espora]

spring tide /spring teyed/ (noun) A spring tide is an unusually high tide that happens at the time of a new moon or a full moon. *page 121* [marea viva]

stage /stayj/ (noun) The stage on a microscope is the place where you put the specimen that you want to look at. *page 8* [platina]

stamen /STAY-men/ (noun) The stamen is the male part of a flower, which produces pollen. Compare pistil. *page 40* [estambre]

star /star/ (noun) A star is a large ball of burning gas in space. Stars appear to us as small points of light in the sky on clear nights. *pages 102, 106, 202* [estrella]

state /stayt/ (noun) When you talk about the state of someone or something, you are referring to the condition they are in or what they are like at a particular time. *pages 162, 164* [estado]

static electricity /STAT-ik ee-lek-TRIS-i-tee/ (noun) Static electricity is electricity which collects on things such as your body or metal objects. *page 218* [electricidad estática]

stem /stem/ (noun) The stem of a plant is the thin, upright part on which the flowers and leaves grow. *pages 34, 38, 42, 62* [tallo]

stimulus /STIM-yoo-luhs/ (noun) A stimulus is something that encourages activity in people or things. *page 94* [estímulo]

stoma /STOH-muh/ (noun) Stomata are the tiny openings on the leaves of plants that allow water and air to enter and leave the plant. *page 42* [estoma]

stomach /STUHM-uhk/ (noun) Your stomach is the organ inside your body where food is digested. *page 58* [estómago]

stop /stop/ (verb) **1.** If an activity or process stops, it is no longer happening. *page 186* [parar]

(verb) **2.** When a moving person or vehicle stops or is stopped, they no longer move. *page 186* [parar]

storm surge /storm serj/ (noun) A storm surge is an increase in the sea level along a shore that accompanies a hurricane or storm. *page 156* [oleaje]

subspecies /sub-SPEE-seez/ (noun) A subspecies of a plant or animal is one of the types that a particular species is divided into. *pages 74, 100* [subespecie]

subtropical /sub-TRO-pi-kuhl/ (adjective) Subtropical places have a climate that is warm and wet, and are often near tropical regions. *page 153* [subtropical]

sucker /SUHK-er/ (noun) The suckers on some animals and insects are the parts on the outside of their body which they use in order to stick to a surface. *page 49* [ventosa]

sugar /SHUG-er/ (noun) Sugars are substances that occur naturally in food. When you eat them, the body converts them into energy. *page 174* [azúcar]

sun /suhn/ (noun) The sun is the ball of fire in the sky that the Earth goes around, and that gives us heat and light. *pages 106, 110, 114, 202, 214* [sol]

sunlight /SUHN-leyet/ (noun) Sunlight is the light that comes from the sun during the day. *pages 28, 34, 42* [luz solar]

supergiant /SOO-per-jeye-uhnt/ (noun) A supergiant is a very large, bright star. *page 106* [supergigante]

supernova /soo-per-NOH-vuh/ (noun) A supernova is an exploding star. *page 106* [supernova]

surgery /SER-jer-ee/ (noun) Surgery is medical treatment in which your body is cut open so that a doctor can repair, remove, or replace a diseased or damaged part. *page 185* [cirugía]

suspension /suh-SPEN-shuhn/ (noun) In chemistry, a suspension is a mixture containing tiny particles floating in a fluid. *page 176* [suspensión]

switch /swich/ (noun) A switch is a small control for an electrical device which you use to turn the device on or off. *page 220* [interruptor]

symbiosis /sim-beye-OH-sis/ (noun) Symbiosis is a close relationship between two organisms of different kinds which benefits both organisms. *page 88* [simbiosis]

symbol /SIM-buhl/ (noun) A symbol for an item in a calculation or scientific formula is a number, letter, or shape that represents that item. *pages 173, 178* [símbolo]

T

taiga /TEYE-guh/ (noun) The taiga is an area of thick forest in the far north of Europe, Asia, and North America, situated immediately south of the tundra. *page 82* [taiga]

tapeworm /TAYP-werm/ (noun) A tapeworm is a long, flat parasite which lives in the stomach and intestines of animals or people. *page 50* [tenia, solitaria]

taste /tayst/ (noun) Taste is one of the five senses that people have. When you have food or drink in your mouth, your sense of taste makes it possible for you to recognize what it is. *page 162* [gusto]

telescope /TEL-uh-skohp/ (noun) A telescope is a long instrument shaped like a tube. It has lenses inside it that make distant things seem larger and nearer when you look through it. *pages 6, 102* [telescopio]

telophase /TEL-oh-fayz/ (noun) Telophase is the final stage of cell division, when two completely separate cells are formed. *page 64* [telofase]

temperature /TEM-per-uh-cher/ (noun) The temperature of something is a measure of how hot or cold it is. *pages 12, 84, 106, 150, 153, 210* [temperatura]

test tube /test toob/ (noun) A test tube is a small tube-shaped container made from glass. Test tubes are used in laboratories. *page 6* [tubo de ensayo]

texture /TEKS-cher/ (noun) The texture of something is the way that it feels when you touch it, for example, how smooth or rough it is. *page 162* [textura]

thermal energy /THER-muhl EN-er-jee/ (noun) Thermal energy is energy in the form of heat. *pages 206, 210* [energía térmica]

thermometer /ther-MOM-uht-er/ (noun) A thermometer is an instrument for measuring temperature. It usually consists of a narrow glass tube containing a thin column of a liquid which rises and falls as the temperature rises and falls. *pages 6, 12, 166* [termómetro]

thunderstorm /THUN-der-storm/ (noun) A thunderstorm is a storm with thunder and lightning and a lot of heavy rain. *page 154* [tormenta]

thymine /THEYE-meen/ (noun) Thymine is one of the four basic components of the DNA molecule. It bonds with adenine. *page 70* [timina]

tidal range /TEYE-duhl raynj/ (noun) The tidal range is the difference in height between the low tide and the high tide at a particular place. *page 120* [rango mareal]

tide /teyed/ (noun) The tide is the regular change in the level of the ocean on the beach. You say the tide is in when water reaches a high point on the land or out when the water leaves the land. *page 118* [marea]

tilt /tilt/ (noun) The tilt of something is the fact that it tilts or slopes, or the angle at which it tilts or slopes. *page 114* [inclinación]

tissue /TISH-oo/ (noun) In animals and plants, tissue consists of cells that are similar to each other in appearance and that have the same function. *page 30* [tejido]

title /TEYET-uhl/ (noun) The title of a book, play, movie, or piece of music is its name. *page 16* [título]

topographic map /toh-puh-GRA-fik map/ (noun) A map showing topographic features, usually by means of contour lines. *page 136* [mapa topográfico]

topography /tuh-POG-ruh-fee/ (noun) The detailed mapping of the features of a small area. *page 136* [topografía]

tornado /tor-NAY-doh/ (noun) A tornado is a violent wind storm consisting of a tall column of air which spins around very fast and causes a lot of damage. *page 154* [tornado]

total eclipse /TOHT-uhl ee-KLIPS/ (noun) A total eclipse of the sun is an occasion when the moon is between the earth and the sun, so that for a short time you cannot see any part of the sun. A total eclipse of the moon is an occasion when the earth is between the sun and the moon, so that for a short time you cannot see any part of the moon. Compare partial eclipse. *page 118* [eclipse total]

trace gas /trays gas/ (noun) Trace gases are gases that make up less than one percent of the Earth's atmosphere, such as carbon dioxide and methane. *page 148* [gases traza]

trait /trayt/ (noun) A trait is a particular characteristic, quality, or tendency that someone or something has. *page 70* [rasgo]

translucent /trans-LOO-suhnt/ (adjective) If a material is translucent, some light can pass through it. *page 202* [traslúcido]

transparent /trans-PAIR-ent/ (adjective) If an object or substance is transparent, you can see through it. *page 202* [transparente]

transpiration /tran-spuh-RAY-shuhn/ (noun) Transpiration is the process by which plants release water vapor into the air through their leaves. *page 92* [transpiración]

transverse wave /tranz-VERS wayv/ (noun) Transverse waves are waves, such as those in water, in which the material that the waves are passing through moves at right angles to the waves. Compare longitudinal wave. *page 198* [onda transversal]

trichonympha /TRIK-uh-nimf-uh/ (noun) A member of the protist family that lives in the intestines of the termite species. *page 26* [trichonympha]

trypanosome /tri-PAN-uh-sohm/ (noun) A protozoan that lives in the blood or tissues of humans and other vertebrates. *page 28* [trypanosoma]

tropical /TRO-pi-kuhl/ (adjective) Tropical weather is hot and damp weather typical of the tropics. *page 153* [tropical]

tropical depression /TRO-pi-kuhl dee-PRESH-uhn/ (noun) A tropical depression is a system of thunderstorms that begins in the tropics and has relatively low wind speeds. It is the second stage in the development of a hurricane. *page 156* [depresión tropical]

tropical disturbance /TRO-pi-kuhl di-STER-buhns/ (noun) A tropical disturbance is a system of thunderstorms that begins in the tropics and lasts for more than 24 hours. It is the first stage in the development of a hurricane. *page 156* [perturbación tropical]

tropical storm /TRO-pi-kuhl storm/ (noun) A tropical storm is a system of thunderstorms that begins in the tropics and has relatively high wind speeds. It is the third stage in the development of a hurricane. *page 156* [tormenta tropical]

troposphere /TROH-poh-sfeer/ (noun) The troposphere is the layer of the Earth's atmosphere that is closest to the Earth's surface. *page 149* [tropósfera]

trough /trawf/ (noun) A trough is a low area between two big waves on the sea. *page 198* [seno]

trout /trowt/ (noun) A trout is a fairly large fish that lives in rivers and streams. *page 54* [trucha]

tsunami /soo-NAH-mee/ (noun) A tsunami is a very large wave, often caused by an earthquake, that flows onto the land and can cause widespread deaths and destruction. *pages 138, 140* [tsunami]

tube worm /toob werm/ (noun) A kind of worm that lives in the sea, often in hydrothermal vent environments. *page 29* [gusano tubícola]

tundra /TUN-druh/ (noun) Tundra is one of the large flat areas of land in the north of Europe, Asia, and America. The ground below the top layer of soil is always frozen and no trees grow there. *page 82* [tundra]

turtle /TERT-uhl/ (noun) A turtle is any reptile that has a thick shell around its body, for example a tortoise or terrapin, and can pull its whole body into its shell. *page 46* [tortuga]

U

unbalanced forces /un-BAL-insed FORS-es/ (noun) In physics, unbalanced forces are forces that are not equal and opposite to each other, so that an object to which the forces are applied moves. *page 186* [fuerzas no equilibradas]

updraft /UP-draft/ (noun) An updraft is a rising current of air, which often produces a cumulus cloud. *page 154* [corriente ascendente]

upper mantle /UP-er MAN-tuhl/ (noun) The upper mantle is the part of the Earth's interior that lies immediately beneath the crust. *page 130* [manto superior]

uranium /yoo-RAY-nee-uhm/ (noun) Uranium is a naturally occurring radioactive metal that is used to produce nuclear energy and weapons. *page 182* [uranio]

Uranus /yer-AY-nuhs/ (noun) Uranus is the seventh planet from the sun. *page 110* [Urano]

V

vacuole /VAK-yoo-uhl/ (noun) A vacuole is a space within a plant cell that contains water, waste products, or other substances. *page 22* [vacuola]

variation /vair-ee-AY-shuhn/ *(noun)* A variation is a change or slight difference in a level, amount, or quantity. *pages 69, 74* [variación]

vascular plant /VAS-kyoo-ler plant/ *(noun)* Vascular plants are plants that have tissues which can carry water and other fluids through the body of the plant. *page 38* [planta vascular]

vegetative reproduction /VEJ-uh-tay-tiv ree-proh-DUHK-shuhn/ *(noun)* Vegetative reproduction is a process by which new plants are produced without using seeds, for example by using cuttings instead. *page 62* [reproducción vegetativa]

velocity /vuh-LAHS-uh-tee/ *(noun)* Velocity is the speed at which something moves in a particular direction. *page 190* [velocidad]

Venn diagram /ven DEYE-uh-gram/ *(noun)* A Venn diagram is a diagram in mathematics that uses overlapping circles to represent features that are common to, or unique to, two or more sets of data. *page 14* [diagrama de Venn]

vent /vent/ *(noun)* A volcanic vent is a crack in the Earth's surface through which volcanic material such as lava and gases are released. *page 138* [chimenea]

Venus /VEE-nuhs/ *(noun)* Venus is the second planet from the sun, situated between Mercury and the Earth. *page 110* [Venus]

vertebrate /VER-tuh-brayt/ *(noun)* A vertebrate is a creature that has a spine. Mammals, birds, reptiles, and fish are vertebrates. *page 54* [vertebrado]

vibrate /VEYE-brayt/ *(verb)* If something vibrates or if you vibrate it, it shakes with repeated small, quick movements. *page 209* [vibrar]

volcano /vahl-KAY-noh/ *(noun)* A volcano is a mountain from which hot melted rock, gas, steam, and ash from inside the earth sometimes burst. *pages 128, 138* [volcán]

volume /VAHL-yoom/ *(noun)* The volume of an object is the amount of space that it contains or occupies. *pages 8, 12, 16, 164, 166* [volumen]

W

wall cloud /wawl klowd/ *(noun)* A wall cloud is an area of cloud that extends beneath a thunderstorm and sometimes develops into a tornado. *page 156* [nube de pared]

warm-blooded /worm BLUHD-ed/ *(adjective)* A warm-blooded animal, such as a bird or a mammal, has a fairly high body temperature that does not change much and is not affected by the surrounding temperature. *page 56* [de sangre caliente]

warm front /wawrm fruhnt/ *(noun)* A mass of warm air rising over a mass of cold air. *page 150* [frente cálido]

warning /WORN-ing/ *(noun)* A warning is something said or written to tell people of a possible danger, problem, or other unpleasant thing that might happen. *page 157* [advertencia]

watch /wahtch/ *(noun)* A hurricane watch or a storm watch is an official announcement that severe weather conditions may soon develop in a particular area. *page 157* [alerta]

water /WUH-ter/ *(noun)* Water is a clear thin liquid that has no color or taste when it is pure. It falls from clouds as rain and enters rivers and seas. All animals and people need water in order to live. *pages 46, 90, 174* [agua]

water energy /WUH-ter EN-er-jee/ *(noun)* Water energy is the same as hydropower. *page 158* [fuerza hidráulica]

waterspout /WUH-ter-spowt/ *(noun)* A waterspout is a small tornado that occurs over water. *page 154* [tromba marina]

water vapor /WUH-ter VAY-por/ *(noun)* Water vapor is water in the form of gas in the air. *pages 146, 150, 154* [vapor de agua]

water wave /WUH-ter wayv/ *(noun)* A water wave is a wave that occurs in water, especially in the sea. *page 198* [ola]

wave /wayv/ (noun) **1.** A wave is a raised mass of water on the surface of water, especially the sea, which is caused by the wind or by tides making the surface of the water rise and fall. *page 140* [ola]

(noun) **2.** Waves are the form in which things such as sound, light, and radio signals travel. *page 198* [onda]

wavelength /WAYV-lenth/ (noun) A wavelength is the distance between a part of a wave of energy such as light or sound and the next similar part. *page 198* [longitud de onda]

weathering /WETH-er-ing/ (noun) Weathering is a process in which rocks near the Earth's surface are broken into smaller pieces as a result of exposure to rain, wind, and ice. *pages 128, 142* [erosión]

weather map /WETH-er map/ (noun) A weather map is a chart that shows what the weather is like or what it will be like. *page 150* [mapa meteorológico]

wedge /wedj/ (noun) A wedge is a simple tool with a thick triangular shape used for raising, holding, or splitting objects. *page 194* [cuña]

weight /wayt/ (noun) The weight of a person or thing is how heavy they are, measured in units such as kilograms, pounds, or tons. *page 188* [peso]

wheel and axle /weel and AK-suhl/ (noun) A simple machine consisting of an axle connected to a wheel. *page 194* [volante y eje]

white blood cell /weyet bluhd sel/ (noun) White blood cells are the cells in your blood which your body uses to fight infection. Compare red blood cell. *page 32* [leucocitos]

white dwarf /weyet dworf/ (noun) A white dwarf is a very small, dense star that has collapsed. *page 106* [enana blanca]

whooping crane /WUP-ing crayn/ (noun) A whooping crane is a rare bird belonging to the crane family that lives only in North America. *page 98* [grulla cantora]

wind /wind/ (noun) A wind is a current of air that is moving across the earth's surface. *pages 146, 150* [viento]

wind energy /wind EN-er-jee/ (noun) Wind energy or wind power is energy or power that is obtained from the wind, for example by the use of a turbine. *page 158* [energía eólica]

wire /weyer/ (noun) A wire is a long thin piece of metal that is used to fasten things or to carry electric current. *page 220* [cable]

work /werk/ (noun) In physics, work is the energy that is transferred to a moving object as the result of a force acting upon the object. *page 196* [trabajo]

worm /werm/ (noun) A worm is a small animal with a long thin body, no bones, and no legs. *pages 48, 78* [gusano]

X

X-ray /EKS-ray/ (noun) **1.** X-rays are a type of radiation that can pass through most solid materials. X-rays are used by doctors to examine the bones or organs inside your body and are also used at airports to see inside people's luggage. *pages 185, 201* [rayos X]

(noun) **2.** An X-ray is a picture made by sending X-rays through something, usually someone's body. *page 185* [radiografía]

xylem /ZEYE-luhm/ (noun) Xylem is the layer of material in plants that carries water and nutrients from the roots to the leaves. Compare phloem. *pages 38, 42* [xilema]

Y

yeast /yeest/ (noun) Yeast is a kind of fungus which is used to make bread rise, and in making alcoholic drinks such as beer. *pages 26, 62* [levadura]

Index

The index for *Gateway to Science* will help you locate the scientific terms and topics quickly and easily. Each entry in the index is followed by the numbers of the pages on which it appears. A page number in *bold italic type* indicates a page on which the entry is used in a graphic or photograph.

Skills Index

Concepts

Critical Thinking

Academic Vocabulary

Credits

Illustrators

Ron Carboni / Anita Grien: pp. 27 (8, 12), 28, 66–68, 70–71

Gary Ciccarelli / AA Reps Inc.: pp. 50–53, 75

Fiametta Dogi / AA Reps Inc.: pp. 46–47, 98

Bruce Emmett / Artworks Illustration: pp. 154–155, 186–188

Dick Gage / illustrationOnLine.com: pp. 182–184

Garth Glazier / AA Reps Inc.: p. 83

Patrick Gnan / illustrationOnLine.com: pp. 42–43, 86–87, 90–91

InContext Publishing Partners: pp. 90 (6), 173, 174 (Word Study top), 178, 179 (11), 180 (bottom), 192 (bottom), 215 (top two formulas)

Sharon and Joel Harris / illustrationOnLine.com: pp. 58–59

Phil Howe / illustrationOnLine.com: pp. 190–191, 192 (top)

Bob Kayganich / illustrationOnLine.com: pp. 110–111

Rob Kemp / illustrationOnLine.com: pp. 150–151

Yvan Meunier / contactjupiter.com: pp. 78–79 (all art except Word Study)

Brandon Pletsch / illustrationOnLine.com: pp. 22–23, 25

Precision Graphics: pp. 4–5, 8 (bottom), 13, 14–17 (except callout 5), 27 (yeast packet), 34, 36, 44–45, 48, 60, 62–64, 73, 74, 76–77, 78 (Word Study), 80, 84, 88, 92–93, 95, 97, 100, 108–109, 112–113, 116–117, 122, 124, 127–128, 132–133, 136, 148–149, 156, 160, 164 (The Senses diagram), 168–169, 170, 172, 174 (4, Word Study bottom), 177, 179 (water molecule), 180 (top), 181, 196, 198–201, 207 (8, 10), 208, 211, 212–213, 215 (bottom two illustrations), 216–217, 220

C.R.É.É. Alain Salesse / contactjupiter.com: pp. 130–131, 138–141

Space Channel/Phil Saunders / AA Reps Inc.: pp. 102–103, 118–119

Studio Liddell / AA Reps Inc.: pp. 10–11

Tony Randazzo / AA Reps Inc.: pp. 114–115

Gerad Taylor / illustrationOnLine.com: pp. 20, 194–195

Claude Thivierge / contactjupiter.com: pp. 38, 40

Ralph Voltz / illustrationOnLine.com: pp. 2–3, 166–167, 202–203, 218–219

Matt Zang / AA Reps Inc.: pp. 30–33, 106–107, 206–207 (background image)

Photos

Unit Icon Photos: Science Basics Unit Icon: ©Photodisc Green/Getty Images; Life Science and Earth Science Unit Icons: ©Royalty-Free/Corbis; Physical Science Unit Icon: ©Stockdisc Premium/Getty Images

4: ©William Leaman / Alamy; 5 (top): ©Vstock LLC / Index Stock; 5 (middle and bottom): ©2006 JUPITERIMAGES and its licensors. All rights reserved.; 6 (1): ©Hemera Technologies / Alamy; 6 (2): ©2006 JUPITERIMAGES and its licensors. All rights reserved.; 6 (3): ©Leslie Garland Picture Library / Alamy; 6 (4): ©Royalty-Free/Corbis; 6 (5): ©Royalty-Free/Corbis; 6 (6): ©Pascal Goetgheluck / Photo Researchers, Inc.; 6 (7 left): ©David J. Green / Alamy; 6 (7 right): ©matthias engelien / Alamy; 6 (8): ©Royalty-Free/Corbis; 6 (9): ©2006 JUPITERIMAGES and its licensors. All rights reserved.; 6 (10): ©Michael Matisse / Getty Images; 8: ©NASA / Photo Researchers, Inc.; 12: ©imagebroker / Alamy; 14 (Word Study image): ©2006 JUPITERIMAGES and its licensors. All rights reserved.; 16 ©Valerie Giles / Photo Researchers, Inc.; 18 (1, 2): ©Jonathan Nourok / PhotoEdit; 18 (3): ©2006 JUPITERIMAGES and its licensors. All rights reserved.; 19 (4): ©Stockbyte Platinum / Getty Images; 19 (5): ©Gabe Palmer / Alamy; 19 (6): ©*Blend Images* / SuperStock; 19 (7): ©*Digital Vision Ltd.* / SuperStock; 21: ©Robert Holmes / Alamy; 22: ©Ilene MacDonald / Alamy; 24: ©Bettmann/CORBIS; 26–27 (background image): ©Kent Wood / Photo Researchers, Inc.; 26 (1, 2): ©Eric V. Grave / Photo Researchers, Inc.; 26 (6): ©Eric V. Grave / Photo Researchers, Inc.; 27 (7): ©2006 JUPITERIMAGES and its licensors. All rights reserved.; 27 (10): ©Steve Gschmeissner / Photo Researchers, Inc.; 27 (bread): ©2006 JUPITERIMAGES and its licensors. All rights reserved.; 28 (top): ©M. I. Walker / Photo Researchers, Inc.; 28 (bottom): ©Richard Kirby/Oxford Scientific; 29: ©Ralph White/CORBIS; 30–31: ©Bill Brooks / Alamy; 34–35 (background image): ©Royalty-Free/Corbis; 34 (Word Study top): ©2006 JUPITERIMAGES and its licensors. All rights reserved.; 34 (Word Study bottom): ©Ilja Hulinsky / Alamy; 34 (1): ©2006 JUPITERIMAGES and its licensors. All rights reserved.; 35 (7): ©Royalty-Free/Corbis; 35 (8, 9): ©Foodcollection / Getty; 35 (10): ©Hot Ideas / Index Stock; 37: ©blickwinkel / Alamy; 38 (2): ©PhotoLink/Getty Images, Inc.; 38 (3): ©2006 JUPITERIMAGES and its licensors. All rights reserved.; 38 (4): ©Christopher Griffin / Alamy; 38 (5): ©2006 JUPITERIMAGES and its licensors. All rights reserved.; 39 (8): ©Peter Arnold, Inc. / Alamy; 39 (10): ©Phil Schermeister/CORBIS; 39 (11): ©2006 JUPITERIMAGES and its licensors. All rights reserved.; 39 (12–14): ©2006 JUPITERIMAGES and its licensors. All rights reserved.; 40: ©Hot Ideas / Index Stock; 41: ©Corbis; 48: ©Anthony Mercieca / Photo Researchers, Inc.; 49 (top): ©Gregory Ochocki / Photo Researchers, Inc.; 49 (bottom): ©Stuart